Preface

A boy in his twenties living somewhere across the border quarrels with his parents, and leaves his home in anger. Unknowingly crossing the Indo-Pak border, he finds himself in the domain of another country. Still seething over his parents' behaviour, he is accosted by a few security personnel. He learns of his mistake as he is arrested and sent to the lockup—he has crossed the borders of his country and mistakenly landed on to the soil of an enemy, a soil that a few decades ago belonged to his forefathers. His pleadings and explanations of innocence fall on deaf ears. The security personnel, though sympathetic, do not allow him to go back as their country's laws do not permit the same. He might be a spy in guise, the personnel conjecture amongst themselves. After spending a sleepless night in a dingy cell at the police station, he is presented to a local court the next day. He is charged with several criminal acts including espionage and waging war against the state. The day ends with his court ordered incarceration. The boy is perplexed. He asks himself, "Why is this an enemy country? Hadn't father often recounted to him that before 1947, it was where they lived? What about those sweet memories of father's youth spent here?" The boy remained imprisoned long after serving his sentence for reasons unjustfied, and when his release and departure to home is finally secured by a self-righteous civil society, he returns to his country, a man deranged.

Every year, hundreds of people, including poor fishermen on the seas, trespass into enemy territory where they languish in jail for years, charged with crimes they never committed, except of wandering into enemy waters which were theirs about half a century ago. At times, they are freed as a part of exchange programmes on the eve of political summits or as diplomatic deals struck upon the meeting of political bosses. They are treated as if they were commodities, not humans—a simplistic negation of human rights.

The Indian subcontinent is inhabited by a large number of poor people. The subcontinent's greatest enemy is backwardness in human development but the political leadership in command, placing this common foe aside, nourishes the enmity between countries, particularly Pakistan and India. The internal insurgencies in neighbouring countries are overtly and covertly supported, resulting in the killing of people at the hands of insurgents. State forces respond with similar ruthlessness, killing, and inflicting hardships on those also who have nothing to do with the insurgencies. Often, political expediency leads to armed clashes and wars, resulting in immeasurable loss to humanity.

Every human has the inherent right to live and enjoy the world, not to die serving the political interests of others. The sorry state of affairs in the Indian subcontinent and our resolve to not let the status quo go unchallenged has inspired us to write this commentary and to identify, assess, and offer the way forward from the present situation. Hostilities, within and without, must end. Expenditure on wars and conflicts must be shifted to activities geared towards economic, social and human development.

As our readers turn to the next page, we humbly remind them that this is not a book on history even though it states and analyses historical facts based on secondary sources. But do bear in mind, that this is not a work of fiction either.

Sudhan Chandra Chandola

July, 2020 **Himadrita Chandola**

Combating Everlasting Tragedy

United Nations of Indian Subcontinent

Sudhan Chandra Chandola
Himadrita Chandola

GYAN

Published, 2021
Published by

Gyan Publishing House
5, Ansari Road
Daryaganj, New Delhi-110002
Phone: 011-47034999, 9811692060
www.gyanbooks.com
E-mail: books@gyanbooks.com

Printed at: G. Print Process, Delhi.

Cataloging in Publication Data—DK
Courtesy: D.K. Agencies (P) Ltd. <docinfo@dkagencies.com>

Chandola, Sudhan Chandra, author.
Combating everlasting tragedy : United Nations of Indian Subcontinent / by Sudhan Chandra Chandola, Himadrita Chandola.
pages cm
Includes bibliographical references.
ISBN 9788121219808 (PB)

1. South Asia—Foreign relations. 2. South Asia—Politics and government. 3. South Asian cooperation. I. Chandola, Himadrita, author. II. Title.

LCC DS431.C43 2020 | DDC 327.54 23

Combating Everlasting Tragedy

Dedicated to the more than one and
half billion people of the Indian subcontinent

Contents

Acknowledgement –Words of Gratitude

The right to life is a fundamental right of every human being and the denial of it the greatest crime to humanity. Birth, as we know, is not a matter of choice but a matter of chance, sometimes defined as 'luck' by some, or 'destiny' by others. One may be born to any parents in any family, of any faith, living in any part of the world. This is the hypothesis underpinning the concept of '*Vasudhaiv Kutumbakam*' (the entire universe is a family), an idea indelibly associated with the Indian subcontinent's culture.

This is the view of life that I imbibed from my parents, Satya Prasad Chandola and Kishori Devi, and it has been my guiding light ever since. And for that I owe a huge debt of gratitude to them.

I and Himadrita have been and remain dedicated students of world history. Numerous scholarly works on the subject have been foundational to our growth as learners and for that, we express our gratitude to the writers, analysts and historians whose works have guided us in our own studies. Their contribution while not always direct to the content of the present work and hence not cited, has been crucial to our understanding.

We are also extremely grateful to the authors and scholars referenced in the notes without whose works it would have been impossible to refine and carve our thoughts.

We greatly benefitted from Katyayani Chandola's critical eye and constructive feedback. We express our thanks to her.

We are thankful to Mr. Dheerendra Kumar and Mr. Anwar Saleem for their computer support.

We are also grateful to Gyan Publishing House and Mr. B.P. Garg, its Editor-in-Chief, in particular, for publishing this book in a short span of time.

Finally, we express our deep gratitude to Sunita Chandola, my wife and Himadrita's mother, whose constant encouragement kept us motivated through the long process of research and writing.

Introduction

This book comprises eight chapters. Chapter-I opens with a discussion on the fateful events that submerged almost the entirety of the subcontinent into a state of bipolarity, ranging from extreme joy to extreme sorrow. The chapter focusses on this situation as an effect of the British decision to leave India and the consequent emergence of the two independent states, India and Pakistan, the latter as a homeland for about 10 crore (100 million) Muslims of the then British India in 1947. The Hindus and Muslims had more or less lived as a composite society till the demand for a Muslim Homeland gained currency in British India. Communal tensions and conflicts in India were not unknown but were also not a common feature of the society. Yet, communal divide and concocted apprehensions of Hindu domination over minority Muslims in an undivided India were assumed. Communal strife and riots became the raison d'etre for separate Muslim homeland. The forefathers of the entire local population, if the popular interpretation is to be believed, came from outside the subcontinent, including from across the Hindukush mountains and through the passes therein that now fall close to the borders of Pakistan and Afghanistan. Historic western migration, from the Aryans to the Turks, Afghans and the Mughals predominantly followed the same route to this land of abundant opportunities. In the words of Maulana Abul Kalam Azad,

> "It was India's historic destiny that many human races and cultures and religious faiths should flow to her (India), and that many a caravan should find rest here.... one of the last of these caravans was that of the followers of Islam.....", and further,
>
> "Eleven hundred years of common history have enriched India with our common achievement, our languages, our poetry, our literature, our culture, our art, our dress, our manners and customs, the innumerable happening of our daily life, everything bears the stamp of our joint endeavour. There is indeed no aspect of our life which has escaped this stamp."[1]

However, those who viewed Islam and Hinduism as different and distinct social orders belonging to two different civilizations, having conflicting and contradicting ideas, prevailed over the concept of governance as laid out in the 'Medina Constitution', which Maulana Abul Kalam Azad had put forth.[2] Lala Lajpat Rai, one of the prominent leaders of Congress and of the Hindu Mahasabha was so afraid of Muslims that once he wrote to CR Das that "I am not afraid of the seven crores of Mussalmans. But I think the seven crores in Hindustan plus the armed hordes of Afghanistan, Central Asia, Arabia, Mesopotamia and Turkey, will be irresistible."[3]

To the greatest exponent of the Muslim homeland, Muhammad Ali Jinnah , "They (Islam and Hinduism) are not religions in the strict sense of the word, but are in fact different and distinct social orders; ....The Hindus and Muslims belong to two different religious philosophies, social customs and literature (s). They neither intermarry nor interdine together, and indeed they belong to two different civilisations which are based mainly on conflicting ideas and conceptions".[4]

On 23 March, the day on which Lahore Resolution was presented before a gathering of more than 60,000 Leagures, Fazl-ul-Haq reading the resolution criticised Maulana Abul Kalam for his address in the capacity of the President of Congress.

India and Pakistan gained independence as per the provisions of the Indian Independence Act of 1947. The directly ruled state of British India was bifurcated into the dominions of India and Pakistan. 'Princely states,' which were around 562 in number, were given the opportunity of remaining independent. None of the 'princely states' were capable of governing themselves as a sovereign unit, and the desire of those aspiring for an independent status was met with armed interventions from either of the dominions. Kalat in Pakistan and Hyderabad in India were among those of the 'princely states' where their refusal to join the respective dominion was put to naught through a direct military action. All 'princely states' eventually had to succumb to the pressures exerted by nearby dominions or by their own subjects.

Unfortunately, soon after their independence, India and Pakistan brawled over the issues of accession of 'princely states', subsequently inviting external powers, including the UN, to intervene in their affairs. Chapter-II addresses the incompetence of the political leaders on both sides, and more significantly, the pain and agony of the people, who, compelled under hellish circumstances, had to migrate from their original homes in search of new ones to the other dominion, leaving everything near and dear behind. They risked their lives, whether they chose to stay or leave. They had to experience a multiplicity of tortures. The most heinous crimes were committed against women. While debates over partition grew from loud to louder since 1940 (when the Lahore Resolution was adopted by the Muslim League and politicians began to affirm or denounce it), the anticipated mass migration of the hapless multitudes—forced to flee on the plank of communal divide—was hardly given any serious thought by those who either were at the helm of power or were to get the reins of the newly born States in their hands. Elites among the British as well as politicians belonging to the Muslim League and the Congress benefitted at the cost of the misery of crores (millions) of the poor in the subcontinent. While the politicians of undivided India were restless to assume charge of the future dominions as early as possible, the poor masses, most vulnerable to communal violence, were left to fend for themselves. The day of independence or deliverance proved to be a doom's day for many.

Chapter-III talks about the hostile relations between India and Pakistan that have never allowed a fair space to the question of economic development of the people. Post-independence, politicians proceeded on a path of territorial aggrandisement by claiming and counter-claiming the acquisitions of the 'princely states'. This was regarded as an act of national integration or nation building. Kashmir was claimed by both the dominions, India and Pakistan, which then became the epicentre of animosity between the two, having culminated in three wars and about a dozen conflicts and clashes at different occasions.

The internal and external rivalries of the two states also combined to birth a new politico-territorial entity in the subcontinent. The year 1971 heralded the emergence of a new State, Bangladesh. The sole India-Pakistan war fought in the eastern horizon resulted in the liberation and birth of a new country. This was perceived as a loss to Pakistan and a strategic victory to India, for Pakistan was cut into two unequal halves in the process. To Bangladeshis, political and territorial independence bestowed them the opportunity of absolute and sovereign self-governance, with no obligation to share power as in the past with anyone else. For the Indian leadership it had inflicted a deadly blow to the strength of Pakistan by creating a State, friend to it and foe to Pakistan. The latter assumption soon turned out to be a myth, as borne out by the political developments in the ensuing years. Within a period of three years, Bangladesh freed itself from the burden of Indian gratitude (and therefore an India expected unwavering friendship) by claiming that the liberation was won by the Mukti Bahini, and not the Indian forces. It was claimed that the Indian forces simply provided them logistic support. Bangladeshis in no equivocal terms got their freedom from West Pakistan's dominance but Pakistan and India both lost the war. More than 11,000 soldiers were killed and many more were left injured in the war. Pakistan also lost more than 10 lakh civilians living in its then eastern wing, now Bangladesh. The trauma of the largescale sexual violence and rapes and the loss of dignity to lakhs of women, inflicted upon them by their own former countrymen, remained unremedied with the Bangladeshi people.

Since independence, India and Pakistan have only occasionally demonstrated good neighbourly behaviour towards each other. Their hostile relations can partly be attributed to their historical conflicts and largely to their inability to identify the real foe. This real foe is within their own system, the system in which concern for human development is relegated to the background in order to make way for personal and political interests of a few. These concerns have been dealt with in Chapter-IV. Reproducing the status of human development indicators (that are at appalling levels in the subcontinent), attempts have been made to compare them with some of the most developed countries of the world. Interestingly, the latter are also the major arms manufacturing and exporting countries of the world. The constituents of the Indian subcontinent are invariably dependent on these for their arms supplies. The treasuries of the developing world get depleted as this trade burgeons, filling up the coffers of the developed arms-exporting countries. It is no surprise then that the developing countries should find themselves short of funds to invest in social and economic sectors, including social assistance. At the same time, the industrialized countries enrich themselves with arms exports, tariffs, patents and royalties; trade strategies that enable them to carry on their own domestic robust social-assistance programmes. This massive outflow of national resources on arms imports has to be curtailed, if not stopped altogether, in the interest of more than one billion poor of the subcontinent. Priority must be given to human development rather than to the procurement and development of the machines of destruction.

Chapter-V is dedicated to the Europe which by now, has travelled a long distance from destruction to construction and from disintegration to unification. Throughout its history during the past millennium till the conclusion of second world war, European countries were continuously engaged in war with each other for the various reasons. The immense losses to Europe in men, money and property in the second world war, led the Europe to understand the futility of confrontations. A small beginning in 1944 by the fugitive kings of three small countries of Europe, in England, came up with the formation of BENLUX Union in 1948, the year in which India and Pakistan were fighting a bitter war over Kashmir. Very soon other nations also joined, to form ECSC first and then European Union. The European Union, a group of 27 countries (before the exit of Britain on 31 January 2020, it was 28), now is a Nation in effect with its own Parliament, flag, national anthem, constitution, currency and other things. The EU members, many of whom were arch-rivals till the first half of twentieth century for territorial claims, today work in unison in all matters ranging from commerce to agriculture and from industry to foreign affairs. In Indian subcontinent, people living together till 1947, began to fight each other under the flags of India and Pakistan, thereafter.

Chapter VI deals with the industrialised world's treatment towards the developing countries. The era of territorial colonialism has been given a good bye by those who once had thrown the whole world to the two Great Wars for the sake of territorial aggrandisement, for ever. A new sort of colonialism with trade, tariff and farm support as the main weapons in the hands of developed world, has taken place. Various world organizations, including UN, IMF, World Bank and WTO, are used by these countries as tools to influence the policies through a sophisticated mechanism to siphon off the economic resources of the developing world. The wealth of the latter is sucked out by the former in a sheer mechanism which prima facie does not appear unfair towards anyone. The world organizations are controlled by the developed world either through quota or votes, or the veto power or through a restricted membership. This world-order ensures an uninterrupted richness to the developed world at the cost of impoverishment of the third world countries.

India and Pakistan were created as British dominions in August, 1947. Before their independence, they had a common history since the Indus Valley civilization or much before that, followed by the immigration of various races to the land commonly referred to as Indian subcontinent. This common history has been revisited in Chapter VII. Way back in the second century BC, Mauryans were able to extend their rule from river Helmund in Afghanistan in north-west to river Penner-Tungbhadra in the South, and from Rann of Kachh-Arabian sea in west to the Padma-Brhamaputra delta and Bay of Bengal in the east. However, Asoka's march for territorial acquisitions was halted by an awakening within his self. He adopted Buddhism after the Kalinga (Odisha in India) war. He shunned violence and propagated the rule of pity, nonviolence and peace not only within his kingdom, but across the borders of his kingdom also. Though Indian history is replete with the stories of benevolent rulers, it was only about 17 centuries later; Asoka was replicated in the personality of Mughal Padshah Akbar. Akbar established the rule of Sulh-i-kul or 'peace to all'. This laid down the foundation of secularism in India, not in words but in practice.

All the tribes and communities that came to India contributed to the development of a common culture of the subcontinent. Even Buddhism which retained its separate identity across the borders of the subcontinent, became an inseparable part of India's culture which later on came to be known as Hinduism. The people who came to India with the invading armies from the north-west in the last decade of twelfth century, came with a distinct faith, Islam, which had its roots in Arabian lands. Islam was a religion in the true meaning of the word. It had a definite ideology with a clearly defined set of its observance and practice. Any deviation from that was a heresy and attracted harsh punishment. The rulers carried on its proselytising spirit and more or less tried to keep its identity separate from the then existing religion, faiths and practices of the land.

The believers of the two dominant faiths, Islam and Hinduism, sometimes clashed and co-operated at the other, with each other. The necessities of the day-to-day life, gradually, brought them closer to each other and very soon they began to learn to live together. The barrier of language in interaction was broken by 'Rekhta' which was an amalgamation of Arabic, Persian and the local languages. A new cultural milieu began to take shape.

The British subjugation of India which started in the second half of the eighteenth century was complete by the first half of the nineteenth century. This was the era of colonialism all over the world. For the first time in its history India came under a foreign rule. Indians had to serve their British masters. Indian soldiers fought in alien lands, during these years to protect and strengthen the British Empire, the empire of their masters. Ironically, when they got independence in 1947, they divided themselves, in categories, groups and communities and started fighting with each other. They followed the democratic model of the governance, albeit leaders utilizing the caste, creed and communal divide at their fullest.

India, through its Constitution in 1950, adopted secular form of democracy. Pakistan very soon succumbed to theocracy by declaring itself Islamic Republic in 1956 vide its first Constitution. Bangladesh swinging between secularism and theocracy, has Islam as the state religion with secularism as one of the four fundamentals of the state policy. However, Nepal boldly has done away with Hindu theocracy by declaring it a secular State in 2007. Bhutan, has given an equal space to all the people by providing equality with Buddhism as the "spritual heritage of Bhutan" in 2008.

While the Constitution of Europe envisages human dignity, freedom, democracy, equality, the rule of law and respect for human rights of persons belonging to minorities, in Pakistan minorities have been put at the mercy of dominant faith. The provisions made in the Pakistan Penal Code regarding Blasphemy Law(Section 295-C), putting restrictions on Ahemadiyas to practice Islam (298-B and 298-C), Diyat ordinance and the Hudoot Laws are not bad in the light of international law and human rights only, but are detrimental to the progress of the Pakistani society as a whole. Adoption of medieval period methods are not to yield fruitful results in the new millennium, as they have lost their relevance in the changed circumstances. Pakistani leadership has to take bold and progressive decisions to relieve Pakistani people from the shackles of such regressive and oppressive provisions.

The last Chapter (Chapter-VIII), 'The Beginning of the Beginning' is an expression of a sincere desire and a pious hope for the beginning of a resurgent Indian subcontinent. The obligation lies on two big nuclear powers of the subcontinent, India and Pakistan. To the disadvantage of the people of the subcontinent, the leaders of these countries, have always found solutions to their ills and failures in the hostilities towards each other. An atmosphere of suspicion and paranoia about a hostile neighbour is fomented among the masses. The scantly-educated and ill informed people are misled by their political bosses to accord highest priority to war preparedness diverting their attention from the daunting problems of economic and human development. People divided in arbitrarily created nationalities through artificial borders, rally behind 'sham patriots' and 'phoney-nationalists' of their countries against a perceived threat from across the borders. Historically, though the people of the subcontinent have many commonalities to bind them together, politicians harp on the differences. Once paranoia and war hysteria is generated, they proceed to purchase killer-machines from industrialized countries. Such purchases, it is speculated by many, at many occasions are accompanied by kickbacks. Anyone who rejects the war threats and speaks against such purchases risks to be labelled as 'Gaddar' (unpatriotic). Those at the helm of affairs spend a huge amount on purchase of killer-machines, putting the daunting issues of human welfare of their citizens aside. Each year a handsome amount from the national budget is allocated to the defence sector.

The question of the territorial possessions in Kashmir or the disputes over the dividing line in the waters of Sir Creek and elsewhere can be resolved with the same spirit which India and Bangladesh displayed in case of their enclaves in one another's territory in 2016. The pathetic state of the human development indicators urgently requires national focus on the investment in human beings, instead of expenditure on the development and procurement of killing techniques. All the countries of the subcontinent need to invest in human beings rather then spend their tax payers money on development and purchases of arms and weapons to keep the territorial disputes alive. For the Indian subcontinent like developing economies the expenditure on former is an investment and a waste on latter.

The Chapter ends with a sort of an appeal to the people of the subcontinent, to forget their hostile past, recognize and respect each other's territorial possessions, bury hostilities and form a politico-socio-economic union on the lines of European Union. A perpetual peace is a prerequisite for the prosperity. It also suggests a joint defence system for the subcontinent encompassing all the five nations of the subcontinent, i.e., Bhutan, Nepal, Bangladesh, Pakistan and India, placing each and every nation at the equal footing.

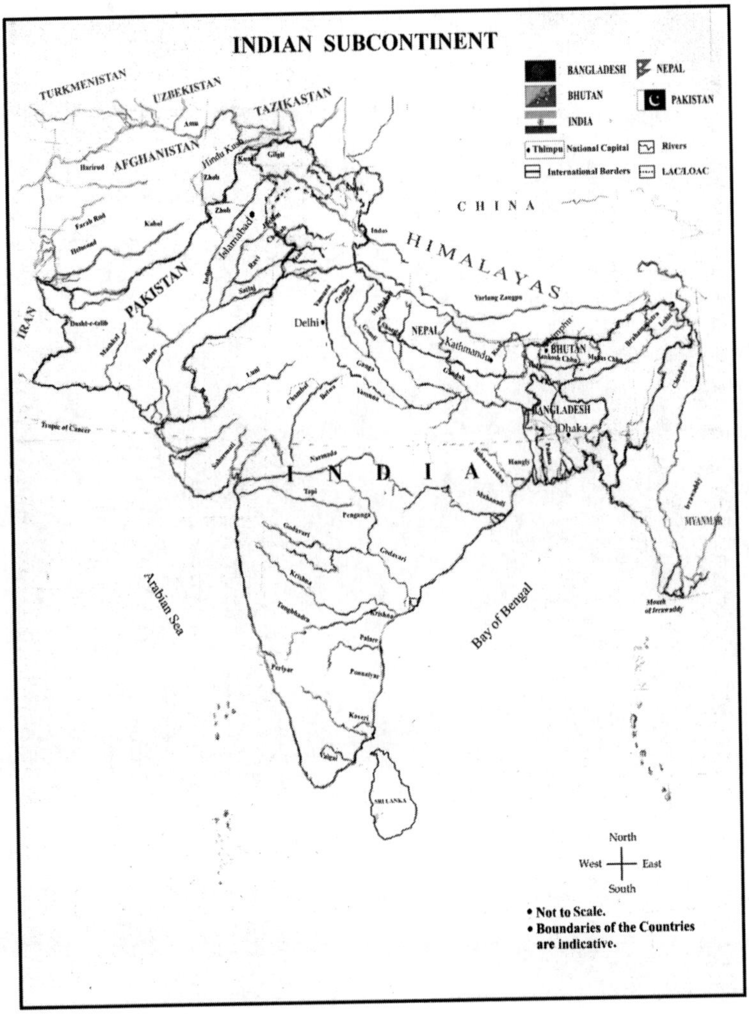
INDIAN SUBCONTINENT
BANGLADESH
NEPAL
BHUTAN
PAKISTAN
INDIA
Thimpu National Capital
Rivers
International Borders
LAC/LOAC
TURKMENISTAN
UZBEKISTAN
TAZIKASTAN
AFGHANISTAN
CHINA
HIMALAYAS
PAKISTAN
IRAN
Islamabad
Delhi
NEPAL
Kathmandu
BHUTAN
BANGLADESH
Dhaka
INDIA
MYANMAR
Arabian Sea
Bay of Bengal
Tropic of Cancer
Narmada
Tapi
Godavari
Krishna
Kaveri
SRI LANKA
North
West
East
South
• Not to Scale.
• Boundaries of the Countries are indicative.

Chapter - I

The Onset of the New Season-
Early Summers

Unable to bear the political, social and economic pressures arising out of the Second World War (September 1939 to August 1945), where Great Britain had a providential escape from defeat, and reeling under an equally massive stress of a steadily increasing demand for freedom from the Indian masses, the British government decided to leave India. Following the American advice to adopt 'twentieth century methods' in governing the British colonies, India in particular, an honourable departure from India was the only logical option available to Britain in the post Great War era.

On 14 August 1941, US President Franklin Delano Roosevelt and British Premier Winston S Churchill met in the Bay of Argentia, off the coast of Newfoundland in Atlantic, to discuss war strategy in order to save Europe from falling into the German hands. The deliberations culminated in the famous Atlantic Charter. Notably, Roosevelt had raised the issue of the Indian independence with Churchill, saying:

"Whichever of your ministers recommends a policy which takes wealth in raw materials out of a colonial country, but which returns nothing to the people of that country in consideration. Twentieth century methods involve bringing industry to these colonies. Twentieth century methods include increasing the wealth of a people by increasing their standard of living, by educating them, by bringing them sanitation-by making sure that they get a return for the raw wealth of their community."[1]

Many Indian Prisoners of War languishing in Japanese jails in Southeast Asia had joined Subhash Chandra Bose's Indian National Army (INA), with the objective to liberate India from the British rule. Defeated though in the battle fields, the INA soldiers had won the hearts of the Indian public when were tried at the Red Fort (November 1945-May1946), after the end of the war. As British Indian government commenced their trials, all leading sections of the Indian society, even those who had hitherto not approved the INA methods, stood up to defend them. The entire nation, cutting across the poltical ideologies, rose in their support. For Britain, India once the "Jewel in the Crown", was increasingly becoming an unbearable burden.

As the British departure appeared a near-reality, the two main political parties of India, the Indian National Congress and the Muslim League, seemed overly impatient to grab their share in the future power structure. Thus, when the Mountbatten Plan was offered to them on 3 June 1947, they after performing some cosmetic formalities, quickly agreed to it. The Plan was to divide India in to two political entities on the basis of Hindu - Muslim identities.

To confirm the partition with a legal instrument, the British Government enacted Indian Independence Act, 1947, on 18 July of the same year. The Act brought up two new Dominions on the world-map.The Act vide Section-1, under the head 'The new Dominions', envisaged that;

> '(1) As from the fifteenth day of August nineteen hundred and forty seven, two independent Dominions shall be set up in India, to be known respectively as India and Pakistan.
>
> (2) The said Dominions are hereafter in this Act referred to as "the new Dominions", and the said fifteenth day of August is hereafter in this Act referred to as "the appointed day"'.

The two dominions did not include the "princely states" that on 15 August 1947, were to become sovereigns. In respect of these states, Section 7 (1) of the Act provided that;

> '(1) As from the appointed day-
>
> (a) His Majesty's Government in the United Kingdom have no responsibility as respects the government of any of the

territories which, immediately before that day, were included in British India;

(b) the suzerainty of His Majesty over the Indian States lapses and with it, all treaties and agreements in force at the date of the passing of this Act between His Majesty and the rulers of Indian States all functions exercisable by His Majesty at that date with respect to Indian states, all obligations of His majesty existing at that date towards Indian States or the rulers thereof, and all powers, rights, authority or jurisdiction exercisable by his Majesty at that date in or in relation to Indian States by treaty, grant, usage, sufferance or otherwise; and;

(c) there lapse also any treaties or agreements in force at the date of the passing of this Act between His Majesty and any persons having authority in the tribal areas, any obligation of his Majesty existing at that date to any such persons or with respect to the tribal areas and all powers, rights, authority or jurisdiction exercisable at that date by his Majesty in or in relation to the tribal areas by treaty grant, usage, sufferance or otherwise'[2]

As the creation of a Muslim homeland on both, eastern and western parts of the British India had become a certainty much before the partition, Hindus living in those areas had started to leave their homes for the future state of India. Though migration was not mandatory, it was forced upon the minorities in the respective Dominions by violent, unprecedented and unanticipated circumstances. While India was conceived as a State for all communities by the Indian leaders, a miniscule number of Muslims left for Pakistan to fulfil their long cherished desire to live in the Muslim homeland. On the other hand, most of the Muslims, much like their Hindu and Sikh counterparts across the border, were traumatised and forced to leave for Pakistan. Clouds of turbulence had begun to gather over the skies of social harmony much before the partition was accepted as the only remedy to cure the disease of communal strife. There had been communal riots in the recent past. The wisest were the first to leave for the land marked for them. Influential and rich Hindu and Muslims anticipating the inevitability of partition swapped their properties with each other in advance. For majority of people, migration was not a matter of choice but a painful compulsion. People had to face an orgy of violence. Many were killed, injured or traumatised at their homes by the maurading crowds of other faith followers.

The Indian Independence Act had created many divides, dominions, princely states and persons with authority in tribal areas. The later events were just following their natural course.

In 1947, there were around 562 princely states, covering roughly 45% of the area of British India[3]. As per the Indian Independence Act, the British suzerainty over the princely states was to be terminated on 15 August 1947. Their loyalty towards British Empire had remained unquestionable throughout the British subjugation of India. As a reward to their loyality, they were given the choice of either remaining independent or to accede to either India or Pakistan.

Insidiously, the international boundary line known as the Radcliffe Line (named after Sir Cyril Radcliffe, the Chairman of the Boundary Commission) was not made public till the very day of independence. It was published only on 16 August, a day after the Independence Day. Till then, the borders between the two Dominions were a matter of guesswork and conjectures, based on the Muslim League's demand and a proposal presented by Mountbatten to the League and the Congress. Pakistan with its two wings, western and eastern, was created on the grounds of Muslim majority areas. Muslim and Hindu population in the princely states was to play an important role in a situation of its ruler being from the minority community. People fled from their homes to the new unknown land, often unseen and alien to them. Many were killed in their own homes, villages and cities while other lost their lives to violent crowds, hunger, thirst and fatigue during their journey. To ensure that they were travelling in the correct direction, people moved in columns. Moving with the people having similar tales of woes was to instil a sense of protection from the marauding crowds of criminals belonging to the faith other than their own.

The 'princes' found themselves in a dilemma. The poignant question was, what to do? Maintaining independent status was their first choice but was beyond their capability. Politically, diplomatically, and militarily, they were weak; tigers on paper, lambs in practice. The Indian Independence Act did not give any say to the people of the princely states and left them at the mercy of their rulers. They were treated nothing more than the property of the 'princes'. The 'Princes' were empowered to take a decision keeping their best interests over and above all other considerations. In the background of a volatile situation within and outside, the option to remain independent was just to live in a fool's paradise. Their subjects had their own aspirations to fulfill in the post-British era. In a monarchical system, there was no place for them in governance while democracy promised them the infinity. In such a situation accession to one of the Dominions seemed the wisest choice to the 'princes'. A wilful acceptance had the fair chances for better deals in favour of the 'princes'.

Lord Mountbatten, about just a month before the independence, had already cautioned them against going solo when they met him at the 'Chamber of Princes' in July 1947. The princes were to face a revolution, he hinted and suggested them to accede to one of the Dominions of their choice. Many of the princes who refused to follow Mountbatten's advice fell to the military might of the Dominion adjacent to them. No 'princely state' had the military or diplomatic capability to resist the territorial aggrandizement of the neighbouring dominion. This became quite evident in the case of the princely states of Jammu and Kashmir including Gilgit Agency in the second half of October 1947, Junagadh in October-November 1947, Kalat in August 1947-March1948 and Hyderabad in September 1948.

Eventually, all independent 'princely states' merged in either of the Dominions. In the event of prince hailing from the majority community of the State, the merger to the dominion having majority of the same community was less difficult. But in cases otherwise, the two Dominions clashed over the acquisitions.

With the 'Great Game' serving as the context, the British government in the year 1935, through an agreement with the Maharaja of Jammu and Kashmir, had taken over the administration of Gilgit and adjoining areas comprising the Gilgit Wazarat, the state of Hunza and Nagar, the Punial Jagir, Yasin, Kuh Ghizr, Ishkoman and Chilas. This arrangement on a lease was for a period of 60 years. In light of the strategic importance of Gilgit as the meeting place of the three great empires, the British government raised a small force 'Gilgit Scouts' from the local Muslim population. This force which was under the command of British officers was to play a decisive role in placing the future of Gilgit, Baltistan and the adjoining areas. When the British government decided to leave India, the process of termination of the lease and the handing over of the administration of the Agency back to Maharaja Hari Singh, was set in motion.

It was the month of July in 1947. Colonel Bacon, the English Governor, handed over the governorship to Brigadier Ghansara Singh who had been sent to Gilgit as the representative of Maharaja of Jammu and Kashmir. The Union Jack was replaced by the flag of the State of Jammu and Kashmir. The handing over of the governorship brought Gilgit Scouts under the command of Ghansara Singh, an employee of the State.

The arrangement was not comfortable for both, Major William Arthur Brown, and his Gilgit Scouts under the command of Subedar Major Muhammad Babar Khan. The transfer of their services from King George VI to one of his erstwhile princes, Maharaja Hari Singh, was taken as a sort of demotion and humiliation. Meanwhile,a few months after, the tribals of the North Western Frontier Province invaded Jammu and Kashmir from the west, which eventually resulted in the formation of Azad Kashmir Government at Muzaffarabad and the accession of Jammu and Kashmir to India. Maharaja Hari Singh signed the Instrument of Accession on 26 October, enabling the Indian forces to land in Srinagar on 27 of the month. These new developments put the Gilgit Scouts into motion as well.

On 31 October 1947, Gilgit Scouts rebelled. The J&K State forces were no match to the disciplined and efficient Gilgit Scouts trained in the British fashion by the army. Brigadier Ghansara Singh, the Governor, was arrested and the troops of Jammu and Kashmir were massacred. A provisional government was formed under the command of Major Brown at Gilgit. On 2 November 1947, Gilgit was handed over by the Gilgit Scouts to Pakistan. The Pakistani army later brought the remaining areas (now known as the Northern Areas in Pakistan comprising Gilgit, Ghizr, Diamer, Skardu and Ganche) under the control of the Dominion of Pakistan. With this, an area of about 28,000 square miles of Jammu and Kashmir became the part of Pakistan.[4]

Parallel to the developments in Gilgit, further in the south-west of Kashmir, in Poonch, a simmering discontent against the high handed policies of the Maharaja was brewing among the locals. The cause was the arbitrary imposition of taxes and heavy-handed realisation of the same by the J&K government. Until 1936, Poonch had enjoyed the status of a semi-autonomous state under a Dogra king, who was unceremoniously ousted by Maharaja Hari Singh in that year. The removal of their King deeply hurt the sentiments of the Poonchis. The King and the Queen had been greatly loved by their subjects, most of whom were Muslims. It is said that the women of Poonch spread out their *dupattas* as carpets on the road for the Queen to walk on when she left the palace on foot.[5] The annexation of Poonch by Maharaja Hari Singh was followed by the imposition of multiple cesses on individual goats, sheep and cattle, and a tax on entering the forest. Hardest hit were the pastoralists of Poonch, again almost all of whom were Muslims.[6] A 'no tax' campaign by the taxpayers in June 1947 was brutally suppressed by the Maharaja. The State forces, consisting mainly of Hindus and Sikhs, burnt houses indiscriminately, irrespective of whether the homeowners had participated in the revolt or not. This was enough to stoke a deep sense of humiliation among the Poonchis. Poonch and the surrounding areas were inhabited largely by the Sudhan Poonchi Musalmans[i-n] who belonged to one of the major tribes living in the districts of Poonch, Sudhanoti Bagh and Kotli.

In the Second World War, the Sudhans had contributed around 60,000 soldiers to the British army. Now demobilized, they were living in their homes in Poonch. The misery brought on by heavy taxation and the royal high handedness agitated the former soldiers. People's resistance was countered with repression by the state forces. Many of the Sudhans fled to nearby tribal areas of North West Frontier Province, which by then had been included in Pakistan. Though National Conference led by Sheikh Abdullah came in support of the Poonchi people, the mood was rebellious, and the rebels preferred weapons over dialogue. They narrated their tales of woes to the other tribesmen, who they shared a cultural affinity with. The ruthless state-response aggravated the sentiments of the tribesmen and pushed them to invade Kashmir. The news of massacre of the Mussalmans in other parts of the country, particularly East Punjab, at the hands of the Hindus and the Sikhs, also served as a contributing factor that further agitated and motivated them. Muslim officers, posted in the NWFP, extended their support via arms and ammunition to the Poonchi rebels. Notable among those officers was Iskander Mirza. Later, Iskander Mirza was to become the Governor General of Pakistan in 1955 and then the first President of the nation in 1956 (only to be deposed by his subordinate, Ayub Khan, in October, 1958). The Prime Minister of NWFP provided all logistical support to the rebels and also as to those who joined them. Meanwhile, by August 1947, as brought to the notice of the Indian government by Major Onkar Singh Kalkat, the Pakistani army under the code name 'Operation Gulmarg' had simultaneously planned the invasion of Kashmir with the objective of its annexation into the dominion of Pakistan. As per this plan, 'Lashkars' comprising Swati, Afridi, Waziri and Mehsud tribesmen (numbering about 5000) backed by Pakistani Army regulars under the command of Major Akbar Khan (codenamed 'Tariq'), eventually invaded the State on 22 October. The same day-Muzaffarabad and Domel, and by 24 October-Baramula (which was less than 50 miles from Srinagar) fell to tribal Lashkars. The Azad Kashmir Government was formed on 24 October[7] at Muzaffarabad.

Maharaja Hari Singh though unable to defend his State was not ready to accede to any of the dominion. He still wanted to maintain the independent status for his State.

However, as the tribesmen entrenched themselves in Baramula and the fall of Srinagar became imminent, Maharaja requested military help from India. The help came instantly but with a heavy price for him. Jammu and Kashmir was to accede to India. And so he had to put his signatures on the Instrument of Accession. Maharaja agreed to and signed the document on 26 October, 1947. The Instrument of Accession signed by Maharaja as 'Shriman Mahender Raj Rajeshwar Maharajadhiraj Sir Hari Singh ji, Jammu and Kashmir Naresh Tatha Tibbet adi Deshadhipati', was accepted by Lord Mountbatten, the then Governor General of India, on 27 October, 1947.

Indian troops landed the same day in Srinagar with the help of Indian Air Force. Tribesmen were held back and Srinagar was saved for India. By then, the tribesmen, and the locals who had turned against Maharaja, with the support of Pakistani regulars had formed the Azad Kashmir Government at Muzaffarabad. War that ensued between the two Dominions, which went on for more than a year, eventually came to an end through a UN sponsored ceasefire on 1 January, 1949.

The ceasefire agreement stopped the war but could not resolve the contentious issue of Jammu and Kashmir. Kashmiri people found themselves divided between two hostile countries as India Held Kashmir (IHK) and Pakistan Held Kashmir (PHK). Their hostile attitude towards each other became a benchmark for the test of their loyalty to their respective countries.

Neither of the countries was satisfied with its acquisitions for both of them wanted the entirety of Jammu & Kashmir (J&K). Yet, the fact is, both of them were in a win-win situation.

They each acquired a sizeable chunk of the territory of J&K, which, as per the Indian Independence Act, did not belong to them. They celebrated their victories by honouring their soldiers with military decorations, though many were awarded posthumously. The Indian government awarded its highest military award, the Param Vir Chakra, to five of its soldiers-Major Somnath, Lance Naik Karam Singh, Second Lieutenant Ram Raghoba Rane, Naik Jadunath Singh and Company Havildar Major Piru Singh (the first three being posthumous). Pakistan honoured Captain Raja Muhammad Sarwar with its highest military award Nishan-e- Haider and Naik Saif Ali with Hilal-e-Kashmir, both posthumously. Some other soldiers were also decorated with a lesser degree of import.

The question *what* and *why* ?

The two Dominions tried their best to uphold their territorial interests. What was forgotten in the episode was the interest of the people of Jammu and Kashmir; they were torn apart, never to meet again. Thousands were killed, displaced, and were made to suffer multiple mental and physical injuries. An unknown number of women were abducted, raped and forced in to brothels. According to some estimates, over 30,000 men, women and children were killed at the hands of the invaders in Rajauri city.[8]

Each country lost about 1500 soldiers.

Presumably, all the soldiers must have fought to their utmost best, but not each of them was rewarded. The fortunate who returned alive, narrated stories of hardships in the battlefields to their kinsmen and acquaintances, who were already languishing in acute poverty at home. The odd circumstances aggravated by the cold weather were no less hostile than the enemy. The two dominions celebrated the valour of those who died for the cause of Kashmir, while their families were to mourn their loss for ever, many of whom were the sole bread earners of their families and the only hope for their future. Soldiers of the erstwhile British Raj fought a disastrous war with their own brother soldiers, albeit divided into two warring States by then. Ironically, the same soldiers about two years ago had been fighting side by side for the British in Europe, Africa and Asia.

The story of a soldier, Brigadier Mohammad Usman, who lost his life fighting for India is an example of the irony of the circumstances. As a soldier of the Raj and a resident of the Indian dominion, he had been given the option of joining the Pakistani army or to remain with India. At the time, Brigadier Mohammad Usman, a resident of Bibipur in the district of Azamgarh in India, was posted in the 10th Baluch Regiment as a Major. The Pakistani leadership tried to persuade him into opting for the Pakistani army but he opted to remain with India. Consequently, he had to leave the Baluch Regiment, which was to become a part of the Pakistan Army. He was transferred to the Dogra Regiment. Unfortunately, very soon, fighting erupted between the two nations over the issue of Kashmir. Usman was posted in the 15th Parachute Brigade at the time. His Brigade had the responsibility of holding back the intruders and regaining the territories of the State of J&K lost to Pakistan. He regained Jhanger and defended Naushera valiantly but was killed by enemy on 3 July 1948. His defence of Naushera earned him the title, 'The Lion of Naushera' or '*Naushera ka Sher*'. Later, posthumous, he was awarded Mahavir Chakra, the second highest gallantry award, by the Government of India.

Had Usman not opted for India and stayed with the Pakistan army, he might have fought against the Indian army, manned by his own brother soldiers, fighting on whose side he eventually sacrificed his life. He is said to be dubbed a 'kafir' by Pakistan. The Azad Kashmir Government had announced a reward of Rs. 50,000 on his head. In India, he was venerated as true symbol of assumed inclusive secularism. His grave was placed next to the grave of Dr. M A Ansari, a renowned Nationalist leader of the pre independence era[9]. It was one of the many other ironies of destiny, friends fought against friends on the basis of their political affinity to India or Pakistan. People's interests were sacrificed at the altar of the false notion of nationalism and patriotism.

Chronologically, Junagarh was the first 'princely state' to spoil the relations, already marred by the partition, between India and Pakistan. Geographically, it was on the Indian side of the Radcliffe Line. However, as per the provisions of the Indian Independence Act, its ruler, Nawab Muhammad Mahabat Khanji III, was free to take any decision. The Nawab took a decision. He acceded to Pakistan on the day India got its independence, 15th August 1947.

After signing the instrument of accession, the Nawab sent the same to Pakistan for approval. The instrument was approved by the Constituent Assembly of Pakistan and countersigned by its Governor General, Quaid-e-Azam Muhammad Ali Jinnah, on 16 September 1947. The accession to Pakistan was objected to by a majority of population of Junagarh, which was Hindu and represented 80% population of the state. As per Indian accounts, a good chunk of the minority Muslims also did not approve of the decision. People rose in revolt.

Unable to suppress the rebellion by his own subjects, the Nawab along with his family members fled to Pakistan on 25 October. Provincial Government was formed at Junagarh which demanded the abrogation of the State's accession to Pakistan. Sir Shahnawaz Bhutto, the Diwan of Junagarh, tried to control the situation in favour of the accession but failed. On the initiative of the Provisional Government, Junagarh was officially incorporated into India through a notification on 8 November 1947 by the Government of India. Next day, the charge of the state was handed over by the state's civil administration to the Indian Government. Indian Army entered the city, Pakistan protested.

A 'princely state' which had already been acceded to Pakistan by its ruler was forcibly included into the Dominion of India in a violation of the Indian Independence Act, Pakistan had argued. By 9 November, for all purposes, Junagarh had become a part of India. About a year later, India held a plebiscite on 28 November 1948. As expected, the vote went in favour of India. With this final approval of the masses, Junagarh was merged into India. Apparently, Jammu Kashmir was not the lone thorn in Indo Pak relations.

This was also the period when thousands of kilometres away, Europe had finally begun to learn the futility of conflicts, clashes and wars fought for territorial gains. It was realised that long-term benefits were not achievable through enmity and fights over territorial expansion but rather through a close and friendly collaboration between countries towards economic development. Now in Europe, foes of yesteryears were turning into mutually understood friends of today. By the beginning of the second half of the Twentieth Century, the Europeans began to sit across the table to discuss issues of mutual economic and social development.

The process was given a kick-start by the three North European countries-the Netherlands, Belgium and Luxembourg in 1944 when they came together to explore the possibilities of a BENELUX Economic Union.

Four years later in 1948, they removed all economic barriers between themselves. The year 1951 ushered Europe into a new era of all round development as Germany, France and Italy, arch rivals for centuries, and BENELUX joined hands to form the European Coal and Steel Community. Past years' enmity was shelved to pave way for cooperation and mutual understanding. In the meantime in the Indian subcontinent, the Indian and Pakistani forces were fighting with each other over the territorial acquisitions in Kashmir. Indian forces' efforts to recapture Muzaffarabad were torpedoed by the British Indian Military Commanders in order to avoid a confrontation between the two armies, which were still manned by British officers.[ii-n] In order to secure Jammu and Kashmir through diplomacy, India moved to the UN Security

Council on 1 January 1948. It requested UNSC to restrain Pakistan from personal, military and civil participation in Jammu and Kashmir and to call upon Pakistani nationals to desist from taking any part in the affairs of the State and to also deny any kind of help, support or aid to the invaders in their Kashmir misadventure. The UN Resolution of the UN Commission for India and Pakistan (passed on 13 August 1948) called first, for ceasefire, second, for a truce agreement, and third, for the determination of the future status of the state of Jammu and Kashmir "in accordance with the will of the people and to that end, upon acceptance of the truce agreement, both Governments agree to enter into consultations with the Commission to determine fair and equitable conditions where by such free expression will be assured".

The Truce Agreement which was stated as 'Truce Agreement' in the UN Resolution as well as Part III, passed on 13 August 1948, was never fully complied with. The Truce Agreement laid down the following principles:

"A

1. As the presence of troops of Pakistan in the territory of the State of Jammu and Kashmir constitutes a material change in the situation since it was represented by the Government of Pakistan before the Security Council, the Government of Pakistan agrees to withdraw its troops from that state.
2. The Government of Pakistan will use its best endeavour to secure the withdrawal from the State of Jammu and Kashmir of tribesmen and Pakistani nationals not normally residents therein who have entered the State for the purpose of fighting.
3. Pending a final solution, the territory evacuated by the Pakistani troops will be administered by the local authorities under the surveillance of the Commission.

B

1. When the Commission shall have notified the Government of India that the tribesmen and Pakistani nationals referred to in part II, A, 2, hereof have withdrawn, thereby terminating the situation which was presented by the

Government of India to the Security Council as having occasioned the presence of Indian forces in the state of Jammu and Kashmir, and further, that the Pakistani forces are being withdrawn from the State of Jammu and Kashmir, the Government of India agrees to begin to withdraw the bulk of its forces from that state in stages to be agreed upon with the Commission.

2. Pending the acceptance of the conditions for a final settlement of the situation in the State of Jammu and Kashmir, the Indian government will maintain within the lines existing at the moment of the cease-fire the minimum strength of its forces which in agreement with the Commission are considered necessary to assist local authorities in the observance of law and order. The Commission will have observers stationed where it deems necessary.
3. The Government of India will undertake to ensure that the Government of the State of Jammu and Kashmir will take all measures within its powers to make it publicly known that peace, law and order will be safeguarded and that all human political rights will be granted.
4. Upon signature, the full text of the Truce Agreement or a communique containing the principles there of as agreed upon between the two Governments and the Commission, will be made public."

The issue of accession of the princely state of Hyderabad to the Dominion of India also became a matter of confrontation. Hyderabad, though ruled by a Muslim ruler, Mir Usman Ali, the seventh in the line of 'Nizam ul Mulk', had about a 85% Hindu population. Muslims were occupying key posts in the administration while the majority Hindus worked as factory workers, artisans, labourers and peasants[10]. It was landlocked, surrounded by the territory of India, and was well within the Indian side of the Radcliffe Line. As it was ruled by a Muslim ruler, Pakistan had its eye on it. India, on the other hand was not to allow it to fall in Pakistan's lap at any cost. For Sardar Vallabhbhai Patel, the then Deputy Prime Minister and Home Minister of India, an independent Hyderabad was like a cancer in the belly of India[11]. Ittihad-ul-Muslimeen and Razakars, though fewer in numbers, stood for an independent Hyderabad state, against the peoples' wishes who were represented by the Communists and the State Congress. The Nizam tried to crush the rebellion with a heavy hand but that only antagonised his Hindu subjects further. A military intervention led by Col. JN Chaudhuri on 13 September 1948, finally brought the 'princely state' under the dominion of India. On 17 September, the Nizam announced a ban on the Razakars in a radio address and appealed to his people to live in peace and harmony. Hyderabad was thus merged with the Dominion of India. Pakistan had no claim over Hyderabad nor it had any reasonable justification to interfere in its affairs.

Geographically, Hyderabad was to India as Kalat was to Pakistan. However, geographically Kalat had an advantage-it had a coast line along the Makran coast. The Khan of Kalat on 11 April 1947, much before Mountbatten presented his plan on 3 June 1947, had announced his decision to make Kalat a sovereign State. Four months later, when Independence of India Act empowered 'princely states' to choose the options given to them, one of them to remain independent, the Khan declared independence of Kalat on 12 August 1947. But it was not accepted by Pakistan and as in other parts of the erstwhile British India, Kalat was annexed to the dominion of Pakistan in a military action on 1 April 1948. The Khanet of Kalat and the Baluchis could never reconciled themselves with their inclusion in the State of Pakistan. The Baluch resistance continued. In September, 1974 Bhutto-government engaged Miraj fighter bombers and Iran supplied Gunship helicopters and around 80,000 troops to suppress the Baluch rebellion spearheaded by Baloach Peoples Liberation Front. The battle took the life of at least 9000 Baluchs. The rebellion was quelled but the discontentment remained simmering beneath the ground of superfluous tranquillity, against the federal government of Pakistan.

Under the Radcliffe Boundary Award, the districts of Gurdaspur and Firozpur in Punjab, despite the fact that they had a Muslim majority, were allotted to Indian side. Firozpur had the headworks of the Upper Bari Doab Canal system which irrigated the lands of Punjab in Pakistan. It also housed an arsenal depot.[12] As per Pakistan's historians, Firozpur had initially been given to Pakistan but at the intervention of

Mountbatten, a few days ahead of the Award becoming public,was shown on the Indian side of the Radcliffe line. Gurdaspur was the district which provided an effective land link between India and Kashmir. The inclusion of Gurdaspur to Pakistan would have deprived India from the only available land route to Kashmir. Thankfully, as many facts and speculations were not revealed till then, the two dominions did not come to fight over such issues of discord.

Chapter - II

The Hot Summer and the Muddy Ground

15th of August – Doom's Day for many a poor

India and Pakistan became independent on 15 August 1947. Lord Mountbatten, the Governor General of undivided British India, addressed the Constituent Assembly of Pakistan on 14 August, stating clearly that Pakistan would be an independent dominion the 'other day'. Pakistan there after celebrated 14 August, as its deliverance day in the ensuing years.

Officially, these dates were the days for celebration observed as such throughout both the dominions. However, for millions of people across the two new States, the days preceding and following their Independence Day were the days of mourning, the days for remembrance. Independence developed a deep connection with their misery and destruction.

Once the British decision to leave India by June 1948 was made public on 20 February 1947, the Muslim League's demand for a separate homeland for Muslims grew loud to louder. An environment of communal disharmony and mistrust began brewing that manifested itself in communal clashes and bloodshed at many places. Hell broke loose in the spring of 1947 on both the sides of the assumed borders of future India and Pakistan. Notably, there were no officially recognised borders between the two till the Radcliffe line came in to effect.

The Radcliffe Award was deliberately delayed by the British and it was notified on 16 August, 1947, only after the two Dominions came into being. Where and who started communal riots first, always remained a big question only to be answered in conflicting and contradicting explanations. As a community, Hindus, Sikhs and Muslims were the perpetrators but also the sufferers. The great Calcutta killings subsequent to the call for "Direct Action" on 16 August 1946, the riots in Bihar, Noakhali, Garh Mukteshwar and Rawalpindi massacres had set the ground for mass exodus much before Lord Mountbatten announced the British Plan for India's partition on 3 June 1947.

The leaders of the Indian National Congress and the Muslim League, who were also the initial and immediate beneficiaries of the plan, agreed immediately. They failed to give even an iota of thought to the problem of shifting a massive population from the territory of one dominion to the the other. On the 3 of June, when Mountbatten announced his plan on All-India Radio, he was followed by Nehru, Jinnah and Baldev Singh (as a Sikh representative) on the microphone.[1]

It has also been claimed that in the beginning, Quaid-e-Azam Muhammad Ali Jinnah, Jawahar Lal Nehru and Liaqat Ali Khan had opposed the migration by urging their terrified populations to remain in place.[2] Yet, it is hardly believable that leaders of such immense ability, who had been instrumental not only in ensuring the exit of as great a power as Britain but also the partition of India, failed to foresee such obvious consequences of the partition. The high-ups among the former subjects of British India joined the race to grab offices of recognition vacated by the British in politics, military, judiciary and bureaucracy.

Not more than half a million Muslims with an allegiance to the ideas of the Muslim League left India for Pakistan. To them, they were *Mohajirs*, just like the men and women who had left Mecca for Medina accompanying Prophet Mohammad (pbh) in 622 AD, in search of better pastures in the new land of promises awaiting them. A majority of the people out of a total of about 72 lakh Muslim migrants (65 lakh to western and 7 lakh to eastern wing of Pakistan) did not leave their erstwhile homeland of their own volition. They were forced to sever all connections including emotional, with their motherland by politically oriented decisions. Hindus and Sikhs living in the lands likely to become a part of future Pakistan, had also to leave their homes for future India. To avoid the risk of being killed and hurt otherwise at the hands of communaly hostile mobs, they preferred another risk of fleeing from their homes, albeit under the shadow of terror. Several of them were killed or injured and many of the women were abducted, molested, raped or sent to brothels. Hindu-Sikh women in order to save themselves from the rampaging Muslim crowds, preferred to commit suicide by jumping into wells. Some hapless women offered themselves to be killed by their own kinsmen. The villages of Thoa Khalsa, Choa, Thamali, Thoa, Nara and Bewal in the Rawalpindi district stand testimony to the inhumane acts committed by the invading Muslim crowds. Their kith and kin who survived the carnage and their descendants were observing those days as "Martyrs' Day" in the successive years. One such day was the 13 of March.[3]

Fleeing people from both the sides took air, sea and land routes subject to availability, approachability and affordability, to travel to the dominion meant for them. Airways were availed by those who were politically and economically powerful or those who were in government jobs. Their numbers were in a few thousand. About one lakh and thirty three thousand travelled through the Arabian Sea in steamers and boats. Trains kept ferrying unfortunate migrants in both the directions. Stories abound of many trains arriving with the corpses of passengers and no passenger left alive to tell the tale of the massacre. Around 28 lakh travelled by train in both the directions across the borders.[4] The majority had to follow the long trails of refugees travelling on foot, the processions growing larger with every new refugee. These were known as '*Karvan*' or '*Kafila*'. The large columns of these people consisted of hundreds of thousands, sometimes three to four lakh of people, spreading to miles in length. Armed gangs were hidden in farms and bushes alongside the roads to ambush them. Women were the most susceptible to these attacks. Many of them were dragged out from the *Kafila/Karvan* who were unable to defend themselves.

The human debris left behind by those columns was terrible, the entire length of roadside from Lahore to Amritsar along which so many passed, became a long, open graveyard.[5]

The leaders of the two Dominions did not seem seized enough of the problem. On 17 August in 1947, two days after the independence, the two Prime Ministers, Jawahar Lal Nehru of India and Liaqat Ali Khan of Pakistan, met at Ambala. The exchange of population was agreed upon. Ironically, by then, an approximate 10 lakh people had already crossed the borders and many others were on their way.[6] Interestingly, they agreed on the issues which had already taken place and had been continuing for months before their agreement. The great deluge, the '*Pralaya*', the '*Dozakh*' or '*Narak*', hell to millions of people who migrated or were unable to migrate was on in its fullest. These victims of freedom ushered in an era which officially is known as Independence but proved a curse upon them for no sin of their commission. The month of August in 1947, was the holy month of Ramzan for Muslims and Rakshabandhan for Hindus. The festivals brought exodus, injury, death, epidemics, hunger, indignity, mental trauma and loss of property, society and motherland to them. Perpetrators and the victims both came from within their own society. Victims and criminals were more or less equally spread in all communities-Hindu, Sikh and Muslims. The perpetrators indulged in the most irreligious acts in the name of their religions. Women, apart from being raped and murdered, were forced to live with the men who were one among their abductors, sold to brothels and kept to entertain the government officials.

Anis Kidwai, who was intensively engaged in the recovery of abducted women in India, wrote in her book, 'Azadi ki Chaon Mein':

> "In all of this sometimes a girl would be killed or she would be wounded. The 'good stuff' would be shared among the police and army, the 'second rate stuff' would go to everyone else. And then these girls would go from one hand to another and then another, and after several would turn up in hotels to grace their decor, or they would be handed over to police officers, in some place to please them."[7]

Women on both the sides of the border met with such intensely barbaric treatment. The independence was no moment of joy for them. They were happy a few days ago as the slaves of their colonial masters, independence ruined their lives forever. They had to carry the burden of their mortal body with a tormented soul like slaves of circumstances, for rest of their life.

Pressed by the public anger, self-righteousness prevailed upon the governments, and operations to recover the abducted women in both the dominions were launched. The Indian government submitted a list of around 23,000 women to Pakistani authorities. Some of them were rescued. But as many abducted Hindu and Sikh women, knowing well that their family members would not accept them, considering them desecrated, chose to remain with their abductors or as they were living in Pakistan. Those who returned to India had to deal with the ignominy and pain of rejection by their family members. Thankfully, the problem was less difficult on the part of Muslim women in Pakistan.

Indian Prime Minister Jawahar Lal Nehru, on learning about the problem of refusal, appealed to people, "unwillingness on the part of their relatives to accept those girls and women back in their homes.....is a most objectionable and wrong attitude to take and any social custom that supports this attitude must be condemned. These girls and women require our tender and loving care and their relatives should be proud to take them back and give them every help."[8] The speech might have enhanced the prestige of Nehru, but was of no avail to the unfortunate women, the victims of independence. Even the pamphlets circulated describing the home coming of Sita from Lanka, rescued from her abductor Ravana and her acceptance by Lord Ram, could not motivate the family members to admit them back into their homes.

The rescued women had the option to, first, join their family, and second, to stay in Ashrams. The third option offered to those who had become mothers was to leave their wards in Ashram and join their families. In practice, the privilege to choose between these options was not of the women but of their families. Out of a list of around 23,000 Hindu and Sikh women submitted to government of Pakistan, only 8,000 returned to India. Many who returned, rejected by their families, had to spend the remainder of their lives in Ashrams established by the government at various places. What left with them were the torturous memories haunting them forever.

The Police forces were not trained to meet such exigencies. Nor did they remain disciplined and impartial in their duties. In many situations, they favoured the looting crowds of their co-religionists. Many of them involved themselves in loot, arson and abductions. One of such recorded incidence is related to Sita Ram, the Dy. Superintendent of Police, Ambala, under whose supervision a refugee train to Pakistan was attacked on 1September, taking the lives of 1000 refugees.[9] Who initiated the attacks always remains a critical question to be answered, but retaliatory actions on the trains carrying the refugees to either side with the complicity of the police forces frequently met with such fates. The railway track of about hundred and seventy kms (106 miles) between Sialkot and Amritsar was strewn with Sikh corps. Both sides of the road from Amritsar to Lahore, a road of about 50 kms. length, too, turned into a massive graveyard[10] .

The Sikh 'Shahidi Jatthas' and 'The Muslim National Guards' became rallying points for attacking on Muslim and Hindu localities respectively. 'Shahidi Jatthas' involvement in burning and plundering of the Muslim villages of Jullandhar and Amritsar in east Punjab was quite visible. The killing and burning of houses of Hindu and Sikhs for twenty four hours on 25-26 August in Sheikhupura were attributed to such Muslim outfits. In Sheikhupura, the Sikh women to save their honour jumped to death in two wells of Namdhari Gurudwaras. As the tales of such massacres of Hindus and Sikhs were narrated by the survivors to their faith followers in India, the hell broke out on Muslims in Delhi. At Karolbagh and elsewhere in Delhi, houses were marked with certain colour marks for the identification of Muslim houses. Mobs of Hindus and Sikhs came in the dark of the night in groups and attacked the Muslim houses. Muslims invented their own security system by guarding the streets themselves and putting red or green lights, former indicating 'A danger' of an attack, the latter 'All Clear'.[11] The hapless Muslim women of Karolbagh had to pay for the sins committed by their faith followers in West Punjab (Pakistan).

Refugees, who were Mohajirs something akin to seventh century migrants to Madina in their own interpretation, were not as welcome guests as they had expected, in Pakistan. In the wake of Hindu and Sikh exodus, since the local Muslim population had occupied the vacated properties, hence did not like to be allotted to the immigrants by the government. The immigrants were to get the properties in proportion to what they had left in India. The powerful and influentials were in quest of getting more and more and in some cases many of them got more than that what they had in India. People living at margins in India, were still to live at margins, most often, in worse conditions in the promised land of Indian Muslims. The provincial governments were not very enthusiastic to accept and settle the refugees. Most of the refugees from east Punjab settled in west Punjab occupying the vacated lands of the fleeing Hindus and Sikhs, with comparative ease. They spoke almost the same language and observed same culture as of the existing local population and many had pre partisan relations with them. But those who were going to Sindh had to confront with an unwelcoming population. Karachi, the capital and the most industrialised city of Pakistan, was most sought after destination for majority of the Mohajirs of north India, Gujarat, Hyderabad and Central India. However, neither the local population nor the state government was enthusiastic to receive them. The opposition came to the fore early in 1948, when Ayub Khuhro, the then Prime Minister of Sindh Province, made it clear that Sindh would not be able to rehabilitate more than 1.5 lakh refugees during the first half of that year. By then, about 4.64 lakh refugees from United Provinces and 3.30 lakh refugees from Delhi had entered Pakistan, majority of them with a hope to settle in Karachi, but only around 3 lakh refugees could be accommodated in the entire province of Sindh. This created a rift between the Federal government and the State government voicing the sentiments of the Sindhi people. Khuhro was rebuked by Raja Ghazanfar Ali, The Minister for Refugees and Rehabilitation, in a meeting on 23 February 1948, for his stand not to receive more refugees. His opposition to accommodate more refugees was termed "against the teaching of Islam and in direct contravention to the principle on which we fought for the achievement of Pakistan". This led the eventual downfall of Khuhro and the beginning of the Sindhi nationalism as against the idea of the Muslim State of Pakistan, simultaneously.[12]

While in 1941 Muslims formed 42% of the total population of Karachi (3.65 lakh- out of which Hindu, Sikhs and other Hindu sects were about 54%), in 1951 Census Muslims were contributing 96.1% to the total population of 10.65 lakh. Out of this population, Mohajirs were 6.126 lakh or 57.55% of the total population. Centrifugal tendencies within the Islamic society of Karachi emerged in two hostile groups, natives and non natives or Sindhis and Mohajirs in other words, began to grow up. Mohajir's population in the major cities of Sindh; Karachi (57.55%), Hyderabad (66.08%), Sukkur (54.08%), Mirpur Khas (68.42%) and Nawabshah (54.79%) was more than 50% of the total population of the respective cities. The demographic change in the population was bound to bring up new political realities and conflicts.[13] Contrary to their expectations, Mohajirs of the deliverance did not find Ansars to welcome them in Pakistan. The divide began to become wide to wider and reached to such uncompromising situation, as early as in 1954, that the Sindhi nationalist leader GM Syed declared that all those who had entered Sindh after 1954 should be depived of their civic and political rights and the influx of the aliens be stopped.[14]

Demand was huge, fulfilment was small. Refugee's demands were not met as per their expectations, elsewhere also. In Multan refugees protested near the residence of Police Superintendent by blocking the road which was responded with police lathi charge upon them. The disenchantment with the new dispensation compelled them to raise anti-Pakistan slogans.[15]

India, owing to its large size, had almost no problem in settling down the population of about 72 lakh migrants from Pakistan. Delhi the capital city of India, itself accommodated about 10 lakh refugees. As per census figures of both the countries in 1951 refugees were 2% and 10% in the total population of India and Pakistan respectively.

The decision to predate the independence to India from June 1948 to 15 August in 1947, about a year earlier, was a decision just to relieve Great Britain from the burden of liability of a land which was gradually proving a costly burden on the British Empire. Lord Mountbatten, the then Viceroy and the British Governor General of India, without assigning any consideration to the mass exodus and the problems arising from it on communal lines, offered the British plan for the partition and consequent independence to India, on 3 June, allowing just two and half a month's time for further deliberations. British leaders seemed in haste to leave, Indian leaders to grab the opportunities in greed. When Maulana Abdul Kalam Azad, one of the most sagacious politicians of the subcontinent, put his apprehensions of communal disturbances arising out of the partition, Mountbatten rejected Azad's apprehensions and boasted, "At least on this question I shall give you the complete assurance. I shall see to it that there is no bloodshed and riot. I am a soldier and not a civilian. Once partition is accepted in principle, I shall issue orders to see that there are no communal disturbances anywhere in the country. If there should be the slightest agitation, I shall adopt the sternest measures to nip the trouble in the bud."[16]

Future events confirmed that Louis Francis Albert Victor Nicholas Mountbatten, First Earl Mountbatten of Burma, better known as Mountbatten was only a soldier, able enough to lead an army at war, but not to lead a country at birth. He failed, though with impunity, to fulfil the loud promises that he had made to Azad. Indeed, the Indian army under the command of General Sir Claude Auchinleck, was a disciplined force and largely stayed secular, even in most adverse situations, was not trained in performing the civilian duties and that too spread over to a large and scattered area. When violence erupted in Sikh populated areas in the Rawalpindi district, and carnage reached to unprecedented proportions in March, 1947 (6-13 March), Nehru requested the British Governor of Punjab to clamp the martial-law, the request was turned down citing the inadequacy of force. As the new state of Pakistan was to come in existence, a new Governor for the province of West Punjab was appointed. He celebrated his appointment by throwing a party on the evening of 15 August at Government house at Lahore. Lahore was engulfed with communal mayhem. As he himself later recalled there was no electricity in the town but the flames of the burning city of Lahore about half a miles away. The volleys of firing was going on. "Who was firing at who, no one knew and no one bothered to ask."[17] Mountbatten probably forgot or deliberately avoided such exigencies and situations to take into account.

Many historians and researchers in the subcontinent find a deliberate well-thought British strategy in delaying the award by one day of independence and pre-ponning the date of independence from June 1948 to 15 August 1947. Radcliffe was ready with the Award, they claim, but delayed its announcement at the behest of Mountbatten. Mountbatten's attitude was callous as he explained the reason for delay:

'without question, the earlier it was published, the more the British would have to bear responsibility for the disturbances which would undoubtedly result.' and 'the later we postponed publication, the less would the inevitable odium react upon the British.' There was a wide gap in what he said to Maulana AK Azad and what he had in his mind.[18] No help coming from the State, people were fleeing from their homes in distress. Easier was to let bloodshed go, difficult was to stop it. Those who were in powers were well aware of it and allowed the things to take their own course.

In the months, that accompanied the independence, the Punjab Boundary Force, created under the command of General Sir Rob Lockhart, was being commanded by Major General TW ('Pete') Rees with a 60,000 soldiers strength, proved insufficient to protect the lives of people from the trouble makers. Founded on 1 August 1947, it lasted only for a month and disbanded on 2 September.[19] Instead of strengthening and streamlining the security mechanism it was done off with its umbilical cord.

Indian leaders, Congress and Muslim League alike, too did not pay due attention to the formidable problem of shifting of such a large population and the violence which was sure to accompany the partition in a communally high charged environment. The writings had already been written on the walls in the communal riots at Calcutta, Noakhali, Mukteshwar, Rawalpindi and at several other places. The leaders in their zeal to enjoy self rule undermined the massacre of Hindu and Sikhs in the villages of the Rawalpindi district in early March and the retaliatory violence against the Muslims elsewhere in the country.

The Rawalpindi violence had been responded by Hindus against the minority Meos in the 'princely states' of Alwar and Bharatpur. By the month of June 1947 about 50 Muslim villages in the two 'princely states' had been destroyed. State forces personnel too involved themselves in loot and arson. Around one lakh Muslims fled from their homes, while around 30,000 lost their lives in the communal frenzy.

'The great Indian people' who had jointly fought the two world wars to save the empire of their British masters, standing together under the same flag (Union Jack), failed the test of unity when it came to their own discretion. Indians lost more than 74,000 soldiers in the first world war and 87,000 soldiers in the second world war, making together a figure of 1,61,000 martyrs for the cause of Great Britain. Around 12 lakh Indians in arms joined the Allied Forces in various continents. During the First World War, they had been exhorted by the British government by issuing a proclamation, that said, "you are descendents of men who have been great rulers and warriors. ....you will recall the glories of your race. Hindu and Muslim will be fighting side by side with British soldiers and our gallant French allies... In battle, your will remember that your religion enjoin on you, that to give your life doing your duty is your highest reward. From Mosques and temples prayers are ascending to the God of all. You will fight for your King Emperor and your faith, so that the history will record the doings of Indian sons......."[20] and they proved themselves worthy of that, the master was saved from the annihilation. But the entire scenario had changed now. The fight, undeclared and unrecognized though, was within. The mortalities of Indians were much more than what they were in the two world wars, a staggering figure of 5 lakh. This was the most conservative estimate. There was no counting of deads. Others assess mortalities up to 10 lakh and even up to 20 lakh. More than one crore and twenty five lakh people rendered homeless. The independence to their countries was meaningless to the victims and families who suffered the carnage, particularly the women who were abducted, raped or pushed to brothels. The children born to mothers as a consequence to rape were fatherless and hence illegitimate, in the context of Indian social system. For them these were the days of hell in their memories.

Mountbatten had his own plans, subjected to British interests. However, the Indian leaders, who after the partition became the proud leaders either of Pakistan or India, had the responsibility to address the problems arising out of partition of the country on communal lines. Partition did not come out of the blue. Many of the Hindu leaders, under the pressurising attitude of separatist Muslims, led by Muslim League, had supported the partition on the lines of Hindu-Muslim divide. Many Muslim individuals and organizations, including political outfits were against the idea of partition. Prominent among those organizations were, Dar-ul-ulum Deoband, Jamait Ulama-i-Hind, Majlis-i-Ahrar and the Khaksar Movement. They believed that Pakistan would not be able to solve the problems of Indian Muslims after the partition; they would be exposed to the Hindus' distrust and suspected of disloyalty to India. Not all Muslims would be able to migrate to Pakistan and the minority Muslims unable to migrate would have no leverage over Hindu majority while at the same time Pakistan being a small and weaker state, would be unable to protect Muslims.[21] But once partition was agreed upon all suffered, as they were termed aliens and Pakistanis by non Muslims in India and those who were not with Muslim League were singled out as anti Pakistanis in Pakistan. For instance in the United Provinces, which was deemed a fortress for separatist Muslims, more than one third of Muslims voted against Muslim League in Muhammadan seats in General Assembly Elections held in 1946.[22] Even in the Muhammadan (MU&MR) seats out of a total of 7.87 lakh votes polled, only 5.13 lakh (65%) voted for Muslim League, having 2.74 lakh (35%) voted for Congress, Nationalist Muslims and independents.

VD Savarkar had termed the partition, "safer to diagnose and treat deep-seated disease than to ignore it" and asserted "Let us bravely face unpleasant facts as they are; India cannot be assumed today to be a unitarian and homogenous nation, but on the contrary there are two nations in the main, The Hindus and Muslims in India."[23]

Baba Saheb Bhim Rao Ambedkar had observed that, there was "no common cycle of participation (between Hindus and Muslims) for a common achievement" and "In fact the heroes of the Muslims were the foes of the Hindus. The factors that divided the two peoples were far more significant than those that bound them together."[24]

Some six years before Muhammad Iqbal's presidential address to the Muslim League in 1930, Lala Lajpat Rai had expressed his views as, "under my scheme the Muslims will have four Muslim states :

1. Pathan Province of the North-West Frontier,
2. Western Punjab,
3. Sindh,
4. Eastern Bengal.

It means a clear partition of India in to a Muslim India and Non-Muslim India"[25]

The Madras Legislative Congress Party on the initiative of Raj Gopalachari, in April 1942, passed the Resolution, "to sacrifice the chances of the formation of a National Government.....and that it has become necessary to choose the lesser evil and acknowledge the Muslim League's claim for separation."[26] The issue of partition had remained a key subject matter in both the national parties' meetings since Lahore Resolution was passed by the Muslim League in 1940 for the creation of a separate homeland for Muslims. Thus, the partition was an outcome of a series of prolonged discussions, centred around the sheer politics of sharing of the power and territories. Communal riots were sometimes used as tools to bolster the arguments in favour of separation. The apathy of the leaders towards the problems arising out of partition to masses who were forced to flee from their homes was quite discernible.

Quaid-e-Azam Muhammad Ali Jinnah, in his Independence Day speech on 14 August 1947, thanked many people, such as His Majesty the King of Great Britain, Lady Mountbatten, the government servants – civil and armed forces and Head of States of USA and Nepal who had sent him the messages of goodwill and friendship. He promised constant efforts to work for the welfare and wellbeing of all communities in Pakistan. But he did not utter even a word about the migration and the hardships faced by the refugees. Sadly enough, in his first Presidential address to the Constituent Assembly of Pakistan on 11 August 1947, he spoke about several issues; bribery, corruption, black marketing, nepotism and maintenance of law and order as the first duty of the government, but escaped from the daunting problem of communal mayhem, exodus and migration and the relief and rehabilitation of the victims of deliverance. Almost at the same time, when Jinnah was delivering his 'thanks giving speech' at Karachi, Jawahar Lal Nehru, the first Prime Minister of India, was rendering his famous speech , 'Tryst with Distiny', during the intervening night of 14-15 August, with his dexterous and impeccable English in his husky yet baritone voice. He promised freedom and opportunity to his people and informed them about their sovereignty. As in the thanks giving speech of Jinnah, Nehru too did not utter even a word in his midnight speech in the Constituent Assembly about the people's suffering due to partition which had thrown them in the worst situation. Probably, knowing well that the migration, as an offshoot of partition, was their own creation, the then leaders of undivided India, found it expedient to ignore it. 'At the stroke of the midnight hour, when the world' was sleeping millions of unfortunates of erstwhile 'India' were 'awoke' to face horror and pain of the Independence - the partition. Nehru missed or deliberately avoided the fact to mention.

The masses indeed, were to get the right to cast their vote, politicians were to enjoy their outcomes. The race among elites was to grab the plum posts in governance, legislatures, executives and judiciary, vacated by the British, poor masses were to struggle to make the both ends meet.

The British officers who played their role in partition received decorations for their indispensable and distinguished services. General Claude Auchinleck, the C-in-C of Indian army was elevated to Field Marshal and Mountbatten to Admiral of the Fleet, the highest post in British Navy.[27]

There was perhaps only one politician in the subcontinent who did not celebrate independence. On the day of independence when all the Congress men and Muslim Leagures were celebrating the independence at various places of the subcontinent, he was on a twenty four hour fast in Calcutta. Earlier on 14 August he had rejected any discussion on the celebration of Independence Day by reacting in disgust, "people are dying of hunger all around, "Do you wish to hold a celebration in the midst of this devastation?"[28] This person was seventy seven years old Mohandas Karamchand Gandhi.

There were many others, who did not like this sort of independence. Even those who expressed their dissent fell dwarfed before the political ambitions of those who had got mandate from the people in the elections held for Council of State and Legislative Assembly of India at the Centre and Legislative Council and Legislative Assemblies at the Provincial Levels. They were elected by an electorate which was conspicuous with the absence of majority of the Indian people. Seats at each level were earmarked as Muhammadan and non Muhammadan and in provincial legislatures Europeans and others also. The composition of electorate was hardly representative of the masses. For instance the population of United Provinces as per census 1941 was 5,65,35,170. In the General Elections held in 1946 only 68,28,778 were enrolled as the voters out of which only 20,48,425 polled their votes. This number of people who voted in the elections of 1946 in the United Provinces, was less than 5% of the total population of the province. They elected the members, whose eligibility was determined on the mandatory requirements of ownership of property and tax paid on income. For example following qualifications were mandatory for the two houses, Legislative Council and Legislative Assembly, of the United Provinces :[29]

The requirement for the three categories are given under the numbers given against them :

The normal qualifications – (I)
Qualifications for SC – (II)
Qualifications for wives of electors – (III)

Sl. No.	*Qualification*	*Legislative Council*			*Legislative Assembly*		
		I	*II*	*III*	*I*	*II*	*III*
1.	Assessed to Income Tax on income of Rs. per annum	4,000	2,000	10,000	Any Income		
2.	Assessed to municipal income tax on income of Rs. per annum	-	-	-	150	-	200
3.	Owner/Occupier of house with rental value of Rs. per annum	-	-	-	24	12	36
4.	Assessed to land revenue of Rs. per annum	1,000	200	5,000	5	-	25
5.	Payment of under proprietary rent in Oudh of Rs. per annum	1,000	200	-	5	-	25
6.	Payment of rent as a tenant of Rs. per annum	1,500	500	-	10	-	50
7.	Kumaun provisions	Payment of rent revenue of Rs. 100 per annum			Holding an estate in fee simple; assessed to land revenue or rent; or having the status of "Khaikar" (=old cultivator, expropriietary cultivator)		

Some additional forms of franchise qualifications were also added for Legislative Council and Legislative Assembly.

These additional franchise were granted to title holders such as Diwan, Sardar, Khan, Rai or Rae Bahadur; pensioners; office holders, judge of the federal or any High Court, chief of Judicial Commissioners courts in India; the Mayor or Sheriff of Madras, Bombay or Calcutta; Non-Official chairpersons of any central co-operative society operating within UP and non-official chairman of a district or Municipal Board in UP for Legislative Council. Likewise for legislative assembly additional qualifications based on education and military retired pensioned and the properly designated representatives of the Shilpkars in Kumaun were also extended in 1946 to make the franchise a little more larger. Thus while the franchise was limited by qualifications the impact was infinite as the decision taken by the people elected by a limited and restricted electorate was to change the destiny of more than 36 crore people of the subcontinent.

Independence was achieved but at a high cost to human lives and values. Disenchanted with the then prevailing state of affairs, Faiz Ahemad "Faiz", a great poet of the subcontinent, lamented in "Subh-i-Azadi" (the dawn of Freedom) as following :

"Ye daag daag ujala ye shab gazida sahar,
Vo intizar tha jiska ye vo sahar to nahin.
Ye vo sahar to nahin jis ki arzoo lekar,
Chale thei yaar ki mil jayegi kahin na kahin.
Falak ke dasht mein taron ki akhiri manzil,
Kahin to hoga shab-e-sust mauj ka sahil.
Kahin to ja ke rukega safinaa-e-gham-e-dil."

(This light, smeared and spotted, this night-bitten dawn. This isn't surely the dawn we waited for so eagerly. This isn't surely the dawn with whose desire cradled in our hearts. We had set out, friends all, hoping We should somewhere find the final destination of the stars in the forests of heaven.)[30]

Enjoying the pre independence days with his friends in Bollywood at Bombay, Saadat Hasan Manto, could not understand which country he belonged to. He was not able to reconcile himself with the idea of partition. As for several others, partition of country meant separation from all of friends and neighbours, left behind. Every Muslim who went to Pakistan, had to leave many of his or her Muslim friends and relatives also, who did not leave India even in the most adverse conditions. The pain of partition finally found expression in Manto's epoch making story "Toba Take Singh". The story is about a lunatic, Bishan Singh, living in a lunatic asylum at Lahore in Pakistan, who was being transferred to India as per agreement between the two governments. Unconvinced with the partition of India the protagonist, Bishen Singh, lies down in the no man's land between the borders of India and Pakistan. He dies there as if he belonged to both the nations.

For Bade Ghulam Ali Khan and Barkat Ali Khan, the two brothers born to Ustad Ali Baksh Khan, a great exponent of Hindustani music, in Kasur near Lahore, the decision to choose between India and Pakistan became a complicated issue. The younger one, Barkat, stayed in Pakistan while the elder one, Bade Ghulam Ali Khan, after an indecisiveness of about a decade, opted for India.[31] But like millions of families across the subcontinent, the partition tore apart the family in to two rival countries.

The people who lost their lives consequent to the independence from the British were the millions of the hapless poor of the erstwhile India. Those wielding political power and influence seldom lost anything substantial. Even now, in the event of war and conflicts between the two countries, they hardly loose anything in men, money or anything else. The poor contribute soldiers to the army and lay their lives in the name of defending their motherlands. Some of them get commendation, citations and medals in lieu of their martyrdom, while majority of the soldiers killed secure only a paltry sum as pensions for their family members. Those wounded are very soon discharged or honourably retired from their services, leaving remaining years of their active life to their destiny. A 'Shaheed' for the media, leaves his parents, wives, sons and daughters in wilderness to struggle with the odds of life.

Chapter - III

Heat, Dust and Devastation Indo Pak Journey- A Saga of Mistrust, Misunderstanding and Misadventures

Mistrust, misunderstanding and misadventures are a few words that can briefly explain the Indo Pak relations. Pakistan was born on the assumption that Hindus and Muslims could not live together. For the supporters of the separate Muslim homeland, Islam was enough to bind a land with a number of sects, various ethnic groups with multiple cultures and diverse languages within it, in a single political entity. A distance of about one thousand miles between the two wings of Pakistan was brushed away as insignificant before the cohesive nature of Islam. A misunderstanding that India was determined to wipe out the State of Pakistan, courtesy to extremists in both the Nations and a sense of loss of Jammu and Kashmir to India, had always been a motivating force to Pakistani leadership to maintain a robust army to defend Pakistan from a monstrous India that was just waiting for an opportunity to swallow it. Added to it, was the desire of wresting India held Jammu and Kashmir (IHK) from India. There was no dearth of contentious issues to flare up the tension between the two. Politicians and the Non-State Actors and Radical groups were always to keep contentious issues alive for their personal benefits. Indian people could never reconcile with the truncation of their motherland known to them as 'Bharatvarsh'. For them it was hard to trust Pakistani politicians who had successfully manoeuvred the partition of erstwhile India on communal lines. These factors have often led to misadventures culminating into armed clashes and wars. Many a time wars and conflicts were averted with the intervention of foreign powers, establishing the inability of Indian and Pakistani leaders to sink their differences in the interest of peace and economic development of their people. From the very beginning of their birth in 1947, they always remained in conflicting terms. Abetment to terrorism and secessionism against each other have always been accorded high priorities. India and Pakistan left no opportunity to let each other down at the international forums. The ability and eloquence of the leaders to spit venom with full throat voices against each other at any forum, bilateral or multilateral, was regarded as an unquestioned credential to their patriotism.

They fought full-fledged wars at four junctures. Apart from the wars their armies clashed or came to very close to war like situations at least at ten occasions. Every time, conflicts were brought to an end through ceasefires, agreements or assurances, leaving the virus of mistrust intact. The interregnums between the two wars or conflicts were just preparation holidays for a new clash. Kashmir remained the reservoir of the issues to flare up the ugly and stupid passions of the people. These people include those also, who had hardly to do anything with the well being of the Kashmiri people. Shelling and the gunfire along the Line of Control (LoC) seldom came to rest. People living in villages close to LoC had no option but to take shelter to save them in their improvised self made bunkers or government buildings, leaving their farms and harvests at the mercy of securities forces.

Wars

1. First war: Over Jammu and Kashmir, 1947-48

In the wake of Great Britain leaving India on 15 August 1947, the 'princely state' of Jammu and Kashmir like other 'princely states' of India, had become free from all British obligations. In consonance to the Indian Independence Act, 1947, the 'princely states' were empowered to take any decision about their political status. But within three months of British departure, an invasion of Kashmir by Pashtoon Tribes of North Western Frontier Provinces of Pakistan, allegedly planned and logistically supported by the Pakistani armed forces, put the very existence of the State at peril. As the fall of State's capital,

Srinagar, became imminent on the intervening night of 25-26 October its ruler Hari Singh fled to Jammu.[1]

The occupation of the state by Pakistani tribesmen meant an end to the rule of Hari Singh and any respectable role to him in the future State of Pakistan. He opted to accede to India, an option to which he had never accorded a damn thought in the past. India accepted his request of sending Indian troops to the state. Crippled by the most adverse circumstances, Maharaja Hari Singh signed the Instrument of Accession with India on 26 October 1947 which was ratified by Mountbatten, the then Governor General of India, on 27 October. Indian army landed at Srinagar with the help of RIAF and started flushing the tribal Lashkars out from the territory of J&K. As the tribal Lashkars had the backing of Pakistani regulars under Major Akbar Khan, fight between the armies of two Dominions ensued, went on for about a year and came to an end by UN sponsored ceasefire on 1 January 1949. Meanwhile, the Government of Azad Kashmir had been formed at Muzaffarabad on 24 October. Seven days later of accession of Jammu and Kashmir to India the administration of Gilgit Agency was transferred by the Gilgit Scouts to Pakistan on 2 November 1947.[2]

By First January 1949 (the day on which UN sponsored cease fire came in to effect), an area of 13,297 sq.kms in Kashmir and 72,971 sq. kms of Gilgit and Baltistan had been occupied by Pakistan leaving an area of 1,35,265 sq.kms. to the former state of J&K which by then had acceded to India. India and Pakistan got a sizeable territory which had not been bequeathed to them under the Indian Independence Act. India was to loose again an area of about 37,300 sq.kms of Aksai Chin to People's Republic of China in 1962.

Judging from the viewpoint of long term repercussions, the Kashmir conflict inflicted a heavy cost in terms of loss of human lives and economic losses to both the countries. The Kashmir created a perpetual cause for conflicts in future. The issue of Kashmir was blown out of proportion by Pakistan. It made Kashmir the central issue before any negotiation putting the agenda of economic and social development to the backburner. Theoretically, as per Indian Independence Act, 1947, and the subsequent termination of the British suzerainty over Jammu and Kashmir, the state belonged to its erstwhile ruler Maharaja Mahender Bahadur Sir Hari Singh, or applying to democratic norms to its people. The territorial lust of Pakistan led it to exhort its Pakhtoon tribesmen to invade the State. The Pakistan plan threw the State in turmoil. It is also on record that much before the invasion by Pashtoon tribesmen; Pakistan had already set the process of its annexation through the policy of its economic strangulation in motion. The account submitted by Major Onkar Singh Kalkat about the Pakistan government's plan of invasion, to Indian Government on 20 October 1947,[3] was almost corroborated by Major General Mohammad Akbar Khan, the Pakistani army commander of the 'Operation Gulmarg'. Few years later in an interview published in the Defence Journal he admitted that within a few weeks of partition he was asked by Mian Iftikharuddin on behalf of Prime Minister Liaqat Ali Khan to prepare a plan (of invasion) for Kashmir[4] The tribal invasion and Pakistan's Gilgit policy to force the State to fall in the lap of Pakistan like a ripe fruit, compelled its ruler to accede to India. Pakistan did not approve J&K's accession to India and resorted to armed action. The armies of the two dominions came face to face against each other within a few months of their friendly parting off.

Had Kashmir remained independent, there would have been no clash over its acquisition between the two states. Pakistan's continued tirade against the accession of Kashmir to India and India's refusal to recognise Pakistan Held Kashmir (PHK) and Gilgit and Baltistan to Pakistan, have become the mother of all conflicts. Kashmir, known for its natural beauty often termed metaphorically as the Switzerland of India, could have been remained independent with a neutral status as Switzerland enjoys in Europe. In that situation, India, Pakistan, Afghanistan, Soviet Union (Tajikistan, separated from Kashmir by Afghanistan's Wakhan Corridor by a narrow land strip of a width of about 20 to 60 kms) and China would have been the guarantors of the independent status of Jammu and Kashmir with people enjoying democratic governance either with a Monarch as a constitutional and ceremonial head of the State as enjoyed by several states in Europe, or a democracy without any semblance of a monarchy .

2. Second war: Over Kashmir, 1965

The second Indo-Pak war had the prelude written over the marshy land of Rann of Kutch. The dispute had the genesis in the pre-independent India. During British time Kutch was a 'princely state' like many other princely states under British suzerainty. After partition the State merged with the Dominion of India. As the Rann was a part of the State it also went to India. Pakistan argued that since the Rann was flooded during the monsoons, the Rann was a sea in real terms and therefore the boundary between both the nations should be half way between the two shores. India maintained that whole of Rann belonged to India. In an armed clash in early months of 1965, Pakistan secured an initial win. Under the British mediation India agreed to a three member Tribunal to decide its ownership. As the case was referred to Tribunal, Pakistan had the reasons to smile and hope for its win with no loss in any case.

A humiliating defeat of India at the hands of People's Republic of China (PRC) and occupation of Aksai Chin in Ladakh in 1962, Pakistan's initial success in the dispute over Rann of Kutch and an assumed internal unrest in India Held Kashmir (IHK), convinced Mohammad Ayub Khan, the first military dictator and self proclaimed President of Pakistan, about the appropriateness of the circumstances to hit at the hot iron. For him it was the most opportune time to wrest it through an armed action and settle the question of Kashmir forever. The Kashmir misadventure was started with the infiltration of Pakistani armed militants in India held Kashmir, code named 'Operation Gibraltar' in July 1965. A similar operation, 'Operation Gulmarg' in the State had yielded good dividend to it about fifteen years back. The 'Operation Gulmarg' had resulted in the annexation of a good chunk of territory later named 'Azad Kashmir' to Pakistan in 1947. For Ayub and his Foreign Minister, Zulfiqar Ali Bhutto, success was sure which eventually was to make them the undisputed leaders of Pakistani people. Their assessment was not entirely baseless. Two important developments were sufficient to embolden their Kashmir enterprise. A few months before in the month of March, Sheikh Abdullah had met the Chinese Prime Minister, Chou En-Lai, and at a separate occasion had expressed his dissatisfaction with the Government of India. In the same month Ayub Khan also had visited China where he had been accorded a warm reception and was assured China's support for a plebiscite in Kashmir[5]. But 'Operation Gibraltar' could not proceed on the expected lines and did not invoke expected response. Radio

Pakistan telecasted a civilian uprising in Kashmir. However, no support was forthcoming from Kashmiri people. There was no Revolutionary Council of Kashmir. It turned a hoax, a creation out of the imagination of Pakistani leaders. In fact people came out to help Indian forces. Indian forces crossed the ceasefire line and cut off the supply lines of militants. Yet Ayub and Bhutto were confident of success. Bhutto advised Ayub that "allowing this movement to die out would amount to debacle which could threaten the existence of Pakistan".

Ayub after the failure of 'Operation Gibraltar', accepting his Foreign Minister's advice launched 'Operation Grand Slam' on 1 September 1965. Pakistani forces made a good start and threatened to cut off Kashmir from the rest of India. India responded with counter offensive on 6 September and crossed the International border. The fall of Lahore, the cultural capital of Pakistan, became a matter of time. The sounds of Indian guns could be heard in the city. To save Lahore from falling in to the Indian hands Pakistani leadership turned towards China. China's threat to India in favour of Pakistan on 16 September 1965 was ridiculous and appeared to be an eyewash. China threatened India with grave consequences if India did not dismantle its military installations in Chinese territory and return 800 sheep and 59 yaks that had been kidnapped by India. Threat did not deter India who, within 3 days replied in unequivocal words that India did not have any military installations within Chinese territory. China, going by geo-political equations and constraints was not ready to take India head on, expressed satisfaction that India had dismantled its military installations in Chinese territory. The demand for return of sheep and yaks were not raised anymore. Bhutto was disappointed by Chou En-Lai with whom he had a very warm meeting less than six months before in April, 1965. History is replete with such instances in which personal friendships and promises were set aside for the sake of national interests.

Both the countries meanwhile had begun to face the side effects of the war that had brought unbearable pressures on their economy. Rationing on food items and commodities of daily use was enforced rigorously in both the countries. Once again, the leaders of both countries agreed to UN brokered ceasefire on 23 September 1965. Ceasefire was followed by an agreement with Soviet Prime Minister

Kosygin acting as the Chief Mediator at Tashkent on 11 January 1966. Both countries agreed to return to their pre-war positions. India returned about 1840 sq. kms of territory to Pakistan, the territory which had been occupied by it during the war. Similarly about 540 sq.kms territory occupied by Pakistan was returned to India.

The issue of Kashmir remained unresolved. Indian people were unhappy over the return of so much territory to Pakistan. This was the first war won by India since its Independence. The war had established the superiority of its armed forces. But the sudden and unexplained death of Indian Premier, Lal Bahadur Shastri who signed the Tashkent agreement on India's behalf, on the intervening night of 11-12 January 1966, saved the day for him. Before he died he told his countrymen that they had to put the same degree of efforts to peace as they did during the war. For Indian people he was the epitome of boldness, simplicity, fairness and honesty. Back in home he was venerated as a Messiah of Peace. His death united the Indian people to rally for peace.

During the war Pakistani leaders had given an impression of tremendous success against India to its people. Pakistani people were dismayed at the betrayal by their own leaders. The expenditure on war pushed back the economies of both the countries for many years. They were not able to meet the food requirement of their people. War was over. The realities of the life had taken over the war hysteria. After the war, people's cry was for bread, cloth and house (Roti, Kapada aur Makan) which both the governments failed to fulfil. Unemployment reached to staggering heights. India signed a public loan scheme with USA, popularly known as PL-480, which enabled India as a 'destitute' to get 15 million tonnes of American wheat. Indian request for an annual commitment of food aid was not met, instead ships with food were released on the monthly basis. Indian leaders had no option but to accept the humiliating terms and conditions, lest their people go empty stomach. The value of Indian Rupee sank low in the international market that forced India in June 1966 to devalue the Indian Rupee in relation to US Dollars. Dollar exchange rate increased from Rs. 4.76 in pre war years to Rs. 7.50 per Dollar after its devaluation[6] in June 1966.

Democracy saved the Indian leaders, dictatorship took the toll of the dictator himself in Pakistan. Zulfiqar Ali Bhutto, Ayub's lieutenant and advisor in the whole misadventure blamed Ayub for all follies, formed his own political outfit, Pakistan People's Party (PPP), and led many of the agitations against the policies of Ayub. Ayub was removed by his protégé, General Yahya Khan, the Chief of Army in a silent coup on 25 March 1969.

India and Pakistan lost about 3200 and 3800 soldiers respectively, in 23 days' War[7]. However, there was no unanimity on the causalities. Both sides exaggerated the enemy losses. According to some other sources Pakistan lost 3000 to 5000 men and India suffered the casualties of 4000 to 6000 men[8]. The war brought no territorial gain to any of the country at war. People were charged with pseudo patriotism throughout the wartime. The war deprived an unknown number of civilians apart from the soldiers of their life and property and led the displacement of thousands of people living in villages and cities close to borders at both sides. Their displacement was necessary to allow the movements of troops. Agriculture, the only source of livelihood for many, was another casualty as the farmers could not harvest their Khariff crops. The sowing of Rabi crop was suffered badly. In short, the people of both the nations were deprived of the opportunity to live with dignity and a life of good quality. It renewed the sense of bitterness, deepened the gulf of mistrust and misunderstanding between the people of the two nations.

The leaders readied them with their begging bowls in their stretching hands for economic aid from foreign countries. The aid came but not without terms and conditions, open as well as hidden, that were to make the future policies of India and Pakistan, subservient to the donors.

3. Third war: Over Bangladesh, 1971

Within 6 years of the Tashkent agreement, propelled by the compelling situations created by the Pakistani rulers , India fished in the troubled waters of Bay of Bengal in 1971. Within six years of their agreement at Tashkent in January, 1966, the two countries plunged into another war. This time clouds of conflict gathered over the sky of Pakistan's eastern wing, East Pakistan.

The problem was internal, caused by the unfair treatment to the East Pakistan at the hands of its own country. From the very beginning of the creation of Pakistan, people of eastern wing were not given adequate representation in almost all the spheres of public life; army, bureaucracy, politics, judiciary or National cabinet. Even their language, Bengali, was seen with contempt in West Pakistan dominated government circles. The discontentment among Bengalis of East Pakistan against the big brotherly attitude of Pakistani leadership, for all the last 24 years since its creation in 1947, reached to a dangerous proportion in 1971. From the very start Qaid-e-Azam Muhammad Ali Jinnah, Liaqat Ali Khan, Nazimuddin to Ayub-Bhutto duo and Yahya Khan failed to realize the economic, social, cultural and lingual concerns of the people of East Pakistan. Instead of bringing Bengalis into mainstream of Pakistan nation they were rebuked, threatened and persecuted for expressing their genuine aspirations.

Their demand to include Bengali language as a national language along with Urdu was not only rejected but was also termed as anti Pakistan and sometimes heretic to Islam. "No No" was the response from the Bengalis to the assertion of Jinnah that the state language of Pakistan was going to be Urdu and no other language, and anyone who tried to mislead them was really an enemy of Pakistan. It had hurt Bengali sentiments to the core of their heart. It was a great denial to the majority of Pakistani people who contributed a population of about 4.20 crore in its eastern wing to a total population of 7.50 crore. They were about 56% of the total population of Pakistan at the time of its creation in 1947. More than 54% Pakistanis were Bengali speakers.[9]

Even after the 1956 Constitution of Pakistan, which has been regarded by many as a sincere effort to establish democracy on a sound footing, proclaimed both Bengali and Urdu as state languages (Article 214;1),yet there were complaints from Bengalis that their language was not being treated at par with Urdu.

The State expenditure too was unfavourable to East Pakistan. The share of East Pakistan in total expenditure was only 20% during 1950-55; 26% during 1955-60; 32% during 1960-65 and 36% during 1965-70, remaining and majority share being spent on West Pakistan.[10] From the very beginning of the creation of Pakistani state, its eastern wing was the major contributor to the national exports, drawing foreign reserves[11] to the Pakistani economy. During 1969-70 while the share of East Pakistan in total import was only35.6%, its share in exports was 50%.

The grievances of the east against the west were further strengthened by the fact that East Pakistan had a poor representation in the power structure of Pakistan. There had been no C-in-C of Army or Navy or Air Force; Finance and Planning Minister from East Pakistan. East Pakistan's representation in government departments was also very low. During sixtees it was only 8.1% in Defence, 22.5% in Home, 27.3% in Education, 19.1% in Health, 21.0% in Agriculture and 35% in Law[12]. Among military officers only 2% and among top bureaucrats only 10% were from East Pakistan. Throughout its history of 24 years only two politicians Khwaja Nazimuddin (1951-53) and Muhammad Ali Bogra (1953-55) from East could get the office of Prime Minister. Khwaja Nazimuddin also served Pakistan as its second Governor General from September 1948 to October 1951. Unfortunately, all of them very soon adopted West Pakistan-centric posture. For instance, even in the matter of Bengali language Khwaja Nazimuddin in a visit to Dhaka as Prime Minister of Pakistan in 1952 declared that 'Urdu will be the State language of Pakistan'. The reaction was sharp. There was a huge pro-Bengali demonstration in Dhaka.[13] It was further followed by a disobedience movement by students of Dhaka University on 21 February, 1952, in defiance of Section 144 clamped by the establishment. Police fired on the protesting students. Police admitted nine deaths in its firing. The day was observed as 'Ekushe' in the following years throughout East Pakistan. In February 1966, Sheikh Mujib-ur-Rahman demanded autonomy for East Pakistan through his 'Six Points'.[14] How could a country that discriminated against its own citizens for the simple reason that, that was about a thousand miles apart, could retain it intact ?

Thus, the simmering discontentment had come to boil at several occasions in the past, but it reached a point of no return after the National Assembly elections of 1971. Awami League, headed by Bengali nationalist Mujib-ur-Rahman, secured 160 seats in the 313 members' National Assembly. Trailing far behind was Pakistan People's Party, led by Zulfikar Ali Bhutto, with only 81 seats. But in spite of this thumping majority, Mujib-ur- Rahman was denied the right to form the government. Bengali disillusion erupted in mass agitations against West's unfairness. Pakistan day, 23 March, was observed as "Resistance Day" in East Pakistan.

Agha Muhammad Yahya Khan, like his predecessor Ayub, a self proclaimed President of Pakistan, acting on the Bhutto's advice, responded with a crackdown on Awami League workers and supporters. The Operation, code named 'operation searchlight', was clamped on the midnight of 25 March. Prior to that, the 'Pakistan Day' on 23 March had been observed as 'Resistance Day' in East Pakistan. Awami League leaders fled to India and established government in exile at Calcutta on 17 April 1971. East Pakistan was declared an independent nation with its new identity as Bangladesh by Mujib-ur-Rahman on 26 March. Pakistani establishment tried to quell the rebellion with its brutal force. People began to flee to save them to their neighbouring country, India. By the month of August 1971 more than 80 lakh Bengalis took refuge in India.

Historically, India had always been sympathetic to the people of East Pakistan. For the people of East Pakistan, Kashmir had never been an issue of much importance which always kept them less concerned with the hostilities with India. By the month of November more than 90 lakh people from East Pakistan had taken refuge in India, which was already grappling with its own economic problems. For India, accommodation and feeding to such a large number of refugees became a big problem. At the other hand, for Indian political establishment, this was the right time to strike and cut Pakistan down to two unequal sizes. Indira Gandhi, the then Indian Prime Minister, tried to draw the world powers' attention to the problem India was facing with the influx of this vast number of refugees. The exodus of the people from East Pakistan was due to the repressive acts and atrocities committed by the Pakistani army, she told world leaders, which was difficult to deny by anyone.

The geo political interests prevailed upon United States of America and China. Both, ignoring the fact that India was sheltering about 90 lakh (9 million) refugees from East Pakistan, stood with Pakistan. The humanitarian concern was taken over by the real politik. This was the time when new equations were emerging between America and China with Pakistan playing the role of facilitator. America by sending its 7th fleet to the Bay of Bengal came forward in defence of Pakistan. It had become apparent that in the event of war with Pakistan, China might engage India at its northern front. India faced with a great threat of being sandwiched between Pakistan from west and east, China from north and US from south. The US President, Nixon, was of the firm view that US could not allow India to use the refugees as a pretext for breaking up Pakistan and Yahya's loyalty to the US must be rewarded by helping Pakistan in suppression of revolt in its Eastern wing.[15] The Indian ships sailing in the waters of Bay of Bengal became unsafe due to the presence of its 7th Fleet in the Indian Ocean moving northward towards the Bay of Bengal.

As India was encircled by hostile forces, it hurriedly concluded the Treaty of Peace, Friendship and Cooperation with USSR on 9 August 1971. This was the time of cold war. The two rival groups were led by the two giants, US and Soviet Union. The treaty was aimed at keeping communist China (PRC) and USA out of the Indo Pak conflict. The Article IX of the Treaty provided that,

> "Each High Contracting Party undertakes to abstain from providing any assistance to any third party that engages in armed conflict with the other Party. In the event of either Party being subjected to an attack or a threat thereof, the High Contracting Parties shall immediately enter in to mutual consultations in order to remove such threat and to take appropriate effective measures to ensure peace and the securities of their countries."

The treaty blocked the possibility of a direct military intervention by any other country in the then Indo Pak conflict. India began lending more and more tactical and strategic assistance to Bangladesh Mukti Bahini. Yahya Khan tried to divert Indian attention from East Pakistan to its western front by attacking India's 9 Air Force bases in north-west India on 3 December. Pakistani attacks on its Air Force bases provided India adequate reasons to declare war on Pakistan.

On 6 December India announced its recognition to Bangladesh as an independent state. As the defeat of Pakistani army became a foregone conclusion, Dr.A.M.Malik, the Governor of East Pakistan, apprehending the massacre of whole Pakistani Army, besieged by the Mukti Bahini fighters, suggested General Yahya Khan to surrender "Unless China or US intervene today with massive air and ground support", but no help was forthcoming from these countries, for the fear of Soviet Union's entry in the war. For India, The Treaty of Peace, Friendship and Cooperation signed with USSR was a clear departure from the fundamental principle of Non Alignment Movement (NAM) but the treaty paid immediate invaluable dividend to India. The war game has turned against Pakistan. Hereafter Pakistani army was at the defending side. General Yahya Khan on 14 December appreciating the heroism of Lt.General Niazi, agreed and sent a message to him to "take all necessary measures to stop the fighting and preserve the lives of all armed forces personnel from West Pakistan"[16] Governor Dr. Malik was so terrified, that following the bombing of the building on 14 December, in which he was holding a meeting, he tendered his resignation.

Pakistan's resistance was over by 16 December 1971. Indian army was to agree only on the terms of not less than the surrender of the Pakistan's army under its Chief of Eastern command, Lt. General AAK Niazi, and that too at a public place. Niazi, listening the terms of surrender with tears in his eyes surrendered along with his 93,000 personnel to Lt. General Jagjit Singh Arora, GoC-in-C of Indian Eastern command.

At home Niazi was criticized by many war hawks, most of whom who had nothing to loose in such a situation. The truth remains that with a sharp presence of mind and providence by surrendering peacefully to Indian forces, he saved the life of more than 90,000 soldiers from being massacred at the hands of Mukti Bahini fighters and locals. He himself defended him by saying that, "I will take 90,000 prisoners of war to West Pakistan rather than face 90,000 widows and half a million orphans there."

Ironically, these 93,000 Pakistani soldiers were Prisoners of War (PoW), in a country which about 25 years ago was their own. Their crime was - murdering their own people at the behest of their political bosses. For a period of about 28 months they had to remain in Indians custody until they were sent back in batches as per Delhi Agreement signed between India, Pakistan and Bangladesh on 28 August 1973. Had Niazi not surrendered and opted to fight till end, there would have been a huge bloodshed at an unimaginable scale. Many of the Pakistani soldiers and Mukti Bahini fighters and civilians would have been killed.

Pakistan lost her Eastern wing, a territory having an area of 1,47,570 Sq. kilometres, an irreparable loss politically. But from the people's perspective, the territorial loss or gain was a hypothetical notion. A nation is made up of people. Political identities are thrust upon them artificially. For the people of erstwhile East Pakistan, their land, property and social fabric remained same. They, hereafter were known as Bangladeshis in place of Pakistanis. It was a change in nationality, asense of pride indeed, but brought no material gain to their lives. India too did not gain anything substantial. Indian people highly charged with patriotism, which is observed in case of Pakistan only, were jubilant over the outcome of the war- the dismemberment of Pakistan. A government friendly to India, came in to power in the newly created State of Bangladesh. Mujib-ur-Rahman became its first Prime Minister. Military dictatorship was replaced by a democratic popular government. Democracy and secularism became the two pillars of the nascent nation. India was satisfied with the above stated outcomes, but this state could not live long.

Within a period of 3 years of its creation, when Indians woke up to celebrate their independence day and switched on their radio sets on 15 August in 1974, they listened the shocking news of a military coup in Bangladesh. Mujib-ur-Rahman along with his entire family, present in his country, had been killed by a group of army officers in the early morning hours of 15 August.

The new government was ethically anti India. It threw the garb of secularism, a fundamental principle of the governance close to the heart of Indian people, through an Amendment to its Constitution in 1977, away.[i-n]

In 1988 Islam was declared State religion. The bonhomie with India was over; democracy was substituted by the dictatorship and secularism by theocracy in practice. In governance Bangladesh rolled back to pre 1971 system.[ii-n]

For the new establishment Bangladesh was liberated by their own people, Indian Army just provided logistic support to Mukti Bahini. In this war India lost about 3,000 soldiers. The loss in military weapons, machines and ammunition and mobilisation of armed forces was unsustainable to a country like India or Pakistan. United States suspended licenses for military sales in the very beginning. India was also deprived with US economic Aid, amounting US $ 87.6 million.

Pakistan, apart from losing its eastern wing, lost about 8,000 soldiers and a huge number of its citizens. The surrender of around 93,000 troops[17] to Indian forces tarnished the prestige of Pakistan and its army in particular. Its atrocious treatment to its own Bengali citizens was received by the world-community with a disbelief, shock, dismay, and disgust. Around two lakh to four lakh women were raped by the Pakistani soldiers and their supporters in the eastern wing. This eroded the credibility and image of Pakistan as a civilized country and army as a disciplined force.

With a view to avoiding a direct confrontation with Indian armed forces United States preferred not to send its formidable 7th Fleet, which was already in the Bay of Bengal, for the evacuation of the besieged Pakistani soldiers. It came heavy on Pakistan after war. It suspended an economic aid worth US $ 75 million, to let Pakistan's poor people go hungry. An embargo on military sales was imposed. The volte-face in the hours of test by the western powers brought disillusion of their friendship in Pakistani minds. A frustrated Pakistan left the British Commonwealth on 30 January 1972 and SEATO security pact on 8 November 1972. The civilian casualties as usual, were seldom counted. Yet the estimates of the total civilian casualties were between 10 lakh to 20 Lakh.[18]

Someone in Pakistani establishment had to be sacrificed for the debacle. If Ayub was held responsible for the Pakistan's defeat in 1965, then Yahya Khan was to be sacrificed immediately to assuage the hurt sentiments of Pakistani people. Bhutto as in the last war of 1965, this time too, encashed the defeat in his favour and managed the resignation of Yahya Khan on 28 December 1971.

It was Bhutto who had not allowed Mujib to assume the Prime Ministership of Pakistan in compliance of 1971 elections' results for

National Assembly. Had Yahya Khan not heeded Bhutto's advice and allowed Mujib to become Prime Minister, Pakistan would have emerged stronger than ever before. This was a war imposed by the self-centred leaders who were at the helm of the Pakistan, upon the people of which more than half did not know even to read or write their names. The Pakistani masses cannot be blamed, either for the molestations of around five lakh (half a million) women or the dismemberment of Pakistan. They had been fed with misinformation about the whole episode. The Shimla Agreement signed by Bhutto and Indira Gandhi on 2 July 1972, paved the way for the release of Pakistani Prisoners of War and return of about 1500 sq kilometres of Pakistani territory which India had won in West Pakistan. The Kashmir issue remained alive to bring two nations to clash in future. The Cease Fire Line (CFL) renamed as Line of Control (LoC), was very soon denounced by successive Pakistani civil and military leadership as a forged border line, agreed by Pakistan under duress under Shimla Agreement. The LoC remained a firing range between the forces of the two nations since its coming in to force in 1972.

Meanwhile, The Sindhi ethnic political giant, GM Syed asked Indian Prime Minister Indira Gandhi, to help him in declaring the independence of Sindhu Desh[19]. However, she declined the request. Had she embarked on the misadventure proposed by GM Syed, it could have been a catastrophe for the subcontinent.

The defeat did not deter Pakistan from its anti India stand, as its dismemberment confirmed its apprehension that India was determined to wipe it out from the map. Pakistan pursued anti India policies with more vigour and technology. India could have replicate the mischief in Sindh or in Balochistan; Pakistan apprehended. Bhutto found atom bomb as the best weapon to take Pakistani military many times ahead of India. Atom bomb has an unimaginable killing power. He exhorted Pakistani scientists, engaged Munir Khan first and then Abdul Qadir Khan as the Chairman of PAEC, but India exploded the bomb first. Pakistan demonstrated its nuclear capability 14 years later when it tested its bombs in May 1998. Mad race for missiles began never to stop. Conflicts and desire to take over each other militarily did not achieve anything, but losses to human development.

The expenditure on war and the sustenance of more than ninety lakh (9 million) refugees from Bangladesh was a heavy burden on Indian economy. Very soon war hysteria was taken over by the realities of the day-to-day need of the Indian people. The prices of food grains and food products soared. Students and labours began to cry for employment which Indian government failed to manage. Student unrest and strikes in Gujarat and Bihar were followed with the call of Jai Prakash Narain, a respected socialist leader and freedom fighter, for Total Revolution in April 1974. A month later following the call the railway employee union went on a nation wide strike. Indira Gandhi tried her best with all her dictatorial attitude to contain the voices of protests against her with arbitrary methods but failed. Unsuccessful on all fronts Indira Gandhi resorted to proclaim national emergency on 25 June 1975 under Article 352 of the Constitution of India.[iii-n] Proclamation of emergency became the most infamous and unpopular act in the Indian politics. It was so unpopular that when the general elections were held in 1977, Congress lost the elections very badly. Even the first atomic bomb detonation in May 1974 and merger of Sikkim to the Indian Republic in September 1974 could not rescue her from her unpopularity. For the first time a non-Congress government was formed at the centre. The chaotic political problems had the genesis in the undue pressures on Indian economy that had been thrust upon it, as an aftermath of the last Indo-Pak war.

4. IV War: Over Kargil Heights, 1999

In early 1999 an honest and positive step to normalise the relations was taken jointly by the Prime Ministers of the two countries, Nawaz Sharif and Atal Bihari Vajpayee. Indian Premier, Vajpayee, on the invitation of Pakistani Premier Sharif took a journey by bus from New Delhi to Lahore, popularly known as "Sada-e-Sarhad" on 19 February 1999, where he was warmly welcomed by Sharif. The conspicuous absence of the then Pakistani Chief of Army, General Parvez Musharraf, in defiance of Sharif's call, was received with a shock by the leadership of both the countries and the people of India.

The conspicuous absence of Pakistan's army chief explained itself when a few months later in May 1999 India learned about the occupation of a number of Indian posts in Kargil sector by Pakistani troops. It was a surprise for both the leaders. Peace efforts had been torpedoed. The plan, keeping Prime Minister Sharif in dark, had already been hatched up in the second half of 1998, much before the 'Sada-e-Sarhad' initiative. There are various opinions about the date of Sharif being informed about the Pak operations. It is said that Sharif was informed about the Kargil operation in February 1999, in ISI office at Lahore. According to some other sources Sharif came to know about the operation only in early May. Some researchers argue that the preparations for Kargil had begun as early as in 1994. In that year Indians had successfully cut the Neelum Valley road off, that falls in PoK. Pakistani army, in view of preventing the supplies to Siachen by Indian forces, concentrated on blocking the Srinagar to Leh Highway. Srinagar-Leh road was the only land approach for the transport of Indian troops to Siachen.[20] The plan was kept so secret that when a Northern Light Infantry (NLI) soldier, Hyder Khan, died in Indian Territory captured by Pakistani troops, his body was handed over to his family at his village in Pakistan's Northern Areas by four of his NLI comrades,[21] without informing where and how he was killed. Meanwhile, ironically, negotiations on the settlement of complex issue of Kashmir were going on between the two representatives of the two countries at Delhi.[22] They too probably were not aware of the developments at the Kargil heights.[iv-n]

The Pakistani Army Chief had crossed his limits. By the month of May 1999, a number of Indian posts along the 120 kilometres wide stretch out of a total length of about 776 kilometres of LOC had been occupied by the Pakistani troops. The infiltration was as deep as 11 km inside the Indian Territory. The closest town to these areas was Kargil which was the headquarter of the district of Kargil. These areas as usual, had been vacated by the Indian troops in the last fall winter only to return in summers. These occupations mainly were in Batalik, Drass and Mushkoh. The fight was nerve-breaking and remained focussed in these areas. The occupation of these posts brought Srinagar-Leh National Highway under the range of Pakistani fires from the hill tops overlooking the highway.[23]

India was in defending position. However, Pakistani onslaught at Turtok had been repulsed. Unable to reoccupy some of the lost Indian posts, Indian Army decided to open new fronts, a strategic move which had proved itself brilliant in 1965 war. In June 1999 Indian Army Chief, General VP Malik instructed all of his commanders to "be prepared for escalation -sudden or gradual along the LoC or the international border and be prepared to go to declared war at short notice."[24]

Indian Navy prepared itself for the blockade of Karachi port and began to concentrate in Arabian Sea while Indian Air force planed for bombing a less defended seaport of Gwadar[v-n] at the Bay of Gwadar in Baluchistan. US was reluctant to help Pakistan as the US leadership was convinced of Pakistani army's role in torpedoing the peace efforts. China, 'the All Weather Friend', also did not come forward to help. In such a situation of being cornered to defeat, US apprehended, Pakistan would be under compulsion to use its nuclear weapons against India. On June 16, Indian NSA had told his US counter part that "India would not be able to continue with its policy of 'restraint' for long and that our military forces could not be kept on a leash any longer."[25] This would have progressed in a nuclear war with the whole of south Asian region facing the consequences of nuclear radiation.

Fear of a conflict emnating from the occupation of just a hundred and twenty posts, turning into a full-fledged war, with the probability of both the countries using their nuclear war heads, led US mediation. The Blair House summit in Washington DC on 4 July 1999, convinced Pakistani Premier Sharif that the conflict leading to a nuclear war "would be a catastrophe". Sharif agreed to pull out from occupied Indian posts. By the time US brokered withdrawal was concluded, as per Indian claims 80% of posts had been recaptured by Indian troops, while as per neutral observers largely based on Pakistani accounts, out of 134 positions occupied by Pak forces only 12 had been taken back by Indian forces.[26]

The pullout from the captured Indian posts was not received in a good spirit in Pakistan. The war won by Pakistan in the battle field was lost to diplomacy in Washington DC. Sharif by accepting the withdrawal of Pakistani forces saved both the countries from an unwarranted war which might have brought unforeseen horror and devastation to the people, many of whom were already dying from hunger. While Parvez Musharraf, the Chief of Pakistani army, had many plans in store, many of the former army officers expressed their resentment in open. Gen.

Mirza Aslam Beg, a former Chief of Army Staff wrote in an article, that 'the end result of all diplomatic, political manoeuvres and military measures has been that it is the Pakistan army whose image is being tarnished. The US media, Israel and India have collaborated in the vilification campaign and Pakistan's bastion of strength - its armed forces stand scapegoated for the Kargil fiasco, and the civil government is being projected as if it was the only responsible entity which saved the country from a catastrophic war."[27]

In an address to the Lahore High Court Bar Association, Lt. Gen. Hamid Gul, former Chief of ISI lamented: "The Mujahideen had won the battle while India was in trouble when our immature leadership tried to turn this victory into a debacle.[28] Sharif had to pay the price of withdrawal. A few months later on 12 October 1999 he was deposed by his belligerent army chief and the Chairman of the Joint Chiefs of Staff, Parvez Musharraf, the architect of Kargil, in a military coup. The coup was preceded by a high voltage drama of check and mate (*shah* and *mat*) in the day.

Other conflicts

1. Siachen Glacier Dispute (1984 -1987)

Siachen glacier is located in the extreme north of India in the State of J&K. The glacier is in the Eastern Karakorams with Saltoro ridge in west and Karakoram in the east. Saltoro ridge itself originates from the Sia Kangri in the Karakoram. It is about 76 km long, the second longest after Fedchenko glacier in Tajikistan (77 kms) among the non polar glaciers. It extends further to the north to Indira Col joining with China and Pakistan. The river Nubra originates from it and takes a westward bend meeting the river Shyok to enter in to Pakistani side.[29] Having an altitude rising from 20,000 feet to 24,000 feet the temperature in Siachen plummets as low as minus 50 degree Celsius. Owing to glacier's peculiar geographical features the borders were never well marked, making the legitimacy of each other's possessions questionable.

India and Pakistan had stationed their troops to guard their positions in the glacier. Prior to the beginning of the conflict, the Indian forces with the onset of winter used to vacate their posts to stay at the stations located at the lower altitudes in safer locations. In April 1986 some of the vacated posts were occupied by the Pakistani troops which came to notice of Indian side one year later[30].

Encouraged by the occupation of strategic locations Pakistani forces started shelling the Indian post of Sonam in April 1987. The captured Indian post had a strategic advantage to Pakistan, which the intruders had occupied one year before and had named "Qaid Post" after Muhammad Ali Jinnah. Fights started under "OPERATION QIADAT" from Pakistani side and "OP VAJRASHAKTI" from the side of India. Indian forces recaptured the Qaid post and renamed it as 'Bana Post', after Naib Subedar Bana Singh, who though was killed in the operation, was instrumental in regaining the post. The hostilities took the life of around 600 soldiers from both sides. The fight ended with the restoration of the pre-1986 positions. Borders remained as undefined as were before the conflict. A few soldiers were decorated with gallantry awards for bravery. Naib Subedar Bana Singh and Captain Iqbal were awarded with the highest military awards, Param Vir Chakra and Hilal-i-Jur'at by governments of India and Pakistan respectively, albeit posthumous.

Hundreds of other soldiers also lost their lives in the operation. They just received last pay of respect from their fellow soldiers. Many could not get even this as they were buried in the glacier and their bodies could not be retrieved. Soldiers who died for the cause of their country left their families behind them to mourn their death throughout their life. They were the hope of their future and the sole bread earner in many cases. Siachen the word meaning "place of the roses" in the local language has turned in to "place of thorns", a volcano ready to erupt any time.

Scores of soldiers lose their life every year not only to the enemy bullets only but also to the vagaries of inclement weather and hostile topography also. The leaders of the two countries are the perpetrators of the crime of blowing up the conflicting issues. They have never proceeded sincerely to solve the contentious issues of occupation of this barren land.

Foresightedness and a genuine concern to the well-being of the people, Siachen demands the demarcation of boundaries settled once for ever instead of fighting with each other. The two countries can jointly develop the area for their mutual economic gains through the promotion of useful activities, such as glacial tourism and games. Siachen, the meeting place of three great nations, Pakistan, India and China, can be restored again, in practice to its meaning in the local language, "place of roses".

2. The Khalistan Movement, late 1970s- 1980s

During the last days of British Raj when the abdication of its Indian possessions by Great Britain had become imminent, there was a demand of separate homeland for Sikhs also. The area proposed was to include the large area of Punjab which now falls in India and Pakistan.

However, the movement died soon largely due to its impracticability and reluctance of the majority of Sikhs in its favour. The demand was raised again in seventies of the twentieth century for the creation of a Sikh State, Khalistan, in the state of Indian Punjab. The demand of separation by Davinder Singh Parmar and Jagjit Singh Chauhan received support from Pakistani establishment which had been taken over by Bhutto's handpicked General, General Zia ul Haq, in an army coup in 1977.

A few years back in 1971 India had supported separatist Mukti Bahini of East Pakistan to secede from Pakistan. Now for Pakistani establishment, it was its turn to avenge what they saw as the Indian mischief. Pakistan, in addition to extending moral support to the separate Khalistan, assisted separatists with weapon and ammunitions to carry out terrorist activities in India.

Indian Punjab owing to the geographical proximity to Pakistan and the fulcrum of the demand, became a hotbed for anti-India activities. The Sikh shrine of Harminder Saheb in Amritsar, popularly known as Swarna Mandir or Golden Temple, was virtually occupied by the Sikh terrorists under the command of Jarnail Singh Bhindaranwala in 1983. This was deemed as a challenge to the authority of the State. The terrorists' effrontery was responded with heavy hand by the government of India. 'Operation Blue Star' carried out by the Indian government in the first week of June 1984 took the life of several militants including their leader Jarnail Singh Bhindranwale. Golden Temple was freed from the militants.

The operation that involved the forced entry of security forces in to the shrine, hurt the sentiments of Sikhs. The then Indian Prime Minister Indira Gandhi, the architect of the operation, was killed by her two personal Sikh guards at the point blank-range, on 31 October 1984. Her murder brought retaliatory attacks on Sikhs throughout India. The separatists earned hatred and antipathy from the Indian public. Further, the blowing up of the Indian Air liner AIC 182 flying from Montreal to London on 23 June 1985, over the Atlantic Ocean, that killed all 329 persons on board, by Canadian Khalistani terrorists, alienated Khalistan Movement from external support. The above developments brought a gradual end to Khalistan Movement. However, Pakistani support to secessionist movement deteriorated Indo-Pak relations further.

3. Operation Brasstacks, November 1986 - March 1987

The 'Operation Blue Star' did not deter Pakistan from extending logistic and moral support to the Khalistan movement. Therefore, India decided to threaten Pakistan with a military showdown. As a prelude Indian Armed Forces started military exercises in its western sector and Arabian Sea close to Pakistani borders.

The exercise codenamed 'Operation Brasstacks', was carried out from 18 November 1986 to 6 March 1987. 'Operation Brasstacks' involved mobilization of about 6 lakh soldiers, about half of the strength of the Indian Army, within 150 km from borders of Pakistan. The movement of Indian Navy appeared targeting Karachi. It terrified the Pakistani political establishment which had by then become a close partner of United States in destabilizing the Soviet installed government in Afghanistan. Pakistan for several reasons was not ready to confront with Indian army. However, sensing the gravity of the situation it geared up its war machines and put its nuclear installations on high alert.

The tension came to an end by March 1987 with the withdrawal of a large part of Indian troops from the border areas. The cost of demonstration of power of Indian Military was high in monetary terms. Apart from a high cost of such a grand mobilization of armed forces the operation brought the displacement, though temporary, of thousands of people living in the border areas across both the sides of the borders. Zia ul Haq's policy of fomenting internal insurgency and supporting the secessionism in India, did not bring any material benefit to Pakistani people or to Zia himself. Indeed, Kashmir's peace was disturbed. 'Operation Brasstacks' could not move Zia-ul-Haq to desist from supporting anti India terror-activities. Contrary to the Indian expectations, its military exercise provided Zia-ul-Haq the raison d'etre to stay in power. Zia-ul-Haq's policy towards India heralded a new era of violence in IHK, with the bomb blasts in Srinagar on 31 July of 1988. India blamed Pakistan for the bomb-blasts.[vi-n]

On 17 August 1988, Zia-ul-Haq was killed in a plane crash along with many high ranking officers of the Pakistani army, US Ambassador Arnold Raphel and Chief of the US military mission in Pakistan, Brigadier General Herbert Wassom[31]. But his legacy was carried on further by the successive Pak leaders. The increased insurgency in Kashmir had its genesis in the "Bleed India" policy of Zia ul Haq. Indian leaders too were to be blamed for the disenchantment of Kashmiri people with the Indian democracy. In the 1987 general elections to Jammu and Kashmir Assembly the ruling National Conference (NC) and its ally Indian National Congress (INC) misused the government machinery in their favour. The opposition blamed the ruling party for widespread poll riggings. NC and INC contested elections in a seat sharing understanding. Out of a total of 76 seats in the Legislative Assembly, the NC and INC managed 66 (40 NC and 26 INC) leaving only 10 seats to opposition (4 went to Muslim United Front, 2 went to BJP and 4 went to independents). The absence of powerful opposition brought further problems to the people of the state. As people agitated, government responded with tough measures.

The suppression of people's voice widened the gap between the people and the government. People could not find legitimate means to ventilate their grievances. Extremism and militancy came to fill up the vacuum. At the face of growing militancy security forces were armed with the provisions of Armed Forces Special Powers Act (AFSPA) in 1990. The emergency law became a permanent feature in the State since then. People found compelled to shut their mouth for the fear from both, militants and security forces. They faced a complex situation, security forces armed with AFSPA provisions interrogating them in the daylight, terrorists barging to their houses in the dark of night. Hapless people became the victim of the lust for power of the politicians and radical non-state actors.

4. First Nuclear Test by India, May 1974

In 1974 on 18 May India detonated its first nuclear bomb at Pokhran Test Range in Thar Desert of Rajasthan. The nuclear test was received with a shock by the Pakistani media and the leadership. The test site was very close to Pakistan, within 100 kms from its borders. The morale of Pakistani politicians and the army was at its nadir owing to its humiliating defeat in 1971, with 93,000 Pakistani PoW in Indian jails. Bhutto, the first civilian Martial Law administrator of Pakistan, had told to his scientists on 28 January, 1972 at Multan that Pakistan had to develop nuclear bomb to guard itself in the wake of India becoming nuclearized. His scientists had assured him to produce an atom bomb very soon.

Further, on 22 February in 1974 in the Lahore Summit of Organisation of Islamic Cooperation (OIC) which was attended by Mujib-ur-Rehman of Bangladesh, Shah Faisal of Saudi Arabia, Anwar Sadat of Egypt, Yasir Arafat of PLO and Muammar Gaddafi of Libya among others, Bhutto described Pakistan's nuclear programme aimed at developing an "Islamic Bomb". Pakistan roped in the services of Munir Khan, who was working with International Atomic Energy Agency (IAEA) and a few years later of Dr AQ Khan who was working in Belgium, to head Pakistan Atomic Energy Commission (PAEC).[32] But by exploding the atom bomb at Pokhran, India had checkmated Pakistan. At individual level, Bhutto had been outsmarted by Indira Gandhi, the Indian Prime Minister. India's politicians celebrated the atomic test as a one step up over Pakistan in the defence preparedness.

The nuclear test accelerated the race for nuclear arms in the subcontinent. Instead of bolstering the Indian defence system, the nuclear test weakened it, as it pressurised Pakistan to develop nuclear weapons and maintain a good stock of nuclear arsenals to over take India in any eventuality of an armed clash. For India, a few years later as Pakistan also developed the nuclear technology, 'Advantage Gain' turned in to 'Advantage Lost'.

Though India found entry in the list of 5 countries US, USSR, China, Great Britain and France who had detonated the N bomb, it was slapped with many kinds of sanctions. United States put sanctions on Indian atomic programme. Apprehending a similar action in Pakistan Canada stopped supplies of nuclear fuel, expertise and spare parts to Karachi Nuclear Plant (KANUPP), which was generating electricity and lighting the houses of thousands of people, since 1971.

5. Second Atomic Test by India May, 1998

By early 1990s Pakistan had developed a typical nuclear device.[33] However, Pakistani leadership avoided atomic test, until India detonated atom bombs for the second time. India conducted 5 atomic tests on 11 and 13 May in 1998 again at Pokhran Test Site in the Thar Desert of Rajasthan. As India detonated atom bombs for the second time, Pakistani leadership came under pressure from its people who were keen to respond India's atomic test with the matching force. The reaction of Pakistani people was obvious. This time too, the Indian leadership and the media celebrated the atomic test as another victory over Pakistan. LK Advani, the Indian Home Affairs Minister sent the shock waves in political circles by asserting that the tests had "brought about a qualitatively new stage in Indo Pakistan relations" and that India was "resolved to deal firmly with Pakistan's hostile activities in Kashmir".[34]

Pakistani Prime Minister Nawaz Sharif was perplexed and indecisive. What to do? Pakistan had the N Bomb, test was a matter of time. Restrain was not just an advice but a veiled threat from international community. 'Explode' was the cry from home crowd. Meanwhile, an intelligence report which later on turned a hoax helped Nawaz Sharif to take decision. It was an information from GHQ of Pakistan DG of military operations on 27 May that Israeli fighter jets were flying from Chennai in India to Kahuta with intention to bomb the nuclear installations of Pakistan.[35]

There were many in Pakistani establishment such as Jahangir Karamat, the Chairman of the Joint Chiefs of Staff, for whom the attack was impossible and unfeasible, yet they were not in a position to express their views against the possibility of an air attack from India. The people like Karamat had the responsibility of defending Pakistan's nuclear facilities and space, which prevented them to deny such unfeasible possibility.

F-16 and Mirage Fighter Bomber planes as also the intermediate-range Gauri missiles, capable of carrying nuclear warheads, were pressed into service to defend the Pakistani airspace. Almost all of the leaders and diplomats of the countries of recognition to Pakistan, including United States' President Bill Clinton and UN Secretary General Kofi Annan were informed on the intervening night of 27 and 28 May of a possible attack from India on Pakistan's nuclear installations.

Indian High Commissioner was woken up from his sleep and informed about Pakistan's anguish.

The intelligence report about the air attack from India later turned fake but it relieved Pakistani PM Nawaz Shariff, from restraining himself to allow the atom bombs to be tested.

On 28 May and 30 May Pakistan detonated its atom bombs in Chagai hills in the province of Balochistan. Interestingly, the test site was within a few kms from the border of Afghanistan.

US imposed sanctions on both the countries. Sanctions were detrimental to their economy, yet the people of both the countries were jubilant. The two countries moved many steps ahead on the road of mutual animosity. The replicas of the tests were erected in many cities in Pakistan. Pakistan celebrated the day 28 May, as 'Youm-e-Takbir' and continued to observe as such since then, every year.

6. Hijacking of Air India flight 814, attacks on Jammu and Kashmir Assembly and Indian Parliament by Pakistan based terrorist organisations leading to 'Operation Parakram' by India in December 2001

The joint Pak-US military venture against the pro communist government in Afghanistan, since late seventies of the twentieth century created several terror-outfits in Pakistan. They were provided moral, logistic and financial support by the Pakistani government. Some of these organisations were just aimed at to carry out terrorist activities in India putting Kashmir at the centre-stage.

About less than three months of Musharraf's takeover of Pakistan's government on 12 October 1999, one of such terror-outfit, Harkat-ul-Mujahideen (HuM), hijacked an Indian Airlines Flight, commonly known as IC 814, shortly after it left Kathmandu airport for Amritsar. HuM was a Pakistan based terrorist organisation which had close links with Pakistani intelligenc agency ISI and Taliban.The hijacking took place on 24 December 1999. The hijacked plane made three brief stopovers, at Amritsar, Lahore and Dubai, refuelled it and finally landed at Kandhar on 25 December. Apart from several demands, the hijackers had also planned to give India a horrific Millennium gift at the midnight of the last day of the millennium, 31 December, as told by one of the hijackers to the pilot of the plane. The gift was: blowing up of the plane along with its 171 passengers and 15 crew members with a bomb. The hijacker told to pilot, "Fly slowly, fly carefully, there is no hurry. We have to give India a millennium gift." To make sure of their brutal behaviour to all crew members and the passengers of the plane, hijackers murdered a young man who had just been married.[36]

Negotiations that followed resulted into the release of three Kashmiri terrorists held in Indian jails, Maulana Masood Azhar, Ahmed Omar Sheikh and Mushtaq Ahmed Zargar. Jaswant Singh, the Indian Minister for Foreign Affairs, flew to Kandahar to handover these terrorists in exchange of the Indian plane along with its passengers and crew members.

Later the Indian government based on the post-hijacking developments accused ISI and Taliban Government of Afghanistan for their complicity in the hijacking. Indian government's accusations had the sufficient evidences. Freed terrorists were accorded warm welcome by no less than the chief of Taliban forces at Kandahar, Mullah Akhtar Usmani and a score of Talibani officials present at the Kandahar airport. Usmani welcomed the hijackers and asked them, "Are you satisfied now?" "Indeed" replied one of them. Al-Qaeda had an office at the airport. ISI had managed weapons to hijackers in Nepal. Indian government alleged that the hijackers were in constant contact of ISI throughout the operation. Shortly afterwards, the freed terrorists surfaced in Pakistan where they did fundraising tours to carry out the terrorist activities in Kashmir.[37]

Pakistan's role in hijacking was not a secret. Masood Azhar, on reaching Pakistan founded his own terrorist outfit, Jaish-e-Mohammad (JeM).[38] Indian sentiments were hurt deeply at this behaviour of their neighbour. Meanwhile, many more groups in Pakistan continued to collect the funds for anti India activities in Kashmir.

Within a year of Masood Azhar's release, his outfit Jaish-e-Mohammad (JeM) carried an attack on Jammu and Kashmir State Legislative Assembly on 1 October 2001. The explosives laden car with three suicide members crashed at the gate of Assembly building killing 36 people.

The Indo-Pak efforts to solve the long standing issues of conflicts in the Agra summit between Musharraf and Vajpayee from 14 to 16 July 2001 had already ended in bitterness. With an attack on J&KAssembly building by aPakistan based terror outfit, there had left no room for any dialogue with Pakistan in Indian mind.

An agitated Chief Minister of the State, Farooq Abdullah blamed Pakistan for attack in unequivocal terms. He demanded that, "the time has come to wage a war against Pakistan and to bomb the militant training camps there". "India cannot accept such manifestations of hate and terror from across its borders" warned Indian Government, "There is limit to India's patience."[39]

The threat did not deter Pakistani establishment from supporting terrorist groups based within and without, and these groups continued to carry on their operations on Indian soil. On 13 December 2001, within one and a half month's interval from the attack on J&K Assembly building, terrorists attacked Indian Parliament's building.

India blamed Pakistan-based terror-organizations, Jaish-e-Mohammad(JeM) and Lashkar-e-Taiba (LeT), for the attack. The session of the Parliament had just been adjourned but still there were about 200 parliamentarians and ministers inside the Parliament building. As the car in which the terrorists were trying to enter in the building was stopped at the gate by security forces a tough gun battle between the terrorists and Indian security forces ensued. Ten Indians (nine policemen and a parliament staff) lost their lives in the operation.[40]

The attack stunned the Indian people; within two months of an attack on J&K Assembly, the Parliament, the highest seat of the Indian governance, had been attacked. The three terrorist operations; hijacking of IC 814 to Kandahar, the attack on the State Legislative Assembly building of Jammu and Kashmir and the terrorist attack on Indian Parliament building, convinced the Indian leadership that any further restraint would be suicidal for India.

Five days after Parliament attack, Indian Prime Minister announced 'Operation Parakram' on 18 December 2001. India demanded from the Pakistan the handover of 20 most wanted terrorists including JeM chief Masood Azhar, Ahmed Omar Saeed Sheikh and five other men involved in the hijacking of the IC 814 in December, 1999. India deployed around 8 lakh troops including its three strike corps along the International border and LoC.

The Eastern fleet was shifted from Bay of Bengal to Arabian Sea aimed at blocking the Pakistani waters.[41] India's initial plan was to make multiple attacks across the LoC and siege the territory in Pakistan held Kashmir (PHK), Leepa Valley and Hajipur Pass. It was to be accompanied by a major commando operation in the first month of 2002 to wipe out the major terrorist launching pads in PHK (AJK). Pakistan too started counter mobilization. It deployed its army on its borders. In some cases the two armies were just within 1600 feet on either side of the Jhelum. Risk of a nuclear war was looming large. Yet, Pakistan was not ready to face India in the battlefield. As reported by Karachi Dawn news paper "all along these nerve-racking months, Pakistan maintained dignified posture of restrain, condemning terrorism repeatedly, offering talks to New Delhi for resolving disputes, including Kashmir and a phased withdrawal of troops by both sides".

Pakistan though did not comply with the Indian demand of handing over of 20 most wanted terrorists, banned LeT and JeM, blamed for the 13 December attack on Indian Parliament, launched nationwide crack-down on terrorist organisations and arrested around 2000 activists.

Musharraf, at the same time, also asserted in his speech delivered on 12 January 2002 that the measures against the Islamic groups did not change his position on Kashmir. "Kashmir runs in our blood" Musharraf told metaphorically, "no Pakistan can afford to severe links with Kashmir. We will continue to give all diplomatic, political and moral support to the Kashmiris."

India being a democratic country was not interested in plunging the nation in to the war, found reasons to evade it in Musharraf's ban and crackdown on terrorist groups. India repeated the withdrawal as done in the time of 'OP BRASSTACS', some sixteen years ago, and avoided a possible nuclear holocaust.

The cost of 'Operation Parakram' was a costly enterprise on all fronts, military, economy and politics. Human losses due to mine explosions and the cost of the de-mining as also the psychological stress aggravated with harsh cold weather conditions were irrecoverable. Defence budgets were increased with additional outlays, shifting from economic and social sectors. The whole operation cost about US$ 2 billion to Indian exchequer.[42] The movement of trains and flow of tourists was affected badly in both the countries. Fortunately, Atal Bihari Vajpayee, the Indian Prime Minister even at the face of a virtual failure of a costly adventure, withdrew 'Operation Parakram' without achieving any substantial gain. It is difficult even to guess how much loss and to whom would have occurred in the event of a full fledged war. In a situation of conflict culminating in a nuclear war, US had estimated one crore and twenty lakh (12 million) deaths and injuries to about seventy lakhs (7 millions).[43]

Neverthless, 'retreat' was better than 'march' in the best interest of the people of both the countries.

7. Musharraf's continuance with terrorism.

On 11 September 2001, the Twin Towers of World Trade Centre at New York were brought down by the two American Airlines Boeing 767, hijacked by the Al Qaeda operatives. America was attacked in its heartland, its economic capital, for the first time in its history. US was convinced of the attack originating from Afghanistan. Al Qaeda chief, Osama bin Laden was operating from Afghanistan in close collaboration of Taliban Government of Afghanistan. US decided to avenge its humiliation by invading Afghanistan with the twin objectives, finish the Taliban regime and the Al Qaida along with its supremo Osama. Pakistan was a close ally to both, Taliban and Osama bin Laden.

Pakistan and USA both were instrumental for the ascendency of Taliban to power in Afghanistan. Now as US interests were hit by Al Qaida and Taliban, they were to be eliminated to keep up the notion of American invincibility unquestioned. Pakistan's support owing to its geographical and political proximity with Afghanistan was necessary to accomplish the US mission.

Pakistan had been US's close partner in the exit of Soviet Union from Afghanistan a decade ago, now Taliban and Al Qaida were to be exterminated.

Next day, early in the morning of 12 September, US deputy secretary of the state, Richard Armitage, called Pakistan's Ambassador to US Maleeha Lodhi and ISI chief Lt. General Mehmood who was at that time in America, to his office. Armitage offered two choices to them, "You are either 100% with us or 100% against us, there is no grey area". The language was terse, the message was stern. It was no less humiliating to Pakistan than the ultimatum given by Austria to Serbia on 23July 1914, that plunged the world in the first world war.[vii-n] Musharraf was communicated with the US options who knelt down immediately before the US dictate and ditched Taliban.

Pakistan was expected to be engrossed with the problem which has emerged at its western front, but it kept supporting terrorists to carry on their activities on the Indian soil. Many of these organisations banned in Pakistan as an aftermath of 'Operation Parakram', had shifted their headquarters to Pakistan Held Kashmir (PHK). The ban was not applicable to PHK and the semi autonomous tribal areas bordering Afghanistan[44]. By the beginning of new Millennium they started targeting Indian Army camps. In one of such attack on 14 May 2002, on the residential quarters of an Indian Army camp at Kalchuk in Kashmir, terrorist killed 35 people, mainly women and children. India within half a year of 'Operation Parakram', once again mobilised its armed forces in war mode. Pakistan began to strengthen its defences along the borders of India.[45]

US, at that time was fighting a war with Taliban and Al Qaeda in Afghanistan, using Pakistani territory for base and transit. Therefore, it did not want a war between India and Pakistan. It wanted Pakistan to remain focused on Afghanistan to serve US interests. The job before

US was to accomplish its mission – finish Osama, Al Qaeda and Taliban rule in Afghanistan, first. The US deputy secretary of State, Richard Armitage, was pressed into service by US President Bush. Armitage reminded Musharraf of his not fulfilling the assurances given to India at earlier occasions. Armitage told Musharraf that if he did not assure India a permanent end to cross border terrorist activities, that would be devastating for Pakistan. On 6 June 2002, Musharraf agreed with Armitage to see a permanent end for cross border terrorist activities.[46] As Armitage conveyed it to India, India sent the signals of abandonment of its plan of attack . The retreat of Indian forces began with the moving of its naval fleet back to its base and opening of Indian space to Pakistani commercial flights. Later on, the diplomatic relations were established between the two Nations.

Pakistan's support to terrorist attack on Kalchuk Army residential camp did not bring any benefit either to extremists or Musharraf or Pakistan. They were threatened with dire consequences rather. In the event of Pakistan's defeat or a nuclear war, Musharraf like Yahya Khan about four decades ago, would have to make a disgraceful exit from power. Though the extremist elements in Pakistan were unhappy with the clear volt face of Musharraf to Taliban, their annoyance was manageable and was managed well at the face of US threat.

As a fall out of a six month (May- October 2002) military stand-off both the countries suffered losses in terms of economy. Most of the European countries, Australia and USA had already put Pakistan in the list of travel advisory to their citizens against travelling there after 11 September 2001, now after 6 June 2002 the travel advisory was extended to India also. The advisories compelled a number of businessmen, industrialists and tourists not to stay further in India. Visits in near future were postponed if not cancelled. The fall in the number of foreign visitors had the adverse bearings on the employment of people, engaged in these sectors. For the good of the subcontinent the withdrawal of Indian forces was followed by a relative calm, for nearly next five years.

Backchannel diplomacy involving the highest level bureaucrats, Tariq Aziz and Brajesh Mishra, on the sidelines of SARC summit in Pakistan in January 2004 led to an unscheduled meeting of Vajpayee with Musharraf at his presidential house on 5 January. Musharraf pledged not to allow Pakistani soil to support terrorism in any manner and Vajpayee agreed for a composite dialogue on all issues including Kashmir. This was taken as a good initiative on the part of both the leaders. India and Pakistan moved ahead with the reopening of the bus service between Srinagar and Muzaffarabad on 7 April 2005. Notwithstanding with the confidence building measures (CBMs) agreed between the two countries, terrorists continued their destructive activities, such as serial bomb blasts in the crowded markets of Delhi in 2005, bomb blasts in Guwahati in 2006, blasts in Varanasi in 2006, blasts at Mecca Masjid and Ajmer Sharif in 2007.

8. The terrorist attack on Mumbai

The terrorist attacks at various places in Mumbai, the economic capital of India, on 26 November 2008, inflicted a fatal blow to the Musharraf-Vajpayee managed peace. A relative peace lasting for about five years came to a tragic end. An attack by 10 member terrorist team, at different places in Mumbai, Chhatrapati Shivaji Terminal, the Taj Palace and Tower, The Oberoi Trident, a cafe; a hospital, Nariman House, the Metro cinema and Saint Xaviers College was carried on between 26 and 28 November 2008. The national security guard's commandos were engaged to flush out the terrorists from Hotel Taj. After a gun battle with the terrorists, the Indian security forces secured Mumbai by 29 November morning.

The three days' operation ended leaving nine of the ten terrorists dead and the remaining one, Ajmal Kasab, being captured alive. The terrorist attack took the life of 174 people and left more than 300 injured. Later, Mohammed Ajmal Amir Kasab, the lone survivor of the terrorist group admitted in an open court hearing that the entire team of perpetrators had been recruited and trained and all equipments including weapons were supplied to them in Pakistan by Pakistan based Lashkar-e-Taiba. An open role of David Coleman Headley, a US citizen of Pakistani decent and LeT operative Zaki-ur-Rehman Lakhvi was established on the basis of further investigations. Indian nation was shocked and agitated. The incident was seen as the betrayal by Pakistan, a volt face from the assurances which Musharraf had made to Indian Prime Minister a few years back.

The disguesting incident united the entire Indian Nation across the faiths, communities, political groups and regions. Muslims refused to grant a burial ground to Kasab anywhere on Indian soil. Four years later, Kasab was executed by hanging in November 2012 and buried by the Indian jail authorities. India suffered losses in human lives and economy. Mumbai, the economic capital remained shut for weeks, recovered from the shock slowly but steadily, though with difficulty, to normalcy. India emerged as a nation more united than ever, since 1971.

As the identity of the terrorists and their affiliation with Pakistan began to be known to the Indian people, the temperature began to turn hot to hotter. An English news paper wrote that India was a victim of a pickpocket (Kasab), but the state was too impotent to respond. A television channel showed in graphic details 'how many minutes' it would take for Indian missiles to 'finish' cities like Lahore, Karachi and Islamabad.[47] Pakistan denied its role and refused to admit that Kasab was its citizen. Later, when pressed with undeniable evidences, Pakistan had no option but to admit Kasab's Pakistani nationality.[48]

However, a silver line was there, this time the public sentiments were highly charged though, India did not threaten Pakistan with an armed-showdown.

9. *Terror-acts of JeM and attack on CRPF Bus at Pulwama, February, 2019*

The relations between the two nations again acquaired perilous dimensions due to terrorist activities in J&K involving Pakistan based terror groups and their local recruits, in the second decade of the twentyfirst century. During a period of about four years from December 2014 to 14 February 2019, eight terrorist attacks were carried out by Pakistan based Masood Azhar's Jaish-e-Muhammad (JeM) on Indian soil. JeM claimed responsibility for an attack on Mohura in December 2014, which took a toll of 17 people including 11 security personnel. It again struck at Pathankot air base on 2 July 2016. As Indian intelligence had specific information about the terrorist bases stationed in PHK, Indian forces launched a targeted strike on those bases in the intervening night of 29-30 September in 2016. India publicised the attack as a 'surgical strike'. Indian media claimed the killing of three to six dozens of terrorists present in the camp. The Indian government headed by Prime Minister Narendra Modi celebrated 30 September as the 'Surgical Strike Day'.

Within two months of the surgical strike JeM carried an attack on Nagarkot Army Camp on 29 November killing 12 soldiers. It struck at Pulwama Police Lines on 26 August and again on 30 December 2017, killing 8 and 5 security personnel respectively. JeM claimed responsibility for the attack on Sunjuwan Army Camp on 10 February 2018 that killed 11 soldiers and once again at Pulwama Police Lines killing 8 security personnel.

The savagery committed by JeM reached to an unprecedented height in the beginning of 2019 when on 14 February a JeM suicide bomber from IHK Pulwama, rammed his vehicle with one of the bus of a convoy of 78 vehicles carrying 2547 CRPF Jawans en route Jammu to Srinagar near Pulwama town. The attack took the tall of forty CRPF personnel.[49] Indian sentiments started boiling at the complicity of Pakistan, as JeM chief Masood Azhar had not only been given the safe asylum but he and his associates were freely roaming and collecting the funds in Pakistan to carry out the terrorist activities in India, Kashmir in particular. All of the Indian political parties were shocked and condemned Pakistan. India expressed its anguish by withdrawing most favoured nation (MFN) status granted to Pakistan in 1996.

10. Brief Indo-Pak skirmishes over the sky of Kashmir, 2019

Fed up with the JeM terror-acts, India decided to destroy JeM camps based in PoK and Khaiber Pakhtoonkhwa (KP) province of Pakistan. Air strikes were conducted by Indian Airforce on 26 February 2019 at JeM training facilities at Balakot in KP. Though no official communiqué was issued on the fatalities but various Indian sources claimed a toll of 250 to 300 terrorists present in the facilities. Pakistan refuted any hit, damage or fatality. Many of the international media groups also agreed to Pakistan's claim. India had elections to its Parliament within a few months. As the ruling political party, BJP, tried its best to showcase the airstrike as its tactical win, many people at home (India) also expressed their doubts over the adventure. Jet fighters engaged each other next day in which India lost one MIG-21 over the sky of Pakistan. Its pilot ejected from the plane and landed in Pakistani territory. He was captured by the Pakistani troops. India claimed that the captured pilot too had shot down a F-16 of Pakistan. Pakistan rejected the claim. However, other sources confirmed the loss of one each fighter planes to both of the countries. As the Indian pilot of Mig-21, that had been shot down by Pakistani airforce, a Wing Commander, was in Pakistan's captivity as a POW, Pakistan was at advantage to show the Indian aggrandizement to the international community. However, Pakistan could not get the expected response from the international community. Most of the countries suggested de-escalation of tension. According to some sources, US exerted pressure on Pakistan to return the pilot in its captivity. Better sense prevailed upon Pakistani leadership and the pilot was returned to India on 1 March, 2019.

BJP, the political party which was the ruling party in India used the release of the pilot in its election canvassing as a victory for its leader, Modi, the Prime Minister of India. This was objected by other political parties and subsequently the Election Commission of India restrained BJP to use the name or photograph of the pilot for election purpose. These manoeuvres of the political party at the helm of affairs in India cast misgivings on the whole Balakot enterprise.

Terrorism the biggest road block to Peace and Prosperity

The terror outfits have never allowed the two nations to create a healthy and friendly environment between them. The radical groups naming themselves as the fighters or saviours of their faiths often strike to foment religious tensions and thwart the peace efforts of their governments. Whenever a terrorist attack takes place, the two states quickly blame each other. The incidence of terror acts, mostly through bomb blasts, in India are promptly attributed to Pakistani Intelligence agency ISI or to Pakistan based terror outfits. Similarly Pakistani establishment and the non-government actors blame Indian Intelligence Bureau (IB) wing RAW's hand in the blasts and internal insurgency in Pakistan.

On 12 March 1993, Mumbai witnessed 12 blasts at BSE and A-1 building, Century Bazar, two 5 Star Hotels and other crowded places, killing 257 and injuring 700 people. On 14 February 1998, 19 blasts at a political rally of BJP left 58 dead and 250 injured. On 29 October 2005, serial blasts in Delhi's crowded Pahadganj, Govindpuri and Sarojini Nagar markets killed 70 people, mostly women and children, when they were shopping for Diwali, the festival of lights in India. On 10 June 2006, five explosions in Guwahati injured 28 people leaving one dead. On 11 July 2006, seven explosions in a local train took the life of more than 100 people. On 7 March 2006, Varanasi witnessed a series of explosions. In May 2007 a blast in the Mecca Masjid of Hyderabad took the life of 14 and left dozens injured. Within three months Hyderabad was again rocked with explosions when an open air auditorium and a chat-bhandar were targeted killing about 32 and leaving 35 wounded. Ajmer Sharif was hit by a number of blasts on 11 October 2007, killing two and injuring 17 people. On 23 November 2007, blasts were carried on at several places almost simultaneously. These blasts took the life of 13 people leaving 66 injured. Arrests were made. Arrested people were Indian citizens, but Pakistan was accused for providing logistics which in many cases was found a mere allegation but with substance in some others. India's police and investigation system is as unreliable as any of the other third world countries including Pakistan. A case of arbitrary behaviour of Police is related with the blasts near Hamidia mosque at Malegaon, about 290 km northeast of Mumbai, in September 2006. The Maharashtra Anti-terrorism Squad (ATS) immediately claimed cracking of the case, blamed SIMMI, an India based terror outfit, and arrested nine local Muslim youths from the area. By the month of November, the Mumbai police linked the terror attack with Laskar-e-Toiba. Most of the suspects were from Malegaon in India. They were arrested and put on trial. They, along with their family members, faced social ostracism, till the police charge sheeted some Hindu radicals for the blasts. Court found the arrested Muslim youths innocent and on the orders of the Court they were released. Police administration in the subcontinent has seldom been found above board when it comes to investigations and arrests especially in terror related cases.

Around half of the subcontinent's terrorism related problems emanate from within. Pakistan has been blaming India and Afghanistan for unrest in its northwest regions, Baluchistan and Khaiber

Pakhtoonkhwa provinces in particular. Pakistan accused India for its complicity in the abortive hijacking of a Pakistan plane PIA-554 (Turbat - Karachi) in May 1998, while it had been made public by the three hijackers, Sabir, Shabir and Shaswar, all Baluchs, that the hijacking was to press Pakistan not to use Ras-Koh in Chagai district for atomic explosion. They were captured and were executed. Pakistan ignoring the local Baluch apprehensions about a possible nuclear radiation and consequent health hazards exploded the bomb on 28 May.

Though, India had the reasons to celebrate the UNSC decision on declaring JeM Chief Masood Azhar 'global terrorist' on 1 May 2019, but it is futile to expect any decrease in the level of terrorism till the terrorism is not rejected by the neighbouring countries. Unfortunately, the indictment of a proven terrorist by the UNSC, was taken with dismay in political circles of Pakistan. Immediately after the UNSC decision, the Pakistan Ministry of Foreign affairs issued a statement that, "The Indian media's attempt to build a narrative claiming it as a victory for India and validation of its stance are false and baseless." Enlisting of a terror group or person in UNSC list is not going to serve any good, unless the country of its origin ensures that no terrorist or terror outfit receives any support from its soil. The problem of terrorism can be erased only with the co-operation and mutual understanding for the mutual economic development, between the neighbouring countries. Pakistan's Foreign Minister's assertion on 1 May in 2019, within half a month of Pulwama attack, that the JeM leader was very well in Pakistan, but Pakistan would act only if India provided evidences of his hand in the terror acts, was intriguing as it established the complicity of the Pakistani establishment in all the JeM led terror acts in India. It is no secret that JeM chief was one of the terrorists whose release was bargained with the life of 171 passengers and 15 crew members of the hijacked Indian plane in December 1999 at Kandahar. On his release he had been given a rousing welcome along with a safe asylum in Pakistan. This policy never helped Pakistan. The emergence of Tahrik-e-Taliban–e-Pakistan as an off shoot of Tahrik-e-Taliban, created and engaged in Afghan War by Pakistan, was one of the living example of such follies. The civic life of Pakistan was taken at ransom by the terrorist organizations claiming affiliations to various schools of Islamic thoughts. Encouraging youths to become fidayeen (suicide bomber) in the name of religion or faith is most inhumane and irrelligious, as it takes away the opportunity from oneself to enjoy the world bestowed upon her/him by the Mother Nature or the God. Peace, friendship and co-operation between the countries of the subcontinent and outside its borders are the most potent inteventions to cure majority of the terrorism related problems of the countries of the subcontinent.

The disease of three Ms; mistrust, misunderstanding and misadventures, carries the virus of backwardness which is more dreadful than any other disease in the subcontinent.

Chapter - IV

Pleasant Rains after a Hot Summer in Distant Lands

European Union- A Paradigm Shift- From Destruction to Construction

The Europe, for centuries has been the house of Christianity, the religion of nonviolence and humility. People followed it in their life and practice but the rulers practiced politics. The result was frequent wars for the political ends of the ruling class. The two main sects within the religion, Catholicism and the Protestantism, drew the dividing line, uniting the same sect followers but trespassing these divisions many a times to suit their political exigencies.

Neither the faith nor Jesus Christ could restrain them from fighting with each other. As before, between sixteenth to eighteenth centuries they largely remained busy in constant and continuous wars. India, during those times was ruled over by Afghans and later on by Mughals in north and Rayas of Vijaynagar kingdom and the Deccan Sultanates among others in south. Kashmir was ruled by Ladakhis, Chaks, Mughals and Afghans. Mughals brought gradual unification of India in the following centuries and established a rule of comparative peace and prosperity throughout the Indian subcontinent. India was then inhabited by the people of two major faiths, Hinduism and Islam. Annexation of the territories was the basic requirement for staying in power but the wars on the basis of faiths were not common in India. The massacre and prosecution of catholic or protestant population by the victorious princes and kings of the rival faiths was the outcome of many of the wars fought on the soil of Europe. In India, Muslim rulers assigned jobs of high rankings in governance and army to Hindus and Hindu rulers to Muslims, vice versa. The armies of Mamluk Turks and successive Sultans of Delhi was composed of high ranking generals from Muslim community, indeed, gradual and increasing induction of Hindu warriors was an increasing trend. Religion largely was a matter of individual faith not of a political doctrine. Europe at the other hand remained divided on the plank of Catholicism and Protestantism during the same period.

Gradually, from eighteenth century onward, Europe began to move towards nationalism shedding the communal divide but the lust for territorial acquisitions dragged them into two great wars in the first half of the twentieth century. Indians as a nationality were not party to those two world wars though more than thirty six lakh Indian soldiers participated in them as the soldiers of British Empire. With the end of Second World War in 1945, Europe began to resurge as a united continent, while in India Hindu-Muslim divide reached the point of dismemberment of the country in 1947.

Europe fought several wars in its history. One of them was Thirty Years War fought from 1618 to 1648. This period was of the golden age in India under the benevolent rule of Mughal Emperors, Jahangir and Shahjahan (1605-1648), continuing the legacy of good governance initiated by Akbar (1556-1605) the Great. In the mean time, the dominance of catholic Habsburgs of Austria and Spain over the protestant population of Bohemia had engulfed almost entire Europe in a war that lasted for thirty years. The war for its duration came to be known as Thirty years war (1618-1648). The catholic dominance was challenged by the protestant rulers and noblemen in the kingdom of Bohemia. In 1618, protestant noblemen of Bohemia revolted against the anti-protestant rule of catholic Ferdinand. The rebellious protestant noblemen elected Frederick, the Calvinistic Elector Palatine, as King of Bohemia. Spain, Austria and the Catholic League combined to crush protestant Christians. Frederick was defeated and the practice of Protestantism was prohibited in Bohemia. Kings and princes arrayed on the basis of schism they followed. German principalities, Bohemia,

Palatinate, Spain, Baveria, Holland, France, England, Austria, Denmark, Norway, Sweden, almost the entire Europe was engulfed in a prolonged war that lasted till 1648. War came to end with the signing of the Treaty of Westphalia in 1648. Spain remained in war for a decade more. The treaty signed in Pyrenees in 1659 between Spain and France, brought the hostilities to an uneasy-cease.[1] More than eighty lakh (eight million) people were killed in the war.

Almost a century later, Europe engaged itself in another war, i.e., Seven Years' War. Once again, almost all from big to small, Prussia, Saxony, Austria, Russia, Bohemia, Great Britain, France and Spain and many other countries got themselves involved in war. The war went on from 1756 to 1763. The war between France and Britain ended with a treaty in 1763 at Paris.[2] Both the countries lost more than 4 lakh soldiers and civilians.

By then the Mughal power was diminishing in India giving rise to region-centric kings, Maharajas, Rajas and Nawabs and the European traders. The Nawab of Bengal, Siraj-ud-Daula was defeated in the battle of Plassey in 1757 at the hands of British traders headed by Robert Clive. Seven years later in 1764 the Mughal Emperor Shah Alam along with his deputy, Shuja-ud-Daula, the Nawab of Oudh, and the fugitive Nawab of Bengal, Mir Qasim was defeated in a battle at Buxer at the hands of Robert Clive, the British Governor of Bengal Presidency. The consequences of the battle of Buxer heralded the ascendency of the British rule in India, in the guise of a trading Company known as East India Company. French had also tried to establish them in Madras, now known as Chennai, but failed.

France and Great Britain, the two main contenders for the territorial acquisitions in India, had to fight a tireless war in Europe in the very beginning of the nineteenth century. The Austrian and Prussian monarchs in their attempt to reinstate the French Monarch, Louis XVI at the throne of France which he had lost to revolutionaries owing to French Revolution in 1789, threatened the French revolutionists with the 'punishment that they merit' which was responded with the imprisonment of the royal family, abolishment of Royality and beheading of Louis XVI on 21 January 1793, by the revolutionaries.

War started between France at one side and Austro-Prussian troops at the other. Napoleon Bonaparte, an offspring of the French Revolution, started his military operations to bring the entire Europe under the French subjugation which brought France at war with Spain, Austria, Prussia, Russia, England and some other countries of lesser importance. War with Britain was also fought in Syria and Egypt and the seas. The hostilities between France and Great Britain remained high from 1806 to 1814, most of the time France aiming at the annihilation of British naval power. France, with the announcement of Berlin Decree(November 1806) followed by decrees at Warsaw in January 1807, Milan in December 1807 and Fontainebleau in October 2010, closed all ports of Europe for Britain and its colonies and threatened such ships sailing to Great Britain. This was the 'continental system' aimed at economic strangulation of Great Britain. The ferocious naval battles at Nile, Copenhagen and Trafalgar went to Britain; Marengo, Austerlitz, Jena and Friedland went to France. Austrian, Prussian and Russian forces acting together inflicted a crushing defeat upon France at Liepzig (Battle of Nations) in 2013, followed by a joint attack with Britain as a leading force. This compelled Napoleon to surrender in March 1814. He was expelled to Elba. His escape from Elba, eventual and final defeat at the hands of British at the battle of Waterloo on 18 June 1815 and final dispatch to the island of St. Helena in exile, was a story of bitter conflicts between Great Britain and France for years to come. Around thirty lakh (3 million) soldiers killed and an equal number of civilians were estimated injured in the Napoleonic wars.

France and Great Britain were to align very soon when were threatened by a common enemy, Prussia, to be known as Germany in future. With intrigues, alliances, secret treaties and agreements, frequent changes in friends and foes, and betrayals focussed on territorial gains within Europe and the colonies, mostly in Asia and Africa, during the nineteenth and early twentieth century's, Europe plunged into another war. This time it was not restricted to European borders but engulfed almost entire world. This came to be known as First World War (1914-1918). By this time the Europe had become the master of the world. The entire Indian subcontinent was under the British subjugation and the colonial slaves had to defend the empire of their masters. Indians were to shed their blood for the sake of Great Britain in distant lands in the process. Europe was sitting on the pile of gunpowder waiting for a spark.

The spark came from a lesser known place, Sarajevo, the capital of a tiny state, Bosnia. Bosnia had been annexed by Austria-Hungary combine a few years back. In 1914, the Archduke Franz Ferdinand, the heir of Austrian throne, was assassinated along with his wife at Sarajevo on 28 June, by a Serbian nationalist. Serbia was blamed for the complicity; hence Austria gave an ultimatum with 11 demands to Serbia to be fulfilled within 48 hours. Serbia failed and on 28 July Austria declared war on Serbia. Russia mobilised its army to defend Serbia and three days later Germany declared war on Russia and 5 days later on 3 August on France. Very soon Great Britain also entered in the war.

The war fought between the 'Central Powers', comprising Austria, Hungary, Germany, Turkey and Bulgaria at one side, and 'Allies' comprising Russia, USA, France, Great Britain, Serbia, and Japan at the other. Towards the end of the war between the month of April and December in the year 1917, Panama, Cuba, CostaRica, Nicargua, Haiti, Honduras, Bolivia, Peru, Uruguay, Ecuador and Brazil joined the 'Allies' in the war against the 'Central Powers'. The war came to end with an armistice on 11 November 2018, signed at 11 a.m. at adhoc head quarter of Foch, the French Marshal and the Commander-in-Chief of the allied forces. The armistice was followed by the Treaty of Versailles on 28 June 1919. Germany, the aggressor in the beginning but vanquished in the end, was humiliated by Allies, the victors. The war theoretically won by allies but the losses were immense throughout the continent and European colonies in other continents, cutting across the dividing lines of winners and losers. About six crore and fifty lakh (65 million) soldiers took part in the war, out of which one crore thirty lakh (13 million) or 20% lost their lives. Two crore and twenty lakh (22 million) were wounded and seventy lakh (7 million) became disabled for life. The number of civilians perished due to massacres, hunger and epidemics was difficult to ascertain, even more difficult to assess were the casualties in colonies spread over in Asia and Africa.

On economic front Europe, though still was the master of the world, had to face unprecedented economic-chaos. The trembling economies of all the countries of Europe came crumbling down with the outset of

Great Depression in 1927. Starting from Germany, the vanquished, the entire Europe had to live on rationing of the food. The onus of throwing Europe in to war had been attributed to Germany and Germany had to pay the war indemnity by surrendering its territory and regular payment of war compensation which resulted in the rise of radical nationalism in Germany and the emergence of Nazism with Adolf Hitler as its leader.

Within two decades of the signing of the Treaty of Versailles, Europe engaged in another world wide war in 1939, greater than the first in every respect, in area as well as in population and devastation. The warring nations were grouped in two blocs, "Axis" and "Allies". The former was comprising Germany, Italy, Romania, Hungary and Japan and the latter was consisting of USSR, USA, Great Britain and France as the leading countries. Across the Atlantic Ocean in Latin America Mexico and Brazil lend their support to 'Allies'. Poland, Greece, Bulgaria, Yugoslavia Denmark, Belgium, Luxemburg, Norway and Holland had to face the brunt of the expansionist designs of the axis powers. The war went for about six years and came to an end with the occupation of Berlin, the German capital, by the USSR, and the Great Britain led non communist Block forces and consequent surrender by Germany on 8 May in 1945. In the far east of the world, the droppings of the atom bombs on the Japanese cities of Hiroshima and Nagasaki on 6 August and 9 August in 1945, respectively, by America, compelled Japan to agree with the terms set by Allies on 14-15 August 1945. The devastating power of the atom bomb had surprised and unnerved Japanese. The Japanese surrender brought hostilities to end in the pacific front.

Once again as in the First World War, the responsibility of waging war was thrust upon Germany. To ensure that Germany may not raise its head again and the allies may get their share in the booty of war, Germany was divided into four regions. Each region was put under the area of influence of big fours; USSR, USA, France and Britain. The strength of army of Italy was curtailed and some of its colonies were taken over by the allies.

As has been stated earlier, the Second World War was more devastating than the first. The war took the tall of about 5 crore

(50 million) people out of which 2.70 crore (27 mllion) were soldiers, more than two fold of the First World War. An estimated 2.20 crore (22 million) civilians were killed in the war. About 1.2 crore (12 million) people lost their lives either in concentration camps or to some other types of killing methods. The losses of Soviet Union were huge. Around 40 lakh (4 million) Soviet soldiers and 60 lakh (6 million) civilians were taken as prisoners and killed. In Leningrad (erstwhile Petrograd founded as Petersburg) alone, owing to its siege and encirclement by German forces for two and a half years around 10 lakh (one million) people died of starvation and diseases. About 40 lakh (4 million) citizens of Stalingrad died due to German attack on it. In all around 10% (20 million) of the Soviet population and 20% (6.5 million) of the Polish population was perished. The air raids of Germany and Britain on one another resulted in indiscriminate killings of the civilians. For instance, the British bombing of the German city of Dresden on 13-14 February in 1945 killed 1,35,000 people. This was a relentless war with no consideration to humanity. Every country was right in its own interpretation. Most of them were the followers of the same religion, Christianity, and were praying Jesus for their victory.

This was the first half of the twentieth century Europe. But the second half was quite different. Forgetting the hostile past, Europe began to unite searching the elements of cohesion, cooperation, collaboration and mutual understanding for the economic benefits of its people. This quest of economic development resulted in the birth of European Union. It was to change the political history of the entire continent as well. The hot summers were over and the pleasant rains began to drizzle.

Let us have a brief look over the journey of this change. Expelled from their own countries by the invading German forces during the Second World War, the governments of Belgium, The Netherlands and Luxembourg in exile in Great Britain, mulled over the economic cooperation for the mutual development of their countries. The discussions resulted in the formation of BENELUX Economic Union which established a customs union. It was signed by them in September 1944 which became operative in 1948. Among other things it abolished pre-union quantitative trade restrictions. Within three years of its signing it got a broad and wider base with the formation of European Coal and Steel Community (ECSC) with France, West Germany and Italy and BENELUX as the members, by the Treaty of Paris in 1951. The basic principle was the promotion of trade through a common market and common institutions. Needless to remind, BENELUX and France had fought a disastrous war against Germany and Italy only seven years ago. Traditional enmity was being replaced by the urge of the economic wellbeing of the people. The ECSC put forward the desire of economic integration of Europe. The desire was further strengthened through the establishment of EC, the Council of EU, the European Court of Justice, the European Parliament with a common Assembly and the economic and social unity. The economic and commercial unity ultimately led the political unity of Europe.[3] Territorial disputes and claims were given a silent burial to usher in an era of economic and social development of the people.

At the other part of the world, some six thousands km east of Europe, the two nations, India and Pakistan in the Indian subcontinent, had emerged on the basis of communal divide on 15 August 1947. They were applying all means to strengthen the animosity, giving no consideration to economic well being of the people. They fought over the issue of the independent 'princely state' of Jammu and Kashmir and quarrelled on several others. In order to compel Kashmir to 'fall like a ripe fruit' in to Pakistan's lap as once told by Jinnah to Agha Shaukat, Pakistan by the month of October in 1947, cut off the supply of fuel, kerosene, wheat, salt and cloths to the independent 'princely state' of J&K and also stopped accepting Kashmiri cheques in Pakistan. The king of Jammu and Kashmir, Maharaja Hari Singh protested to Pakistan, but was given no heed. In Europe BENELUX has moved to economic cooperation, Pakistan at this part of Indian subcontinent had resorted to economic strangulation of its neighbour, J&K. Moreover, Pakistani leadership extended covert support to Pashtoon tribesmen from the North Western Frontier Province (NWFP) to invade the state of J&K.[4] As the princely State acceded to India, and war broke out between the two nations, India stopped the water supply from Upar Bari Doab canal system to the Dipalpur and Bahwalpur canal taking water to Pakistan, on 1 April 1948. This stoppage of water rendered about 5.5 percent of the total sowing area of Pakistan without water and deprived Lahore from its water requirement.[5] People living in the same plains during Raj days found themselves in two different camps, hostile to each other. The British had drawn the battle lines by drawing Radcliffe line.

The scenario in Indian subcontinent was in stark contrast to the Europe's economic cooperation. Europe was marching ahead on the way of European integration inventing new instruments of cohesion. A Common Market Treaty was signed in March 1957 by the six member ECSC countries. The treaty was signed at Rome. It aimed at, first, abolition of tariffs and quotas between the members, second, application of a common tariff against all non members, and third, extension of the provision of no tariff to the overseas territories of the six member countries.[6] The economic objectives of the Common Market Treaty of Rome were also aimed at political integration, rejecting any future armed conflict between the member countries. "We are not just integrating economies, we are integrating politics" said Walter Hallstein, the first President of the European Commission, "we are not just sharing furniture. We are building a new bigger house." In the words of French Foreign Minister, Robert Schuman, the foundation of a European Federation was "indispensable to the preservation of peace." Europe moved one step further when the European Union Treaty (EUT) was signed on 14 February 1984. Within three years a Single European Act (SEA) was ratified in July 1987.

The unification of Europe became a popular subject of common debate across the Europe. Meanwhile, in Indian subcontinent Pakistan was meddling in the affairs of its neighbour, Afghanistan. In close collaboration of America, it created and supported first, Mujahideens and then Taliban to throw out the then Afghan government. India and Pakistan had opened a new front of conflict at Siachen glacier at an altitude of more than 22,000 feet resulting in the armed clashes over the acquisitions in 1984. The fighting for possesions went for three years from 1984 to 1987. The 'Bleed India' policy enunciated by President Zia-ul-Haq was ill conceived and was not to bring any benefit to the people of Pakistan. India's 'OP BRASTTACS' worsened Indo-Pak relations further. Indian subcontinent and Europe were following different paths, the former-to economic impoverishment, the latter to economic enrichment.

The German people had to navigate through the troubled situations until the Berlin Wall was razed to dust by themselves on 9 November, in the year 1989. The Wall had artificially divided the people of Berlin in to two rival political power blocks. Within a year of fall of the Berlin wall, people with their concerted efforts, reunited two politically estranged Germanies, GDR and FRG, on 3 October 1990. Within two months of the reunification, the country wide elections brought a coalition government to the power. The Germans divided in 1945, got themselves reunited, within 45 years of separation. British India was divided in to two independent dominions, two years later in 1947, far from being reunited, continued drifting apart from each other, inventing new areas of disputes and methods to perpetuate them. India's anti Pakistan stand in the war of liberation of Bangladesh, Pakistan's covert support to 'whip up anti-Indian feelings amongst the students and peasants preferably on some religious issues' in J&K, alleged harbouring and providing logistic support to anti India terrorist groups; India's alleged manoeuvring of terrorist activities on Pakistani soil, especially in Baluchistan, are a few examples of continued bitter relations between the two nations. There exists no reinforcement-cement-concrete wall between the two nations, as was in Berlin, but the wall of hate, mistrust, mischief and misunderstanding, becoming harder to hardest.

The 1973 Declaration of European Identity that "Europe must unite and speak increasingly with one voice" "to make itself heard and play its proper role in the world" was received as a new Gospel in Europe. Since the Treaty of Maastricht (7 February 1992) which brought EU in to existence, it has grown up as a collective force in international affairs and a single entity to any outsider. It shows this spirit when it comes to a trade agreement or disbursement of aid.[7] The economic and political success of the EU has always been a temptation to neighbouring non-member countries to join it. In July 1997, five countries of the eastern Europe, i.e., Hungary, Poland, Estonia, The Czech Republic and Slovania were found qualifying the parameters in the Luxemburg Council and subsequently were admitted to EU. Two years later some more countries, i.e., Bulgaria, Latavia, Lithunia, Romania, Slovakia, Cypress and Malta were given entry by the Helsinki European Council negotiations in 1999.

With a view to give EU a kind of national entity 'Constitution for Europe' was finalised in a Treaty, signed in Rome on 29 October 2004, and published in the 'Official Journal of the European Union on 16 December 2004. The significance of the 'Constitution of Europe' lies in the fact that its Preamble was signed by the Presidents or Prime Ministers along with their Foreign Ministers of Belgium, Czech Republic, Denmark, Federal Republic of Germany, Republic of Estonia, Hellenic Republic, Spain, French Republic, Ireland, Italy, Republic of Cypress, Republic of Latavia, Republic of Lithunia, Luxemburg, Hungary, Malta, Netherlands, Republic of Finland, Republic of Poland, Portugual, Republic of Slovania, Slovak Republic, Sweden and United Kingdom of Great Britain and Northern Ireland.

The Member States were well aware with their bitter past, but now were determined to make future better than ever.

"BELIEVING that Europe, reunited after bitter experiences," reads the Preamble of the Constitution of Europe, admitting the hostile past, "intends to continue along the path of civilization, progress and prosperity, for the good of all its inhabitants, including the weakest and most deprived; that it wishes to remain a continent open to culture, learning and social progress; and that it wishes to deepen the democratic and transparent nature of its public life, and to strive for peace, justice and solidarity throughout the world," and further that the establishment of the European Union, was the "reflection of the will of the citizens and states of Europe to build a common future." The Constitution of Europe provided further that the Union was founded on the values of respect to human dignity, freedom, democracy, equality, the rule of law and respect for human rights of person belonging to minorities.

Strangely and sadly enough, in 1973 when the European Community was proclaiming the "Declaration of European Identity", Pakistan proclaimed its new Constitution, third in line since 1956, on 12 April 1973, granting freedom, equality, tolerance and social justice but only "as enunciated by Islam.", depriving others from these fundamental rights to citizens. While the declaration of European Identity moved ahead with 'Constitution for Europe' in 2004 to grant all, including minorities equal rights, Pakistan moved ahead with the Constitution (Second Amendment) Act, 1974 taking away Quadianis

(Ahemadias) from the list of Muslims. Hereafter, Quadianis were declared non Muslims. Quadianis were denied to practice Islam in a land which for many of them was a 'Muslim Homeland'. They had already began to experience discremination from the very beginning of the new State. There were anti-Ahemadiya riots in and around Lahore in 1953.

Pakistan in Article-1(1) of its Constitution, reiterated that, "Islam shall be the State religion of Pakistan". While in European Parliament, as also in India, any person belonging to any community or faith can be appointed or elected to any office, the Pakistan Constitution bars all non Muslims as per State's interpretation from the high offices such as President, Prime Minister and Chief Justice. A clause was inserted in Article 260, clause (3), which says, "A person who does not believe in the absolute and unqualified finality of the Prophethood of MUHAMMAD (peace be upon him), the last of the Prophets or claims to be a Prophet, in any sense of the word or of any description whatsoever, after MUHAMMAD (peace be upon him) or recognise such a claimant as a Prophet or religious reformer, is not a Muslim for the purposes of the Constitution or Law." As State was empowered with the right of interpreting Islam, the extremists among Sunnis began to demand to declare minority Shias as non Muslims, which gave rise to militant outfits across both the communities. In September 1996, Shia and Sunni students of Parachinar high school of Kurram valley clashed. Both the factions in the valley were equipped with Kalashnikovs. They fought for about a week leaving at least 100 dead. Prior to it in 1995, a group of army officers led by Zaheer ul Islam Abbassi plotted a coup which was to declare Pakistan a Sunni Islamic State. The coup, however, failed to materialise. If majority population was a justification to declare Pakistan an Islamic Republic, then Sunnis who constitute more than three fourth of the total population, too had a logic to declare it a Sunni State. One wonders, was that Jinnah's Pakistan, which he had promised on 11 August in 1947 in his Presidential address at Pakistan Constitutional Assembly to his people. The religion, cast or creed, spoke he, "has nothing to do with the business of the State".

The persecution of religious minorities in Pakistan, Bangladesh and Afghanistan and their exodus to India led the government of India to amend its Citizenship Act of 1955 in December 2019 to extend citizenship to such minorities. The amendment popularly known as CAA {Citizenship (Amendment) Act,2019.}, did not include Muslim immigrants, generating fear among the Indian Muslims of being forced to prove their Indian citizenship. It was apprehended in many quarters that CAA provisions were to become the basis for the National Population Register (NPR) and National Register of Citizenship (NRC). The determination of citizenship on the basis of the provisions of CAA and consequent entries in above-stated registers were seen as harassment to Muslims. There were widespread anti-CAA demonstrations throughout India. The Government did not succumb to the public protests and went ahead with its policy.

In the Constitution of Europe, rights were categorised in 'Subjects', vested in the Union and shared by the member states. Common foreign and security policy, including the progressive framing of a common defence policy were allotted to the Union. Custom Union, rules to guide internal market, monetary policy, conservation of marine biological resources, and a common commercial policy were exclusively allotted to the scope of Union. In short, the Constitution addressed almost each and everything to the satisfaction and agreement of all the member states.

Thus, a union of a continent, unheard ever before in the world history, with an Anthem of Union, 'Ode to Joy', drawn from the Ninth Symphony of Ludwig Van Beethoven, a flag having a circle of 12 golden stars on a blue background, a common currency, Euro, and above all with a Constitution like a nation, emerged which ensured peace and better life to its people. Today, EU's member countries are free from any external or internal threat or aggression, unimaginable in the first half of the twentieth century Europe. In the Union, which has grown up to 27 member entity, the independence of every member state is ensured. Unlike Indian subcontinent, there is no neighbours' paranoia in the Union.

Can the countries of Indian subcontinent take some lessons from that distant land and apply the twenty first century methods to rescue themselves from the vicious cycle of poverty and backwardness, remains a big challenge to be accepted by them.

EUROPEAN UNION
2020
MEMBER COUNTRIES
Candidate Countries
Potential EU Countries
Brexit 2020
ICELAND
NORWEGIAN SEA
NORWAY
SWEDEN
FINLAND
EST ONIA
LATVIA
LITHUANIA
Russia
Atlantic Ocean
IRELAND
DENMARK
Belarus
POLAND
GERMANY
NETH.
FRANCE
CZECH REPUBLIC
SLOVAKIA
Ukraine
AUST.
HUNGARY
Moldova
CASPIAN SEA
ROMANIA
ITALY
CROATIA
Serbia
SPAIN
PORTUGAL
BLACK SEA
BULGARIA
Albania
GREECE
Turkey
MEDITERRANEAN SEA
MALTA
N
E
S
Not to scale
Boundaries of the countries are indicative

Chapter - V

World's Rich's Enrichment - The Poor's Impoverishment

Around two-third of the people of the Indian subcontinent live in rural areas. The people living in rural areas are broadly engaged in agriculture or in agriculture-allied activities. Country-wise, a population of about 65% in India, 65% in Pakistan, 64% in Bangladesh and 72% in Nepal, of the total population, stay in rural areas, rendering them dependent on agriculture and agriculture-related activities. Agriculture sector consists of poorest of the poor, yet contributes about 24% to the Gross Domestic Products (GDP), of their respective countries. As of 2017 it was feeding a population of around 173 crore (1.73 Billion), taking India's 133.91 crore, Pakistan's 19.70 crore, Bangladesh's 16.46 crore, Nepal's 2.93 crore[1] and Bhutan's 0.08 crore population put together.

As a policy, subsidy to purchase seeds, pesticides and fertilizers as well as farm loans are admissible to farmers but the mechanism is so cumbersome and complicated, and rigged with corrupt practices that the actual farmers get a little benefit from such so called farmer-friendly schemes. Muhammad Ali Jinnah, the first Governor General and the President of the Constituent Assembly of Pakistan identified "bribery and corruption" and the "black marketing" as the two curses on India and warned his countrymen to desist from them in his first Presidential address to the Constituent Assembly on 11 August 1947. The three curses instead of vanishing in the subcontinent are ever increasing since then, agriculture sector being one of the victims.

The farmers of developing countries are betrayed at home by their own policy-makers, the one hand, and exploited by the economy-conglomerates of the industrialised countries, which often act collectively, at the other. Even while dealing in their individual capacity, industrialized countries are powerful enough to carry on the business in their best interests pushing back the farmers of developing countries to disadvantage. They oblige the decision makers of the developing or underdeveloped countries for their own benefit. World Bank with its two arms, International Bank for Reconstruction and Development (IBRD) and International Development Agency (IDA), at the request of the loan/credit seeking countries, advance loans to them for the developmental activities but not without terms and conditions that favour the industrialized countries. Industrialized countries also advance financial assistances in the form of Aid programmes. These debts in the garbs of Loans and Aids are laden with conditions which influence the economic and political policies of the Aid receiving countries. These terms and conditions, most of the times are not conducive to the national interests of the receiving countries, yet are accepted gladly by their leaders to relieve them from the then prevailing grave economic problems. The long-term repercussions are deliberatly rejected for the immediate political and economic benefits.

The developing countries are always ready with their begging bowls to seek financial help from the International Monetary Fund (IMF). IMF is supposed to help the countries to stabilize the financial instability through monetary co-operation, balanced growth of trade and payments, exchange rate stability and orderly Balance of Payments (BoP) adjustments.[2] But owing to its governance structure, it has a pick and choose method for the advantage of member-countries having large voting powers in its governing body. The countries of lesser political importance have naturally fewer chances to get a better deal from IMF. The 182 member IMF's governing structure is dominated by group of 7 countries, i.e., US, Germany, UK, France, Canada, Japan and Italy. United States has the maximum voting powers. By virtue of the votes needed to pass important decisions, and with 17% of voting power with US, it also enjoys the Veto power. As per IMF policy a major change or decision requires 85% majority in its favour, which cannot be obtained without US which has 17% votes with 17.5% quota.

EU has about one third of the total quota. Despite the quota increase to other countries in compliance of Governance Reforms agreed upon in 2010, the situation in the voting shares has not brought any substantial change to the voting powers of the developing countries. US even after its decreased quota at 17.45% retains 16.52% votes.[3] The voting power based on quota system ensures the post of MD going to EU and next highest post, First MD, going to US. By this system of voting share, the US with its ally EU rules over the world. No other country enjoys the veto power. Other member-countries have to garner the support of USA and EU, even for the matter of little importance. Putting together BRICS countries (Brazil, Russia, India, China and South Africa) have only 14% voting power.[4] As of January 2020 it has a marginal increase of 0.17 votes. Thus in the absence of US agreement even the consensus decision of BRICS has a little meaning. Contrary to it, the US with its allies in European Union ensures the passage of any of the resolution in favour of a country which suits to its geo economic and political interests. The countries of Indian subcontinent are not able to get a resolution passed in their favour with a small percentage of votes; 2.63 to India, 0.43 to Pakistan, 0.24 to Bangladesh, 0.03 to Bhutan and 0.06 to Nepal. The loans to the countries such as stated above are sanctioned only on the terms and conditions agreed upon somewhere else.

A clear instance of discrimination was witnessed in the sanction of IMF loans to Greece and Pakistan during recent past. While Greece, an EU member country, was sanctioned a loan of $1.8 billion in 2017, the third loan since 2010, Pakistan was denied in 2018. The denial was a warning to Pakistan for its joining China led "One Belt One Road" initiative. Before Pakistan's proposal could be tabled in IMF, US raised apprehensions that "there is the chance that tax payers' dollars are going to go towards Chinese directed companies as part of that bailout". The efforts of newly elected Pakistani Prime Minister, Imran Khan to seek a loan of $10 - $12 billion from IMF to save Pakistan's dwindling economy from crash, were nipped in the bud. The message was very clear "either with us or without IMF bail out".[5]

Pakistan, like Greece, had received IMF loans at several previous occasions. These loans as well as economic aids were initially helpful in improving the States' ability to cope up with the adverse monetary situation but could not bring prosperity and human wellbeing to its people.

The agricultural policies are formulated by the industrialized countries, such as USA with its ally Canada, and the European Union (EU), in such a way that while there are no trade barriers within the member countries, other countries' imports are subjected to the harshest of the tariff-conditions. The waivers from such tariffs are dependent to the political interests. This can be understood well in the functioning of the Common Agricultural Policy (CAP) of the European Union. Conceived by the Treaty of Rome (1957) the CAP was introduced in 1962. CAP applies various instruments to control the world market. One of the instruments is price support which in common parlance is known as farm support. This is supplemented with import tariffs, which through a comprehensive measure ensure that the EU farmers maintain a high price and export it to the member states without any export support. The member states do not impose any tariff on the produce of another member state. At the same time if any non-member country exports any agriculture produce at the prices lower than the EU output (prices), a heavy levy is imposed. This results in keeping import price much higher to EU market price. This mechanism blocks the import from a non member country at cheap prices to the EU nations. By this system of tariffs while the farmers of EU are encouraged to grow more and more, the farmers of the developing countries in the absence of the buyers are unable to get even the cost price of their produce, are discouraged to carry on the farming any longer. Consequent to the farm support and favourable tariff (export and import) policy EU farmers get the prices many times higher than the cost of production. Increased production in EU countries generates surplus which may lead to the fall in prices. This danger of fall in the prices is averted by fixing floor prices which are much higher to the cost of production, by the government. In the event of a fall in prices below the floor prices, the produces are bought by the government.

Prima facie, CAP appears quite similar to Minimum Support Price (MSP) mechanism adopted in India. But they are different a lot from each other in object, price determination mechanism and practice. In India MSP takes the care of cost of production that includes the cost of inputs such as, seed, fertilizers and pesticides, and labour at the minimum wages, but does not take the rental value of the land into account.[6] In India, the government buys the food grains at MSP for its Food Security Programme, through state owned agencies. The foodgrain then is sold on fixed prices with or without subsidies through Public Distribution System (PDS) from Fair Prices Shops directly to the consumers. The MSP enables Indian farmers just to avoid starvation and carry on his/her traditional occupation of farming. The export subsidy given on the export of rice and cotton by government of Pakistan is no match to EU's CAP. The subsidy is pocketed by big land holders, while the small farmers have to sell their produces in the local markets only. Likewise the reimbursement of Goods and Services Tax (GST) paid on the export of food grains in India, benefits the export conglomerates in the agricultural sector who have very often, seldom to do with the farming.

The EU CAP supports a sector, agriculture, which accounts for less than 2% of employment but absorbs more than 40% of the EU budget. Ironically, in the Indian subcontinent while more than half of the workforce and three fourth of the population depends on agriculture sector, it was attracting only about 2.2 to 2.4% of the annual budget in the recent past. In India, the largest country of the subcontinent, agriculture sector could receive only about 5% allocation in the Union budget for 2020-21, which was acclaimed a progressive budget with such high sounding words 'Sabka Saath, Sabka Vikas, Sabka Vishwas'.[i-n]. As against a 2% in EU, in India agriculture has a share of 43% in total employment generation. Out of total employment generation, 42% in Pakistan, 39% in Bangladesh, 57% in Bhutan and 72% in Nepal goes to Agriculture sector.[7]

US Cotton and Rice Policies have direct ill-effects on the farmers of cotton and rice growing countries in the third world. As explained in Human Development Report, 2005 the US policies in terms of cotton and rice work like EU's Sugar Policy. Under the policy the US farmers receive a hefty amount which is equivalent to the market value of the crop. Once the actual price is secured, the US farm produces like cotton and rice are sold in world markets at the prices cheaper to the prices of local producers. This mechanism throws the local producers out from the market. "Price distortions caused by the US subsidies" states UN HDR- 2005, "have a direct impact on these small holder producers.

These subsidies lower world prices by 9% to 13% and enable US producers to dominate world markets, accounting about one third of total world exports. These exports are not possible without subsidies."[8] Pakistan which has rice and cotton as its major exports among farm produces, has to compete in this unfavourable trade environment. India is one of the largest producer of the cotton yarn. India exports about $4.7 billion and Pakistan $3.5 billion every year making them 3rd and 4th largest exporter after China and US of cotton yarn.[9] In rice India at about $5.5 billion and Pakistan at about $1.7 billion worth of exports are the 1st and 4th largest countries among the rice exporting countries.[10]

Apart from acting individually, US combined with its neighbours, Canada and Mexico, signed North American Free Trade Agreement (NAFTA), which came in to force on 1 January 1994. The agreement was aimed at, among other things, establishment of a free trade regime between the member states while imposing trade barriers to others. NAFTA was updated and replaced by a new agreement, US–Mexico-Canada Agreement (USMCA) in September 2018. USMCA covers a population of about 50 crores, about 23% of Indian subcontinent's population, but controls more than one fifth of the world trade. The agreement protects Canada's supply-managed dairy system, which sets production quotas and the price of the milk, raises prices for the consumers but provides farmers with a stable income. To protect the dairy industry at home from cheaper foreign milk, tariffs of up to 275% are imposed on the imports of foreign milk. At the same time a tariff free access is provided to American farmers by fixing a quota of 3.5% to Canadian dairy market. The car industry of Mexico and Canada has been protected by assigning a quota of 2.6 million cars to them for export to US. At the same time 40% of the car parts of the cars manufactured in three countries are must to be made in North America. Labourers have been protected by making the payment of $16 per hour mandatory.[11]

India and Pakistan, whose agricultural economy is dependent on the exports of such items as cotton and rice, face such unfair practices in world trade. The farm policies adopted by the industrialized countries, US and EU in particular, creates adverse state of balance of payments and consequential monetary crisis in the developing country that depends on the export of such produces. To save the situation from becoming economically and politically worse, the affected countries go for Aids and Loans to the same countries and institutions who were responsible for their economic exploitation through a sheer mechanism of unfair tariff and trade policies, up to a large extent. It has been estimated that between 2002 and 2003 rice grown in the US at a cost of $415 a tonne was exported at a price of $274 per tonne.[12] The bill of the subsidy extended to the US farmers is footed through a complex and complicated mechanism by the developing countries such as India, Pakistan, Nepal and Bangladesh. This mechanism of economic imperialism is hardly to be understood by the common man. The developed countries with a number of international market regulating institutions at their hands do not allow the poor countries to impose import duties on their produces. Equipped with such arbitrary tariff policies the developed countries sell their agricultural produces at the prices cheaper than the prices in local markets of the developing countries. A few glaring examples of such unfair practices are being reproduced below from the UN sponsored Human Development Report, 2005 : "US rice policies harm domestic produces in many countries. .....In countries such as Ghana and Haiti rice farmers have been pushed out of national markets by US imports"[13]. Subsequent to these US rice policies "In Ghana rice farmers in the poorest northern part of the country have seen market squeezed by cheap imports. The IMF has opposed the use of tariffs to restrict these imports on the ground that there is no evidence of unfair competition."[14]

The most vociferous countries of the third world have raised their voices against this unfair practice of farm subsidies and trade barriers at various WTO forums such as Doha and Uruguay Rounds of talks but in vain. The industrialized countries promised to slash them down in WTO meetings but had never complied with the decisions in practice. On the other hand WTO fixed the ceiling of subsidies on the basis of the prices of 1986-88, the decade in which the developing countries like India just began to advance subsidies to farmers. The limit is not in terms of a unified currency, like dollars, but in the national currencies which limits developing nations eligibility of extending subsidies to its farmers. In Pakistan, farmers were able to get agricultural credit and increased support prices only after 1993, that too after a severe crop failure. India's Food Security Act of 2013 has drawn eyebrows from the consortium of the developed countries. The Act is aimed at providing food grains to meet two ends need of its 37% poor population. It also covers partially a population of additional 20% which was living just above the poverty line. The food security involved a cost of $ 21 billion in 2014, an increase of just $ 5 billion over the level of 2013. Thus while in India only $21billion was spent on the food security of a population of about 84 crore out of which about 45 crore were living in acute poverty, the US was making $5.0 billion as payment for farm support to its 20,000 farmers only. None of these US farmers was poor. As against India's food security's bill of about $21 billion, it was $140 billion in US during the same year, 2013.[15] It was disgusting that India had to defend its food security programme focussed at mitigation of hunger at the world-forums.

However, malice is within the Indian subcontinent. EU and USMCA, the two biggest economic conglomerates in the world, have given a goodbye to the hostilities within the respective Unions, and have turned their borders tariff free to member countries. All members have been protected by erecting trade barriers to non members. Ironically, in Indian subcontinent new ways to fuel hostilities are searched and doors for trade and commerce with neighbours are shut. Rich countries get them enriched further, as the poor countries allow them to be exploited in order to keep their neighbours impoverished. Poor or developing countries, while close their doors for trade and commerce to their neighbours, allow themselves to be exploited by industrialized countries, succumbing to their unfair farm and trade practices.

Chapter - VI

State of the People of the Indian subcontinent

The ailment

In 1951, when the first censuses of India and Pakistan were held, they had a population of 36.11 crore and 7.50 crore, respectively. In case of Pakistan its eastern wing, now Bangladesh, had the greater share at 4.20 crore with western wing contributing a population of 3.30 crore. Within a decade there was a sharp increase, with India reaching to 45.0 crore and Pakistan to 9.30 crore, an increase of around 24.50%. By 2017, the population of India risen by 270 % to 133.92 crore and Pakistan by 432.43 % to 19.70 crore and Bangladesh by 292 % to 16.47 crore.[1] Area as obvious, remained unchanged with a few exceptions such as inclusion of Sikkim to India in 1975 and Gwadar to Pakistan in 1958, India at about 32.87 lakh sq kms, Pakistan at about 8.82 lakh sq kms, Nepal at about 1.47 lakh sq kms, Bhutan at about 0.38 lakh sq kms and Bangladesh at about 1.43 lakh sq kms.[2]

However, the official figures of the countries may differ due to their claims and counter claims in respect to territories claimed by them, J&K in particular.

The food grain production could not increase to meet the food requirement of ever-growing population. While the death rate was brought down, the fertility rate remained high at 2.5 in India, 2.2 in Bangladesh and 3.7 in Pakistan during the year 2010 to 2015.

The Gross Domestic Product (GDP) once regarded as an important parameter to judge a Nation's development, too remained at a very low level when seen in the light of population. The growth in the per capita purchasing power parity (PPP per capita) in the subcontinent, from the level of 2001 to 2004 was between US$ 260 to US$ 335.

In a sharp contrast the per capita purchasing power parity (PPP per capita) in most of the countries of North and Western Europe recorded an increase of not less than US$ 3,000 during the same period.

Moreover, PPP per capita is just an average, obtained from total GDP divided by the mid-year population. Nowhere in the world the PPP per capita is equally distributed. The difference of income between various sections of the society or individuals in the Indian subcontinent is vast and a sizeable population has to adjust their lives to arrange two times' meal.

Very soon, people began to question the relevance of GDP and PPP per capita to judge the wellbeing of a nation. Economists realised that just national income or GDP were not the true indicators of development. These two parameters did not reflect the real state of the life of the people. Voices for change in the development indicators were raised from the Indian subcontinent.

The two Economists, one from Pakistan, Mehboob ul Haq and another from India, Amartya Sen, together advanced the notion of Human Development. "The real wealth of a nation is its people. And the purpose of development is to create an enabling environment for people to enjoy long, healthy and creative lives. This simple but powerful truth is too often forgotten in the pursuit of material and financial wealth" asserted Mehboob ul Haq.[3]

Based on the various world human development reports since their first publication in 1990, first penned by Dr Mehboob ul Haq, an attempt has been made in this Chapter to analyse the state of Human Development indicators of the nations of the Indian subcontinent vis-a-vis the status of human development in the countries of Europe and USA which are the most developed countries of the world and most of them are also the original manufacturers and exporters of the arms to the developing countries, including India and Pakistan, having bellicose relations with each other.

The political scenarios in the above stated two categories of countries are in sharp contrast. While the countries of the Indian subcontinent are characterised with external conflicts and clashes, and insurgencies and conflicts within their own political domains; the developed countries are characterized by cooperation, collaboration, mutual understanding with almost no external or internal strife or threat. This political stability in developed countries is instrumental for the better status of life of their people which is reflected clearly through human development indicators. During last seven decades India and Pakistan kept themselves engrossed in clashing with each other and within, while Nepal, Bangladesh and Sri Lanka were wasting their resources in combating internal insurgency, a fight with their own people in unequivocal terms.

Internal insurgency in India held Kashmir (IHK) and left wing extremism in more than half a dozen provinces of India and political unrest in some of the pockets of provinces in north- east India; ethnic unrest in Balochistan, Pakhtoonkhwa, Gilgit-Baltistan and Sindh in Pakistan; Maoist insurgency in Nepal and a war with Tamil secessionists in Sri Lanka, organised terrorism by the state or non state actors in the name of religion, faith and the ethnicity in India, Pakistan, Nepal and Bangladesh; and State's failure in meeting people's aspirations for equal treatment and non discrimination irrespective of caste, creed, community and region have always been the reasons of continued people's discontentment in these countries. The interests of minority communities are more often overlooked in order to appease majority communities and secure their support in the elections to form the government.

The notion of human development as the best parameter to judge the prosperity of a country, propounded by the two economists was not given even a little thought in practice in their home States.

Pleasantly, Imran Khan, the Prime Minister of Pakistan, surprised the world on 14 August 2018, when in his maiden speech as the Prime Minister to his nation he, drifting from the conventional rhetoric, reminded his people about the poor conditions of human beings in Pakistan.

Pakistan is "among those top five countries in which most of our children die before the age of five due to diseases caused by contaminated water" spoke Imran, "where female mortality is very high, where children die because of malnutrition resulted in stunted growth."

Inadvertently, he was addressing the real problems which all of the nations of the subcontinent were facing with. It was not he, but the UN report, which had brought that poor state of Pakistan to every ones notice, Imran said in his address.

The Human Development Reports sponsored by UNDP bring the state of human development indicators and the factors which prevent the people of developing world such as of Indian subcontinent, to enjoy the benefits of a developed society. The countries of the Indian subcontinent have always had the poor ranking among the nations of the world. In 2003 HDR, India was at 127, Pakistan at 144 and Bangladesh at 139 ranks in an order of best to the worst. In 2016 among these three, only Bangladesh maintained its ranking at 139, while India and Pakistan slipped to 131 and 147 place, respectively. These two countries in order to keep the hostilities alive at highest level wasted huge amounts of money on defence preparedness by importing weapons from the weapon manufacturing countries. The latter, the suppliers, interestingly, were enjoying very high level of Human Development indicators like health and education. Norway, Sweden, United States, United Kingdom, France, Germany, Spain, and Italy are some of them, which have been included in this Chapter to compare with Indian subcontinent countries namely, India, Pakistan, Bangladesh, Nepal and Bhutan, the first two had also close ties for import of weapons with Russian Federation and People's Republic of China, respectively. This has necessitated to refer the status of Russian Federation and China also. To facilitate an easy comparison between the countries of Indian subcontinent and the developed countries, to reach to conclusion, figures wherever felt necessary have been given in tabular forms.

India and Pakistan have a long history of armed clashes and wars, prompting them to spend more and more on defence. East Pakistan which parted its ways with Pakistan to become Bangladesh in 1971, largely has friendly relations with its neighbours, India and Myanmar, avoiding armed conflicts and clashes with them. This policy of friendly relations towards its neighbours, adopted by Bangladesh, made a good space for interventions in the human development. Less expenditure on defence paves the way for more expenditure on socio-economic development. Bangladesh appears to have done so, up to a large extent.

India has the burden to sustain an army of 13.25 lakh personnel, Pakistan of 6.19 lakh personnel and Bangladesh of 1.26 lakh personnel. Taken together the combined army of these three countries, i.e., 20.7 lakhs would be the second largest army after People's Republic of China.[4] The total population of these three countries (India-135.3 crore, Pakistan-21.2 crore and Bangladesh-16.1 crore) was around 172 crore in 2018.[5] Thus the percentage population in the aggregate strength of army is; 78% for India, 12% for Pakistan and 10% for Bangladesh. The percentage of army personnel is 64%, 30% and 6% respectively, in an aggregate strength of an army of 20.7 lakh. The figures show the vast difference in the proportion of share in total strength of the armies of these nations. More differences appear between the population and the army personnel when compared with each other.

India has the problems at its north eastern and northern frontiers along the Mac Mahon Line and the Line of Actual Control (LoAC) with China and at its north western border along the Radcliffe Line and LoC with Pakistan. Pakistan has also border problems at its north-west frontier for its borders, along the Durand Line with Afghanistan. All these border lines, except LoC and LoAC, were drawn by British Masters and were agreed upon by the then counter dispensations. At its northern frontier Pakistan has successfully solved all its border problems with China way back in 1963 and has turned a potential foe in to an "All Weather Friend". Yet, it maintains an Army of 6.19 lakh strength which is 30% of the aggregate of three countries sprang from erstwhile India. It also tops the list among the three nations in the ratio of persons per soldier. Ratio of the soldier and the people is 1:343 in Pakistan, 1:1021 in India and 1:1278 in Bangladesh. In other words, Pakistan has one soldier after every 343 persons which is more than three times of India, one soldier after 1021 persons and four times of Bangladesh, one soldier after 1278 persons. Probably a perceived threat from India and a bid to wrest J&K from India with an armed action, coupled with Pakhtoon demand for unified Pakhtoonkhwa, drives Pakistan to maintain an army in such a proportion. Bangladesh maintains one soldier per 1278 persons, the lowest among all three.

Larger is the army larger are the expenses. Same is otherwise with Bangladesh, smaller is the army smaller are the expenses. Since its creation in 1971, Bangladesh, first, did not come to any armed clash with its neighbours, second, was able to solve all its border problems with its neighbour, India, through dialogues. People's problems related to its enclaves in Indian territory and India's enclaves in its territory too were solved in 2016. Keeping the strength of its army as low as one per 1278 persons, lowest in the subcontinent, Bangladesh was able to pay more attention on its economic and social development rather than on defence, a non economic activity. Bangladesh's growth in human development indicators over the years owes much to above mentioned factor.

India and Pakistan in a bid to overtake each other militarily are continuously upgrading their armies with newest weapons of destruction. They are spending a large chunk of their resources on the import of conventional and non conventional weapons. This tendency has led to the neglect of investment in the economic and social sectors. Sophisticated war machines such as air fighter bomber jets, AWACS, self-guided and cruise missiles, missiles defence systems, battleships, submarines and various conventional arms are purchased at the exorbitant prices. These purchase contracts, are accompanied by hidden terms and conditions, that serve the vested interests of arms-suppliers only. This results in augmentation to the enrichment of arms supplying countries at the cost of hard-earned money of the taxpayers of the arms purchasing countries. The latter are invariably in the third world. Pakistan and India are one of them. The hungry people of the third world, like India and Pakistan, are not fed with food but with the war-prospects with the countries across their borders, by their leaders. A weak military, can lead to national humiliation, leaders hypnotize people to agree. This phobia breeds an ugly form of nationalism and patriotism that never allows people to move forward on the path of economic development.

Politicians suck the resources of their own countries through the corrupt means and are benefited by keeping hostilities with the countries identified as enemies, alive. History is rewritten and taught to uneducated masses in a manner that suits the interests of the unscrupulous individuals, groups or radical politico-communal outfits, wielding influence and power in the governance.

As percentage of GDP, India spent 2.5% and Pakistan spent 4.5% in 2001 on their defence.[6] In the developed world only USA and Russian Federation spent more than 2.5% of GDP that is 3.1% and 3.8%, respectively, on defence during the same year. Still, Pakistan was much ahead of them in percentage expenditure of GDP on defence. USA and Russian Federation were followed by Great Britain and France with 2.5% each. None of the developed countries of recognition, spent more than Pakistan in terms of percentage expenditure of GDP.[i-n]

There are clear distinctions in the nature of expenditure on defence between the developed and the developing countries like India and Pakistan. **First**, the high level of per capita purchasing power parity (per capita PPP) with respect to GDP, allows a handsome amount of money for the programmes of socio economic development while in developing countries the low per capita purchasing power parity (per capita PPP), does not leave enough money to be spent on the programmes of socio economic development. In 2001, among the countries having high per capita PPP, US had $ 34,320; France had $ 23,990 and UK had $ 24,150 while India and Pakistan had as low as $ 2,840 and $ 1890, respectively.[7] **Secondly**, in developed countries a major portion of the defence budget is converted back to National Income by exporting the manufactured arms, while in developing countries including India and Pakistan, a good portion of their defence budget is spent on import of arms, siphoning out the public money to arms exporting countries. **Thirdly**, sale of arms is accompanied by various hidden terms and conditions which influence the economic policies and governance of the arm purchasing countries for the advantage of arms-supplying countries.

During the year 2013-17 in the global trade of arms and weapons among the exporters, USA had the largest share at 34%, followed by Russian Federation at 22%, France at 6.7 %, Germany at 5.8 %, China at 5.7 %, UK at 4.8 % and Italy at 2.5 %. India and Pakistan were not among the exporters nor any other country of the Indian subcontinent. Ironically, far from being among the exporters, India was the largest importer at 12% and Pakistan was at ninth place with 2.8 % of the total imports of the arms.[8]

Three-fourth of the arms and ammunition produced by the developed countries is purchased by the countries in Oceania, middle

Asia, and Asia including India and Pakistan.[9] Status of largest arms-exporters and importers and their percentage share in the world trade during 2013-2017 as given in the SIPRI yearbook 2018 is being reproduced in Box No.1.

Box No. 1: The Largest arms Exporters and Importers and their percentage share in the Global Market during 2013-2017.

Major Exporters			*Major Importers*		
Sl. No.	*Countries*	*Share %*	*Sl. No.*	*Countries*	*Share %*
1.	USA	34	1.	India	12
2.	Russia	22	2.	Saudi Arabia	10
3.	France	6.7	3.	Egypt	4.5
4.	Germany	5.8	4.	UAE	4.4
5.	China	5.7	5.	China	4.0
6.	UK	4.8	6.	Australia	3.8
7.	Spain	2.9	7.	Algeria	3.7
8.	Israel	2.9	8.	Iraq	3.4
9.	Italy	2.5	9.	Pakistan	2.8
10.	Netherlands	2.1	10.	Indonesia	2.8

Fear from neighbours and consequent war rhetoric centred around them, in the developing world, is directly proportionate to the intervention of developed countries in their affairs. The interventions come through arbitration or military assistance. The developed world reaps good harvests from the hostilities in the developing or under developed world. People of developed world enjoy the prosperity from the misery of the people of developing world.

Many a time arms purchases are shrouded with the allegations of receiving kickbacks by persons in office and authority, which create political and public uproars against the government. In India, the purchase of 155 mm Bofors Howitzer field guns from Sweden in 1986, Augusta Westland AW101 VVIP Helicopters deal in 2006-07 (later on terminated in 2014) and Rafael fighter bombers from France in 2016 are some of the examples which brought serious allegations of corruption and consequent embarrassment to the governments. Across the borders, Pakistan's paranoia of a hostile India and Afghanistan, speaks the reasons of its never quenching thirst for upgrading its army with most recent sophisticated weapons. Unfortunately, this has led Pakistan often with begging bowls at the doors of the countries, who ever were ready to provide it military aid which earned it the epithet of a "beautiful bride available to highest bidder".

The non-acceptance of the validity of Durand line, drawn by Sir Mortimer Durand, a British officer in India, in 1893, by all Afghan governments including Pakistan supported Taliban regime, is an issue of concern to Pakistan. Its efforts to install a pro-Pak government in Afghanistan have met with successive failures. The US-Pak joint venture in Afghanistan inflicted heavy cost on Pakistani army, economy and society. Pakistan suffered human, economic and political losses in this venture which brought terror and Jihad to home, in the process. The billions of dollars aid to Pakistan from the Bretton Woods Institutions and the individual countries, overburdened it with huge foreign debt and failed to bring peace, prosperity and improved status of life to its people.

The GDP per capita PPP and the Myth of fast growing economies

The leaders of the countries of developing world boast their achievements by presenting the figures in a way that are no less than to befool their people about achievements brought about by them during their tenure in office. The economic growth is shown in terms of percentage growth over the absolute figures of the previous years. The growth seems impressive because even a little growth in absolute terms over the past year which was already very low, comes high in terms of percentage. However, the truth of this percentage growth can be understood by comparing the growth in developed countries in absolute terms.

While the per capita purchasing power parity (per capita PPP) in relation to GDP, increased from the level of 2001 to 2004, in India by US$ 299, in Pakistan by US$ 335, in Bangladesh by US$ 260 and in Nepal by US$ 180, the growth was between 10 to 20 times higher in developed countries, many of them were arms suppliers to third world countries including India and Pakistan. For instance, the per capita PPP over the same period increased by US$ 5361 in Sweden, US$ 5356 in USA, US$ 5310 in France, US$ 6661 in UK, US$ 3510 in Italy, US$ 4897 in Spain and US$ 2953 in Germany.

The people of "All-weather Friends" and major arms suppliers to India and Pakistan, Russian Federation and China, respectively, got their per capita PPP increased by US$ 2802 and US$ 1876 during the same period. The growth can be understood in a tabular form given in Box No. : 2

Box No. 2: HDI Ranking, Military Expenditure and GDP PPP per capita.

HDI Ranking as per		*Country*	*Military Exp. As % of GDP*		*GDP per capita (PPP US$)*		
HDR 2003	*HDR 2006*		*1990*	*2001*	*2001*	*2004*	*Increase in GDP PPP, per capita from the level of 2001 to 2004*
127	126	India	2.7	2.5	2840	3139	299
144	134	Pakistan	5.8	4.5	1890	2225	335
139	137	Bangladesh	1.0	1.3	1610	1870	260
136	135	Bhutan	NA	NA	NA	1969	NA
143	138	Nepal	0.9	1.1	1310	1490	180
		Arms Producing/ Exporting Countries					
3	5	Sweden	2.7	2.0	24,180	29,541	5,361
1	1	Norway	2.9	1.8	29,620	38,454	8,834
7	8	USA	5.3	3.1	34,320	39,676	5,356
13	18	UK	3.9	2.5	24,160	30,821	6,661
17	16	France	3.5	2.5	23,990	29,300	5,310
18	21	Germany	2.8	1.5	25,350	28,303	2,953
19	19	Spain	1.8	1.2	20,150	25,047	4,897
21	17	Italy	0.5	2.0	24,670	28,180	3,510
63	65	Russian Federation	12.3	3.8	7,100	9,902	2,802

Source: HDR, 2003 and 2006.
1. HDR, 2003, Priorities in Public Spending, pg. 295-298.
2. HDR, 2003, Human Development Index, pg. 237-241.
3. HDR, 2006, Economic Performance, pg. 331-334.

Although, Indian leaders highlighted their achievements by boasting India as the third largest economy of the world with a GDP of US$ 8,606.5 billion next only to China with US$ 21,223.9 billion and USA with US$ 17,662.3 billion in 2017, India was able to increase the per capita purchasing power parity only by US$ 697 as against US$ 1909 of China, and US$ 1,676 of USA from the level of 2015.

Same was in the case of other countries whose figures are given in the Box No. : 3. Pakistan, Bangladesh and Nepal remained at a sorry level with an increase of US$ 290, US$ 387 and US$ 130, respectively.

Box No. 3: GDP and PPP per capita in 2015 and 2017 and Increase in PPP per capita

HDI Rank per HD-2018	*Country*	*GDP Total (2011 adjustments) ($ billion)*	*GDP Total ($ billion)*	*Increase in GDP from level 2015 to 2017 ($ billion)*	*GDP per capita (2011 adjustment) PPP per capita ($)*	*GDP per capita PPP ($)*	*Increase in per capita PPP from level 2015 to 2017 ($)*
		2017	*2015*		*2017*	*2015*	
130	India	8,606.5	7,512.5	1094	6,427	5,730	697
150	Pakistan	991.9	896.4	95.5	5,035	4,745	290
136	Bangladesh	580.3	505.0	75.3	3,524	3,137	387
134	Bhutan	7.0	5.9	1.1	8,709	7,601	1,108
149	Nepal	71.6	66.0	5.6	2,443	2,313	130
7	Sweden	472.7	443.9	28.8	46,949	45,296	1,653
1	Norway	342.3	334.9	7.4	64,800	64,451	349
13	USA	17,662.3	16890.2	772.1	54,225	52,549	1,676
14	UK	2,624.6	2518.1	106.5	39,753	38,658	1,095
24	France	2,591.2	2492.3	98.9	38,606	37,306	1,300
5	Germany	3740.2	3586.5	153.7	45,229	44,053	1,176
28	Italy	2,132.6	2042.2	90.4	35,220	33,587	1,633
49	Russian FED	3,636.6	3498.4	138.2	24,766	23,895	871
86	China	21,223.9	18374.7	2849.2	15,309	13,400	1,909

Source: HDR 2016, Table 10.
Source: HD Statistical Update 2018.

However, Bhutan free from internal conflicts and clashes with other countries registered much higher increase in GDP per capita PPP of US$ 1108, more than four times of Pakistan during the same period.

Further, a comparison between the figures of the Year 2001 and 2015 period, first 15 years of the new Millennium, substantiate the above conclusion. The increase in per capita PPP, taking adjustment of 2011 into account, was US$ 2890 in India, US$ 2855 in Pakistan,

US$ 1003 in Nepal and US$ 1527 in Bangladesh. The increase seems impressive, but lags far behind, when compared with the increase in developed countries. People of Norway enjoyed an increase of US$ 34,831 followed by Sweden of US$ 21,116, Germany of US$18,703, USA of US$ 18229 and Russian Federation by US$ 16,795. The comparative figures are given in the Box No. : 4.

Box No. 4: A Comparative Chart of Status and Increase in GDP (Total GDP in $ Billion from 2001 to 2015 and GDP per capita PPP increase in $ from 2001 to 2015)

HDI Rank per HDR 2016	*Country*	*GDP Total (2011 adjust) ($ billion)*	*GDP Total ($ billion)*	*Increase in GDP $ billion from level 2001 to 2015*	*GDP (2011 adjust) PPP per capita 2011 ($)*	*GDP PPP per capita ($)*	*Increase in GDP PPP per capita from level 2001 to 2015 ($)*
		2015	*2001*		*2015*	*2001*	
131	India	7,512.5	477.3	7,035.2	5,730	2,840	2,890
147	Pakistan	896.4	58.7	837.7	4,745	1,890	2,855
139	Bangladesh	505.0	46.7	458.3	3,137	1,610	1,527
132	Bhutan	5.9	0.5	5.4	7,601	NA	NA
144	Nepal	66.0	5.6	60.4	2,313	1,310	1,003
14	Sweden	443.9	209.8	234.1	45,296	24,180	21,116
1	Norway	334.9	166.1	168.8	64,451	29,620	34,831
10	USA	16,890.2	10,065.9	6,824.3	52,549	34,320	18,229
16	UK	2,518.1	1,424.1	1,094.0	38,658	24,160	14,498
21	France	2,492.3	1,309.8	1,182.5	37,306	23,990	13,316
4	Germany	3,586.5	1846.1	1,740.4	44,053	25,350	18,703
27	Spain	1,523.2	581.8	941.4	32,814	20,150	12,664
26	Italy	2,042.2	1,088.8	953.4	33,587	24,670	8,917
49	Russian FED	3,498.4	310.0	3,188.4	23,895	7,100	16,795
90	China	18,374.7	1,159.0	17,215.7	13,400	4,020	9,380

Source: 1. HDR 2006.
2. HDR 2016.

Note: GDP has been calculated for 2015 as expressed in 2011 international $ using PPP rates.

Living at the edge

Notwithstanding their leaders' loud claims a large population is living at the edge in the developing countries.

In the beginning of the present millennium, at the global norms of the poverty, out of every one hundred people about 35 people in India, 17 people in Pakistan, 36 people in Bangladesh and 24 people in Nepal were living at less than US$ 1 a day which means that above stated percent of population was hardly able to meet the minimum requirement of two times meal a day. A total population of 79.9 percent in India, 73.6 percent in Pakistan and 82.8 percent in Bangladesh was living with a maximum income of $2 per day.[10]

Almost none of the country in north or western Europe, USA or Australia had the people with such low income. People of Indian subcontinent had to suffer due to the maverick and unscrupulous practices of their political masters.

Expenditure on Military overshadowing Education and Health of the people

Health and education, the fundamentals for human development have been ignored in the subcontinent to serve the interests of political masters. Hostile treatment towards their own citizens clamouring just for an honourable treatment and inimical response to the neighbouring states have resulted into an unbalanced growth of military power affecting the two important interventions in human development, health and education, badly.

While the health issues cannot wait for long, the neglect to education, the mother of holistic and inclusive development, keeps people entangled in the vicious cycle of backwardness.

As strengthening of the armed forces was the first priority to the governments of the Indian subcontinent, military had always consumed maximum percentage of the GDP leaving scant resources for the improvement in health and education sectors. While the percentage military expenditure of the GDP in Pakistan was 5.8% in 1990, 4.5% in 2001 and 3.4% in 2004, the education sector received only 2.6% in 1990, 1.8% in 2000 and 2.0 percent in 2002-04. Health got much less than the military 1.1 % in 1990, 0.9% during 98-2000 and 0.7% in 2003-04.

In India expenditure on military was 2.7% in 1990, 2.5% in 2001, and 3.0% in 2004. Health was given a little importance with a meagre expenditure of 0.9% in 1990 which remained same in 2001 and 1.2 % in 2003-04. Education however, got more than military 3.9% in 1990, 4.1% in 1998-2000 and 3.3% in 2002-04.

Box No. 5: Percentage Expenditure of GDP on Education, Health and Military and Total Debt Service

HDI Rank, HDR 2003	*Country*	*Public Expenditure on*				*Military Expenditure as % of GDP*		*Total debt Service as % to GDP*	
		Education as % to GDP		*Health as % of GDP*					
		1990	*1998-2000*	*1990*	*2000*	*1990*	*2001*	*1990*	*2001*
127	India	3.9	4.1	0.9	0.9	2.7	2.5	2.6	1.9
144	Pakistan	2.6	1.8	1.1	0.9	5.8	4.5	4.8	5.0
139	Bangladesh	1.5	2.5	0.7	1.4	1.0	1.3	2.5	1.4
136	Bhutan	-	5.2	1.7	3.7	-	-	1.8	1.2
143	Nepal	2.0	3.7	0.8	0.9	0.9	1.1	4.7	4.0
3	Sweden	7.4	7.8	7.6	6.5	2.7	2.0	-	-
1	Norway	7.1	6.8	6.4	6.6	2.9	1.8	-	-
4	Australia	5.1	4.7	5.3	6.0	2.2	1.7	-	-
7	United States	5.2	4.8	4.7	5.8	5.3	3.1	-	-
9	Japan	-	3.5	4.6	6.0	0.9	1.0	-	-
13	UK	4.9	4.5	5.1	5.9	3.9	2.5	-	-
17	France	5.4	5.8	6.7	7.2	3.5	2.5	-	-
18	Germany	-	4.6	5.9	8.0	2.8	1.5	-	-
19	Spain	4.4	4.5	5.2	5.4	1.8	1.2	-	-
21	Italy	3.1	4.5	6.3	6.0	Less Than 0.5	2.0	-	-

Source: HDR, 2003. (Table: 17)

During the period of 2012-17 better deal was awarded to education by raising the expenditure between 3% to 4%, with Bhutan leading the subcontinent at 7.4% which was more than several countries of the Europe.

In this subcontinent military is attached with national pride leaving education and health to the mercy of the God. People's health and education are sacrificed on the altar of pseudo patriotism based on ill-conceived notions of enmity and perceived threats from across the borders.

Education

Inefficacy and inadequacy of Government schools has compelled people of the subcontinent to send their wards to schools run by private institutions and individuals. In Pakistan it paved way to the mushroom growth of madarsas, majority of which turned into nursery of jihad and terrorism. Madarsas and Sanskrit Vidyalayas, in the earlier times, were the institutions to impart the education to students in the subcontinent. They were generally attached to Masjids or Mandirs. The Christian agenda of proselytization of Indian people, led various Christian sects to open schools, even in the farthest and most neglected areas of the country. In common parlance, these schools were known as 'Mission Schools'. The literacy rate at less than 16% in undivided India in 1947, had the reasons in the dearth of educational institutions. The British masters were not much interested in making education approachable to Indian masses. There were a few private schools at the time of independence. But it is difficult to ascertain their authoritative numbers.

According to some estimates, there were around 245 madarsas at the time of independence in Pakistan. Within three decades their number increased to around 2800. Every sect or sub sects of Islam, Deobandi, Bareilvee, Ahle-Hadith, Shia, and Jamait-i-Islami had their madarsas.[11] These madarsas not just imparted the knowledge on Islam but also created hard core students repudiating and condemning all other thoughts and beliefs. In India also madarsas grew up at a fast speed but owing to the secular nature of the state, they became an alternate source of education to the government schools. Government of India came forward to assist madarsas in various ways. Unfortunately in Pakistan, madarsas, from the very beginning of the Afghan war in seventies of the last century were used as the nursery of jihad and the repository of the jihadi soldiers to fight in Afghanistan. These students (Talibs) were exploited first to fight as Mujahideens led by Gulbuddin Hekmatiyar and Rabbani and finally as 'Talibanis' of Mullah Omer led Taliban. These students known as Taliban became pariah internationally.

The Bhutto-dictated third Constitution of Pakistan (1973) bestowed powers upon the majority sect through the State to declare any other sect Non-Muslims. The apprehension of being declared as non-Muslims further gave rise to growth of Madarsas, indoctrinated with hard core beliefs of various sects. In straight words by not providing good and functional institutions of education to its children, Pakistan's leadership left youths to the mercy of terror groups who were determined to give a death blow to the modern education. Girls were entirely barred from going to schools in its restive north western frontier province. As against the dictates of Taliban-elements the quest and struggle of the local Pashtoon girls to get the modern education was epitomised in the story of struggle of Malala Yusufzai. While many of the Muslim girls wanted modern education, Taliban shut the doors of schools to them by threatening them and their family members with severe corporal punishment.

In India politicization of education sector has contributed to the absenteeism among teachers from schools discouraging parents to send their wards to schools. Mid-day meal scheme, one of the largest schemes of its kind in the world in education sector, had a catalytic effect in increasing the enrolment and attendance during mid day meal hours. The Right to Education (RTE) Act of 2009, ensured that every child receives free and compulsory education up to the eighth standard. To achieve that goal as per provision made in section 16 of the RTE Act, no child was to be failed up to the senior primary level. Contrary to the expectations of the planners, this provision encouraged the poor parents to engage their wards as daily wage labourers rather than to send them to schools. Children too preferred not to attend the classes as they were sure to get promotion to next class at the end of the session. The quality of education was the biggest fatality of this provision. The Constitution of Pakistan also promises to remove the illiteracy and provide free and compulsory education up to Secondary education level (Article 37(6)), but no time limit has been fixed. Despite such loud promises in its Constitution, about 2.5 crore children between the age of of 5 to 16 were not attending schools in 1918. At the eastern part of the subcontinent Bangladesh did not make such loud promises in its Constitution, yet its pro-human development policies have resulted in the maximum literacy rate (72.8%) in the subcontinent.

In the Indian subcontinent in 2016, Pakistan topped the list of illiterates at 43%. Other countries too were not good, with Nepal at 40%, India at 30% and Bangladesh at 27%. In the developed world there was no illiterate. In 2016 out of the secondary school going age children only 46% in Pakistan, 69% in Bangladesh, 71% in Nepal and 75% in India were enrolled in secondary school classes.[12] The percentage of literates during the last 25 years from the level of 1990 could be improved from 35.4 % to 57% in Pakistan, 49.3 % to 69.3% in India and from 34.2% to 72.8% in Bangladesh. Bangladesh, indeed made an impressive progress. Country-wise status of some of the key indicators are given in Box No. 6

Box No. 6: Status of Education related indicators in Indian subcontinent-countries and a few Developed countries

Country	*Mean years of Schooling (Years)*			*Literacy Rate (Age 15 & Older)*
	1990	*2001*	*2017*	*2006-16*
India	3.0	4.8	6.4	69.3%
Pakistan	2.3	3.8	5.2	57%
Bangladesh	2.8	5.2	5.8	72.8%
Bhutan	-	2.1	3.1	57.0%
Nepal	2.0	3.6	4.9	59.6%
Sweden	10.5	12.5	12.4	Almost 100%
Norway	11.5	12.6	12.6	
USA	12.3	13.4	13.4	
UK	7.9	12.8	12.9	
France	7.1	11.3	11.5	
Spain	6.0	9.7	9.8	
Germany	8.8	13.6	14.1	
Italy	7.3	10.0	10.2	
Russian	9.2	12.0	12.0	
China	4.8	7.6	7.8	95.1%

Source: 1. HD 2018 Statistical Update (Table 1 and 9).

It is saddening, that by 2017 the two Nations, India and Pakistan each had a stockpile of around 140 to 150 nuclear warheads[13], sophisticated fighter bombers like, F16, Mirage, Rafel, Sukhoi and Migs and missiles that can fly at a speed of 4 mach and hit the targets as far as 5000 kms. and battleships, did not pay attention to the most important issues of Human Development. The countries of the subcontinent house a large number of illiterates. The apathy on the part of the Governments leaves more than 40% in Pakistan and 30% people in India, unable to read and write.

It is unfortunate that in Pakistan, among the people of tertiary education age 90% are not enrolled to graduate classes. More unfortunately, Pakistani election laws that were operative for a period of about 6 years (2002-2008) debarred the people without a graduate degree to contest the elections to Parliament, Legislative Assembly and the Local governments. This provision consequently debarred majority of people, perhaps around 90%, from contesting the elections, weakening the foundation of the democracy. People need to fight against such provisions which debar them from participation in democratic governance. Interestingly, the opposition did not come from the people, but from the Pakistan Peoples' Party (PPP) which got the mandate in 2008, to declare the provision null and void, and that too when its leaders faced disqualifications owing to this provision.[i-n]

Health

The status of health and health related components in most of the countries of the subcontinent are as bad as placing them just above the most backward countries of the world. The percentage expenditure accorded to this sector as against GDP has been given in the earlier paragraphs. The infant mortality rate, under five mortality rate, maternal mortality ratio and the percentage of malnourished children are very high in all of the countries of Indian subcontinent.

The status of the above stated health indicators in the countries of this subcontinent and the countries in the developed world for the purpose of comparative understanding is given in Box No. : 7

Box No. 7: U5MR and MMR

Country	*U5MR per 1000 live births*		*MMR per 1,00,000 live births*	
	1990	*2016*	*1995*	*2015*
India	123	43.0	440	174
Pakistan	128	78.8	200	178
Bangladesh	144	34.5	600	176
Bhutan	166	32.4	500	148
Nepal	145	34.5	830	258
Sweden	7	2.9	8	4
Norway	9	2.6	9	5
USA	11	6.5	12	14
UK	9	4.3	10	9
France	10	3.9	20	8
Spain	9	3.3	8	5
Germany	9	3.8	12	6
Italy	10	3.3	11	4
Russian Fed.	21	7.7	75	25
China	49	9.9	60	27

Source: 1. HDR 2003.
2. HD 2018 Statistical Update.

In the year 2000, the United Nations adopted UN Millennium Declaration with 8 international goals (MDGs) to be achieved by 2015. The goals set were to eradicate extreme poverty and hunger, to achieve universal primary education, to promote gender equality and empower women, to reduce child mortality, to improve maternal health, to combat HIV/AIDS, malaria and other diseases, to ensure environmental sustainability and to develop a global partnership for global development.

Two of the targets were to reduce child deaths before reaching the age of 5 years (under five mortality rate-U5MR) by two third and maternal mortality ratio(MMR) by three quarter between the years 1990 and 2015. Under 5 mortality rate is taken deaths per one thousand children before attaining the age of 5 years and MMR is death of mothers due to pregnancy related causes per one lakh live births. By 2016 while Bangladesh, Bhutan and Nepal almost achieved the target by bringing U5MR down to between 31 to 34, and India with 43, Pakistan trailed far behind at 78.8.

In 1990 Pakistan had a U5 MR less than that of Bangladesh, Bhutan and Nepal and almost equal to India at 123, it could reduce the under five mortality rate only by 50.8 per thousands children, having an under five mortality rate of 78.8 per thousand children by 2016. The reasons are found easily in Pakistan's involvement, A) in Afghanistan, B) in fighting terror groups within and C) war or warlike situations and frequent clashes at borders with India.

Absence of democratic governance and political upheaval in Pakistan might be other contributing factors. Pakistan was unsuccessful in bringing down the infant mortality rate (children dying per 1000 live birth) to the targeted level. Even in 2016, the IMR remained high at 64.2 per 1000 live birth, almost twice of India's 34.6 and more than twice of Bhutan (26.8) Bangladesh (28.2) and Nepal (28.4). However, in comparison of developed countries the IMR in India, Bhutan, Bangladesh and Nepal too appear appalling.

With a share of 34% in global export of major weapons USA had an infant mortality rate at only 5.6, MMR at 14 and U5MR at 6.5 compared to Pakistan's IMR at 64.2, MMR at 133 and U5MR at 78.8. Sweden, France and Italy from whom the purchases of weapons rocked the Indian politics with allegation of corruption and bribes in the past had an IMR of 2.4, 3.2 and 2.8, a MMR of 4, 8 and 4 and under five mortality rate of 2.9, 3.9 and 3.3, respectively. India who had the purchase deals of Bofors Hawitzer guns with Sweden, Rafel fighter bombers with France and Augusta Westland helicopters with Italy had IMR at 34.6, MMR are at 127 and under 5MR at 43.0 by 2016. Russians had brought down the IMR to 6.6, MMR to 26 and U5MR to 7.7.[14] The difference between Indian subcontinent Nations and some of the developed Nations as also the major arms suppliers in respect to IMR and children with stunted growth, may be understood by the figures given in Box No. : 8

Box No. 8: IMR and Stunted Growth in Indian subcontinent countries and a few of the Developed countries

Country	*IMR per 1000 live births*			*Children under height for age/Stunted growth (% under age 5)*	
	1990	*2001*	*2016*	*1995-2001*	*2010-15*
India	80	67	34.6	46	37.9
Pakistan	96	84	64.2	NA	45.0
Bangladesh	96	51	28.2	45	36.2
Bhutan	75	74	26.8	40	33.5
Nepal	100	66	28.4	51	36.0
Sweden	6	3	2.4	-	-
Norway	7	4	2.1	-	-
USA	9	7	5.6	2	2.1
UK	8	6	3.7	-	-
France	7	4	3.2	-	-
Spain	8	4	2.7	-	-
Germany	7	4	3.2	-	-
Italy	8	4	2.8	-	-
Russia Fed.	17	18	6.6	13	-
China	38	31	8.5	17	8.1

Source: HDR 2003 and HD 2018 Statistical Update.

Health of the children is a mirror of the health of the nation. This can be measured through the weight and height at the different stages of the age of the child. Out of every one hundred children under the age of 5 years, 45 children in Pakistan, 38 in India, 36 each in Bangladesh and Nepal and 33.5 in Bhutan were found with stunted growth during 2010-2015.[15] Again in most of the developed countries stunted growth was not a problem owing to the absence of the problem of malnourishment. A sizeable number of people die of the communicable diseases, such as typhoid, hepatitis, diarrhoea, malaria, dengue, encephalitis, tetanus, STDs, influenza, measles, chicken pox, tuberculosis and others in the countries of Indian subcontinent. These diseases can be prevented before their occurrences. They are largely related to insanitary practices and lack of facilities for scientific disposal of excreta, pure and potable water for drinking purposes and a general cleanliness at home and outside in the environment. These diseases on the basis of mode of spread are classified in four broad categories, i.e., human intestine borne, vector-borne, human respiratory tract borne and the surface borne diseases. Sadly enough, even after seven decades of self rule, the Government of India, Pakistan and Bangladesh and all other ever independent countries of Bhutan and Nepal were not successful in providing the two basic public amenities, sanitary toilets and pure drinking water, to all of their citizens.

As in the absence of education and the availability of sanitary toilets and pure drinking water the diseases spread, people do not get adequate medical facilities to cure them. As for the availability of physicians at the population of each ten thousands Pakistanis had just around 8, Indians had just around 7, Drukpas (Bhutaneis) as well as Nepalis had a little above 2 and Bangladesh had only 3.6 physicians during the period 2001-14 to address the medical problems of the people.[16] The number of physicians per ten thousand people in the countries of Indian subcontinent, judging from the international standards, was too low.

Box No. 9: Health Outcomes

HDI Rank HDR 2016	*Country*	*Deaths due to (per 1,00,000 people)*		*Physicians per 10,000 people (2001-14)*	*Public Health Expenditures % (2014)*
		Malaria	*TB*		
		2012	*2014*	*2001-14*	*2014*
131	India	4.1	17.00	7.0	1.4
132	Bhutan	0.0	9.5	2.6	2.6
139	Bangladesh	13.9	51.0	3.6	0.8
144	Nepal	0.2	17.0	2.1	2.3
147	Pakistan	1.8	26.0	8.3	0.9

(Contd...)

(Very High Human Devp. Index)					
1	Norway	-	0.2	42.8	8.3
2	Switzerland	-	0.1	40.5	7.7
3	Australia	-	0.2	32.7	6.3
4	Germany	-	0.4	38.9	8.7
5	Denmark	-	0.4	34.9	9.2
7	N. Lands	-	0.1	28.6	9.5
17	Japan	-	1.8	23.0	8.6
27	Spain	-	0.5	49.5	6.4
26	Italy	-	0.4	37.6	7.0
10	USA	-	0.1	24.5	8.3
16	UK	-	0.5	28.1	7.6
21	France	-	0.6	31.9	9.0

Source : HDR - 2016.

During the same period, in the developed countries the availability of physicians was more than three times of India. In the developed world, Spain was at the top with around 50 physicians at every 10,000 people, United States had around 25, France had 32, and Italy had 38 physicians per 10,000 populations. With the availability of doctors and, sanitary facilities and practices along with the facility of pure drinking water, the developed countries were able to eradicate a number of communicable diseases. Malaria has become unheard while tuberculosis is at the verge of extinction. Several other communicable diseases, nightmarish to people in developing countries, are going to become a part of forgotten history.

The saddest part of this analysis is that despite this dismal state of health, the countries of the Indian subcontinent, over the past three decades, with the exception of Bhutan, have never made adequate budgetary provisions in their annual budgets for public health.

It was sad that, as stated in HDR- 1990 "only 2.2 % of Pakistan's GNP went for education and health in 1986 compared with 6.7 % for military expenditure"[17] This was the time when Pakistan had willfully engaged it in Afghanistan's internal affairs through Mujahahideens, Siachen glacier through its armed forces and separatist Khalistan

Movement in India, inviting 'Operation Brasstacks',a full scale war-threat, from India. All these enterprises demanded shifting of expenditure from socio-economic sectors to the defence. In a sharp contrast, the developed countries were spending 6 to 8 times more, in terms of percentage expenditure of GDP on health. To be specific, while India, Pakistan, Nepal and Bangladesh spent a meagre 0.9%, 0.9%, 0.9% and 1.4%, of GDP on health in 2001, Germany spent 8%, France spent 7.2%, Sweden and Norway spent around 6.5% and other industrialized nations spent around 6% of GDP on public health in the same year. Percentage expenditure on military in comparison to health was more than two fold, 2.5% in India and more than fivefold, 5% in Pakistan.[18]

As the race for stockpiling of the nuclear heads increased, more and more delivery mechanism to inflict devastation on each other was sought from the arms producing countries. A look at the availability of delivery vehicles as given in the SIPRI,2018 Report, is reproduced in Box No. 10 and Box No. 11. The table is sufficient enough to show the dependency of India and Pakistan on arms producing countries and the huge amounts spent on their purchases and maintenance.

Box No. 10: Indian nuclear forces, January 2018

Type (US/Indian designation)	*Launchers deployed*	*Year first deployed*	*Range (km)[a]*	*Warheads x yield[b]*	*No.of warheads[c]*
Aircraft[d]	48				48
Mirage 2000H	32	1985	1 850	1 x bomb	32
Jaguar IS	16	1981	1600	1 x bomb	16
Land-based ballistic missiles	60				60
Prithvi-II	24	2003	250	1 x 12 Kt	24
Agni-I	20	2007	>700	1 x 10-40 Kt	20
Agni-II	8	2011	>2000	1 x 10-10 Kt	8
Agni-III	8	2014	>3200	1 x 10-40 Kt	8
Agni-IV	0	(2018)	>3500	1 x 10-40 Kt	0
Agni-V	0	(2020)	>5200	1 x 10-40 Kt	0
Sea-based ballistic missiles	14				16
Dhanush	2	(2013)	400	1 x 12 Kt	4[e]
K-15 (B05)[f]	(12)[g]	(2018)	700	1 x 12 Kt	(12)
K-4	(4)[g]	..	3500	1 x 10-40 Kt	0
Cruise missiles	..	..	..	..	..
Nirbhay ALCM[h]	..	..	(>700)	..	..
Total					**130-140[i]**

The explanations as given by SIPRI are given at reference no. 19.

Interestingly, this shopping spree of weapons also starts rivalries among the arms manufacturing countries to woo the arms purchasing countries. The latter are even bullied and threatened with the dire consequences if they go to purchase from a rival country.

An example of such threatening acts is US Act known as 'Countering America's Adversaries through Sanctions Act' (CAATSA). Under CAATSA, enacted by the US itself, it can impose sanctions on the country purchasing defence equipments from Iran, Russia and North Korea. India was one of the countries to be severely affected by this law as majority of the defence material was purchased by it from Russian Federation. Countries of Middle East, Africa and South Asia including India and Pakistan were just pawns in the chess board of international politics played by the super powers.

Box No. 11: Pakistani nuclear forces, January 2018

Type (US/Indian designation)	*Launchers deployed*	*Year first deployed*	*Range (km)[a]*	*Warheads x yield[b]*	*No. of warheads[c]*
Aircraft	36				36
F-16A/B[d]	24	1998	1600	1 x bomb	24
Mirage III/V	12	1998	2100	1 x bomb or Ra'ad ALCM	12
Land-based missiles	102[e]				102
Abdali (Hatf-2)	10	(2015)	200	1 x 12 Kt	10
Ghaznavi (Hatf-3)	16	2004	290	1 x 12 kt	16
Shaheen-I (Hatf-4)	16	2003	750	1 x 12 kt	16
Shaheen-IA (Hatf-4)[f]	..	(2017)	900	1 x 12 kt	..
Shaheen-II (Hatf-6)	12	2014	1500	1 x 10-40 kt	12
Shaheen-III (Hatf-6)[g]	..	(2018)	2750	1 x 10-40 kt	..
Gauri (Hatf-5)	24	2003	1250	1 x 10-40 kt	24
Nasr (Hatf-9)	24	(2013)	60-70	1 x 12 kt	24
Ababeel (Hatf-..)	0	..	2200	MIRV or MRV	0[h]
Cruise Missiles	12				12
Babur GLCM (Hatf-7)	12	(2014)	350[i]	1 x 12 kt	12
Babur-2 GLCM (Hatf-..)	..	..[j]	700	1 x 12 kt	..
Babur-3 SLCM (Hatf-..)	0	..[k]	450	1 x 12 kt	0
Ra'ad ALCM (Hatf-8)	..	(2017)	350	1 x 12 kt	..
Ra'ad-2 ALCM (Hatf-..)	..	(2018)	>350	1 x 12 kt	..
Total					**140-150**

The explanations as given by SIPRI are given at reference no. 20.

Thankfully, in 2017, owing to many factors, including international awakening brought in by MDG's and Universal SDGs, all the countries of subcontinent increased the share of public health in public spending. Health sector attracted 6.1% in Nepal, 3.9% in India, 3.5% in Bhutan, 2.7% in Pakistan and 2.6% in Bangladesh of the total annual budget. Though this increase still seems dwarf in comparison to the developed countries which spend between 9% to 17% on health, yet the tendency to allot more in terms of percentage to health sector, appears a positive step in a right direction.

The life expectancy of the people has increased in the subcontinent, with people of India enjoying an average age of 68.85 years, Pakistan an age of 66.65 years, Bangladesh an age of 72.9 years, Nepal an age of 70.6 years and Bhutan an age of 70.6 years by 2017. Yet, the level of life expectancy achieved by these countries, does not appear to be satisfactory when compared with the developed World.[21] The truth is that, life expectancy at birth has already crossed eighty years of age in almost all of the developed countries by the year 2017.

The unchecked growth of population aggravates the problem of hunger as the food grain production fall short to the growth in population. The food grain production in India which was 213.27 million metric ton in 2001-2002 increased just to 244.77 million metric ton in 2010-2011 registering an increase of 12.87% as against a decadal growth of 17.7 percent in population during the same period. In other words the increase in foodgrain production could not keep pace with the ever increasing population. India produced extra 31.50 million metric ton food grains to feed about 17 crore new bellies. The fertility rate in the countries of the subcontinent is very high with Pakistan leading at 3.7 followed by India at 2.5, Nepal at 2.3, Bangladesh at 2.2 and Bhutan at 2.1 during the year 2010-15. Foodgrain production has several natural checks, flood and droughts being the most prominent, while population growth goes unchecked.

The five countries of the Indian subcontinent referred in this work contributed about 23% population i.e., 173 crore, to the total world population of 753 crore in the year 2017, with no less percentage of malnourished children and poor. Ironically, issues of human development have never been accorded serious thought by political parties in their election manifestoes. No Indian politicians ever talked about the poor status of human development indicators in public debates or canvassings in 2019 General Elections for the Lower House of the Parliament. Most of the debates on the electronic media were centred around those issues which had hardly to do anything with the issues of human or economic development. The intensity of antagonism towards Pakistan was the most sought after subject to prove one's patriotism towards his or her country. The non-invitation to his Pakistani counterpart, Imran, by Narendra Modi, the Indian Prime Minister elected for the second term, to attend his swearing-in ceremony on 30 May 2019, was publicised by the Indian electronic and print media as a tough and appropriate gesture of newly elected Indian government, to Pakistan. The reason was Pakistan funded and abetted terrorism in India, J&K in particular.

Chapter - VII

Indian Subcontinent-a Common History

The Indian subcontinent encompasses a land bounded by the Himalayas in the North, the Bay of Bengal in the South East, and the Arabian Sea in the South West. It is flanked by the Makran and Hindukush mountains and mountain passes such as Khyber, Gomal and Bolan in the North West and the Arakan hills in the Far East. At present, this land mass consists of five sovereign nations-Pakistan, India, Nepal, Bhutan and Bangladesh, and the island of Sri Lanka at the confluence of the Bay of Bengal and Arabian Sea.

For the purpose of this book, we have focussed on the three big nations of the subcontinent, Pakistan, India and Bangladesh, which till the mid-twentieth century were the parts of erstwhile British India. The history of these nations till they parted their ways in 1947, was more or less the same.

The subcontinent was ruled over by different rulers with various centres of power spread over this land mass. The Turks came to India in the last decade of the 12th century, established their rule to which they called 'Sultanate', with Delhi as their seat of governance. Qutubuddin Aibak laid the foundation of the independent Turks' rule in India in 1206 AD. Though the Turks and the successive dynasties, the Khaljis, Tughlaqs, Sayyeds and the Afghans were not successful in bringing the present days' three nations under their command, their desire to bring the entire area under their governance tended towards the process of unification of India. Mughals were successful, in giving a national identity to this land mass, geographically known as the Indian subcontinent. The concept of India as a coherent nation came on a sound footing with the establishment of British rule in India. The British, under the banner of East India Company, inherited the political legacy of the Great Mughals (1556 AD-1707 AD), though by the time the British began their conquest-spree, the Mughal empire had been fragmented into a number of kingdoms. But the concept of a unified India had begun to take shape under the unifying spirit of Akbar and the quest for territorial expansion under Aurangzeb. The fragmented Mughal India, more or less, was stretched up to Gilgit, Baltistan, Ladakh and Kashmir in the north, to the north of Tamil Nadu in the south, and from Baluchistan in the west to Chittagong in the east. The Mughals had been addressing themselves 'Padshah', since 1507 when Babur, the founder of the Mughal dynasty, assumed this title at Kabul. Sometimes they referred to themselves as '*Shahenshah-e-Sultanate Al Hindiyyah wa Al Mughaliyyah.*' But they never defined the area as Hindustan. India too was unheard of, then. Historians trace the word 'Hindustan' to the first century AD. Even at that time, the term was used to identify the region situated south of the River Indus or 'Sindhu'. During the time of Delhi Sultanate (1206 AD-1526 AD), Hindustan with Delhi as its seat of governance, stretched at most from Punjab in the north-west up to Karnataka in the south. British came to India with an idea of India in their mind, to trade in the very start of seventeenth century.

The British East India Company received a Royal Charter from Queen Elizabeth on 31 December 1600 AD. They began to refer to their possessions here with the prefix 'Indian'. The Government of India Act of 1833 also known as the Charter Act, as its name implies, re-designated the 'Governor General of Bengal' as the 'Governor General of India' and the 'Governor General's Government' as the 'Government of India'. The identity of an Indian nation thereafter became official. By the mid-19 Century, the entirety of modern India had come under British subjugation. A rebellion or war of Independence waged by the erstwhile rulers who had been dethroned, and officials who had been deprived of their privileges, supported by common people (both from the Hindu and Muslim communities) against the British in 1857, failed. The 'Mughal Padshahat' with the dethronement, expulsion and imprisonment of Bahadur Shah II, the last Mughal, was ended forever.

The emperor was exiled to the Rangoon prison in Myanmar as a punishment for leading the rebels against the British in Delhi. Bahadur Shah II, as a shorn of power and living a life almost as of a pauper during his kingship, yet with the prefix 'Padshah' enjoyed the semblance of Indian's sovereignty. The failure of an armed insurrection in 1857, sealed the possibilities of any armed struggle against the British rule in India in near future.

The rule of East India Company was replaced by the rule of British Crown by the Government of India Act, 1858. Those who supported British in suppression of the revolt were rewarded generously with principalities, fiefdoms, zamindaris and other like entitlements to realise land revenue, and titles. The highest were rewarded by recognizing them as 'princes' under the British suzerainty. About ninety years later, they became sovereign under the Indian Independence Act, 1947, with the right of self determination when British left India, forever. India though subdued and enslaved for the first time in its history, attained the nationhood. The enslavement of India, the process of which had started a hundred years before with the defeat of Siraj ud daula at the hands of Robert Clive at Plassey in 1757, came to completion in 1858. Indians, irrespective of their faith, cast and community had to work for their British masters. A nation, however, has taken a birth albeit under the debris of slavery and humiliation. Unification of India, though effected by foreign masters, became a boon for the future India. Today what one read as the history of India is denoted by the land ruled over by Great Britain and bequeathed to Pakistan and India in 1947.

According to the majority opinion the humans were living in Indian subcontinent since Palaeolithic age, also known as Stone Age for the use of stones for their tools. Moving ahead through the ages they began to use copper and bronze in Chalcolithic. This was when Indians were enjoying the Harrapan or Indus Valley civilization. The above named civilizations, synonym to each other, flourished in and around the above stated areas which now fall in Pakistan. The reminiscences have been discovered by the archaeologists in addition to above mentioned areas at Kalibangan, Chanhudaro, Lothal, Sutkagen-Dor close to Makran coast, Sotka Koh near Pasni, Balakot, Kalsi and others. As civilizations moved on, people of various races continued to immigrate to India.

There is no consensus on the issue of the original habitants of India. The most popular view that no man originated in India had also been countered by many other researchers on various grounds.

People of various races from negroids to australoids, proto australoids, mongoloids and Aryans are said to have come from outside, through the western borders of the subcontinent. The stronger people pushed the weaker ones to southward resulting in their spread throughout the Indian subcontinent. The Indus valley people had to flee from their homes for the fear of Aryan's ruthlessness. Aryans were superior not only in the art of warfare but were also well informed to keep the vanquished in the state of perpetual subjugation through institutionalisation of the victor and vanquished in to classes. They called that system '*Varna Vyavastha'*. The victors, Brahmins and Kshatriyas, were at the top of the four 'Varnas' followed by the business and trading class. Vanquished, as always happened, had to accept the lowest rung of the society or to take asylum in forest to continue the resistance. This was between fifteenth century BC and first century AD. The period was intercepted intermittently by two main thoughts enunciated by Buddhism and Jainism among others. However, nothing can be interpreted with surety as no contemporary document spells such reasons for the division of Aryan dominated society on the basis of victors and vanquished.

Rigvedic people inhabited the area watered by Gomati (Gomel), Krumu (Kurram), Kubha (Kabul), Suvastu (Swat), Saraswati (now extinct), Drishadwati (Ghagar), Shutudri (Satlej), Vipas (Beas), Purushni(Ravi), Askini (Chenab), Vitasta (Jhelum), and Sindhu (Indus). This was the area which also comprises the area now known as Pakistan. As the time passed Aryan invaders marched further south-eastward and subjugated Gangetic plains. By sixth century BC they had reached to Arabian Sea in the south-west and Bay of Bengal in the east and up to rivers Krishna-Godavari in the south. A nation with the same culture, Bharat, had been born under the umbrella of Aryavart. Based on Rigveda, Atharvaveda, Buddhist and Jain literature it is believed that early Indians followed the democratic system of governance among others. Many centuries before the Greek 'City Republics', Aryans were governing themselves through *'Sabha'* and *'Samitis'* and sixteen

Republics (*Mahajanapadas*) throughout India. India, then known as Bharat, was a nation based on uniform cultural ethics, politically it was a divided land mass.

India or Bharat witnessed two great monarchs, despots in theory, benevolent in practice, adorned with the adjective 'The Great' by the western oriental historians, Ashoka the Great (273BC-232BC) and Akbar the Great (1542AD-1605AD) who had a gap of 1774 years between them. Ashoka, the son of Bindusara and the grandson of Chandragupta Maurya who founded the Mauryan Dynasty in about 322 BC, is said to crowned himself as the king of Magadh with Patliputra (Patna) as its capital, by eliminating all other claimants to throne in the year 268 BC. He followed the policy of expansion by waging relentless wars against his neighbours, most famous of which was the Kalinga war. The war was fought in 260 BC, eight years after his ascendancy to the throne. The war was brutal. In the words of Asoka himself, "a hundred and fifty thousand people were deported, a hundred thousand were killed and many more died." Led by a Buddhist monk the indiscriminate killing under his command brought remorse to Ashoka. Following the teachings of Lord Buddha he shunned violence and adopted Buddhism, the *'Dhamma'* of *'Ahimsa'*. In the words of DN Jha, "Ashoka's insistence on abstinence from killing, considerable relationship between parents and children, elders and young people, friends, masters and servants, various religious sects and his excessive concern for the general welfare of the subjects suggest that his *dharma* was an ethical code aimed at building up an attitude of social responsibility among the people. The policy of '*Dhamma*' sought to make a strong case for the recognition of the dignity of man, inculcation of virtuous behaviour transcending all social, religious and cultural barriers. By pleading for consideration towards slaves and servants, Ashoka sought to promote harmony."[1]

No doubt he attained a vast empire from north-west of river Helmund in Afghanistan to river Brahmaputra in Bangladesh and river Jhelum and Indus in Pakistan to the river Ponnaiyar in South India, but his greatness did not lie in his conquests and territorial acquisitions, but in the policy of '*Dhamma*' based on non violence and peace for all.

INDIAN SUBCONTINENT UNDER ASHOKA 273 - 232 B.C.

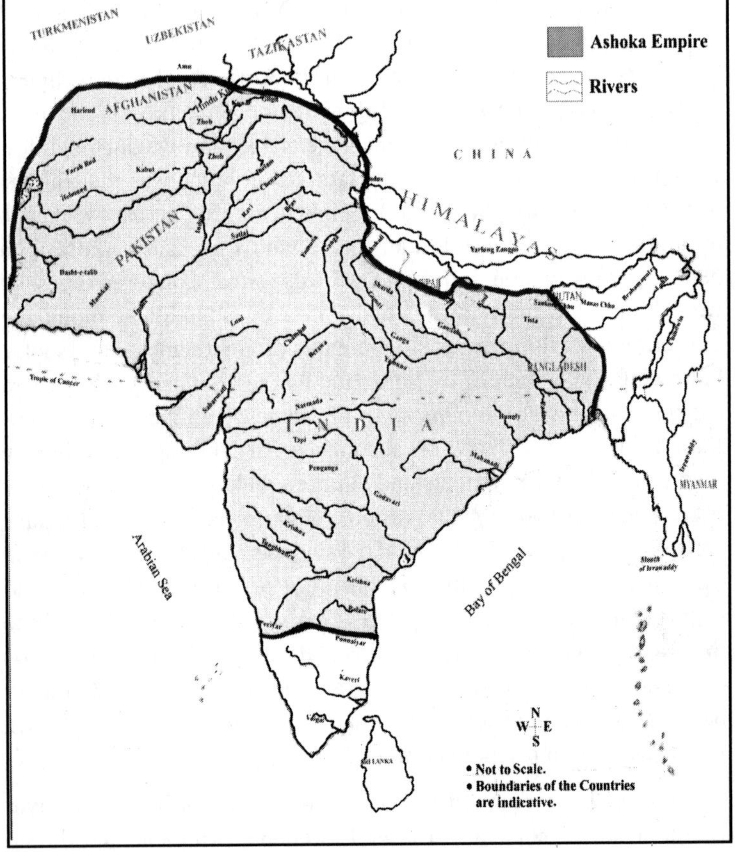

Ashoka's propagation of *'Dhamma'* was much alike *'Sulh-i-kul'* ofAkbar, more than one and a half millennium after him. Born in 1542 in Amarkot (now in Sindh Province of Pakistan) to fugitive Mughal Padshah Humayun, he made a notable dent in India's politics by defeating the forces of Hemu, the king of Delhi at the battle field of Panipat on 5 November 1556 AD, almost at the same place where his grandfather Babur, some thirty years ago in 1526 AD, had defeated Ibrahim Lodi, the last king of the Lodi dynasty. Akbar led many successful expeditions to extend the boundaries of his kingdom. When Akbar died in 1605 AD, the Mughal empire encompasses, with a few exceptions, the land from Kandahar-Kabul provinces of Afghanistan in the west to the Chitogong division of Bangladesh in the east and from the province of Srinagar in the north to the province of Maharashtra of India in the south. His territorial limits were not as large as of his greatgrandson, Aurangzeb, but his benevolent governance was unparallel to any other statesman in the medieval world.

Akbar with the able assistance of Abul Fazal and Faizi and interface with the intellectuals drawn from all faiths prevalent in the then India, found the answer in the oneness of all human beings.

It was Akbar who laid the foundation of secularism in India when the Europe was fighting wars within and committing atrocities against those who did not conform to their own faiths, Catholism or Protestanism, within the Christianity. No one should be barred from worshipping the God in the manner and way whatever one liked, was the principle of Akbar. He abolished the pilgrim tax, imposed on Hindus, throughout his empire. He was just a lad of 20 years when he began to feel the oneness of all human being. "Formerly" once told Akbar to Abul Fazl, "I persecuted men in to conformity with my faith and deemed it Islam. As I grew in knowledge, I was overwhelmed with shame. Not being a Muslim myself, it was unmet to force others to become such. What constancy is to be expected from proselytes on compulsion?"[2]

Akbar was much ahead of his time in many respects. His respect towards women was quite evident in his discourses with his courtiers. "To seek more than one wife is to work one's own undoing." he expressed his views, and further regretted, "Had I been wise earlier. I would have taken no woman from my own kingdom in to my seraglio,

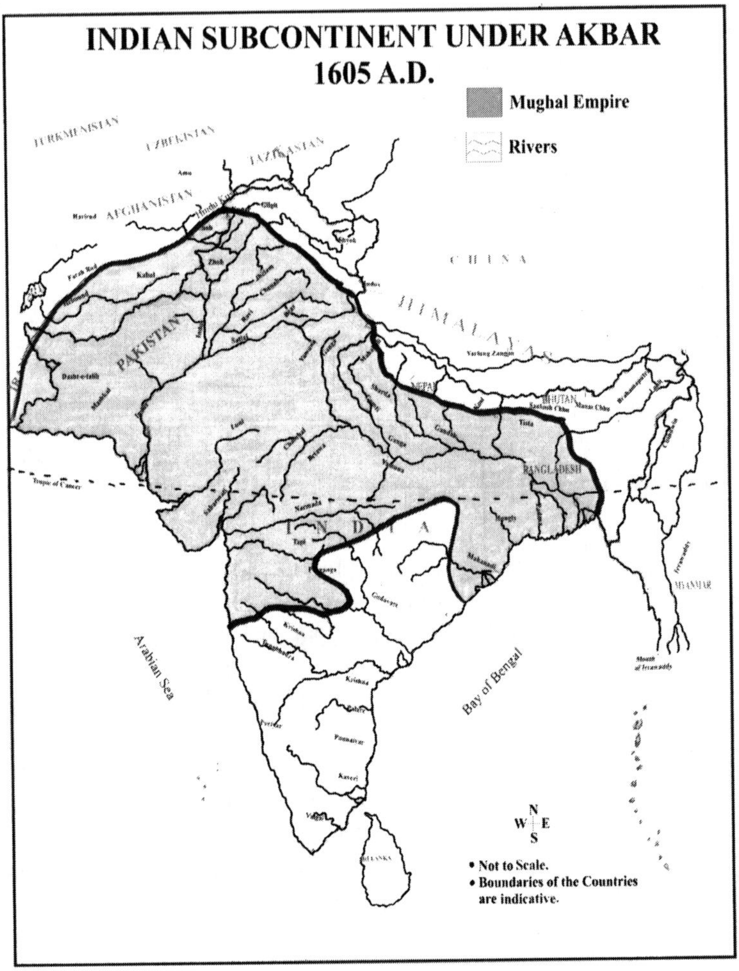
INDIAN SUBCONTINENT UNDER AKBAR
1605 A.D.
Mughal Empire
Rivers
AFGHANISTAN
PAKISTAN
CHINA
HIMALAYAS
NEPAL
BHUTAN
BANGLADESH
INDIA
Arabian Sea
Bay of Bengal
N
W E
S
• Not to Scale.
• Boundaries of the Countries are indicative.

for my subjects are to me in the place of children." He advised Hindus to desist from the practice of wife burning at the funeral pyres of their dead husbands. "It is an ancient custom in Hindustan for a woman to burn herself however unwilling she may be, on her husband's death and to give her priceless life with a cheerful countenance, conceiving it to be a means of her husband's salvation." In no unclear terms he denounced the then prevalent belief of salvation of husbands through the sacrifice of the life of their wives, among Hindus. "It is strange commentary on the magnanimity of men" asserted Akbar, "that they should seek their deliverance through the self sacrifice of their wives."[3] Kindness to all living beings was the foundation of his governance. He advised people to refrain from animal killings and not to turn their stomachs into grave of animals. He even asked them not to eat meat at least once a month in a year. As he understood the oneness of the God there remained no reason for religious discrimination in his kingdom. For him "Each person according to his condition gives the Supreme Being a name, but in reality to name the Unknowable is vain."[4]

However, not in the time of Akbar only, whosoever, Hindu or Muslim, was at the helm of affairs, theocracy in the true sense of the word and governance, was seldom practised in medieval India. For European traders who traded with India in the seventeenth and eighteenth century India, it was a strange phenomenon.

In the second decade of thirteenth century Iltutmish, the second Sultan of Delhi, was asked by some of the Ulemas of Delhi to enforce Shari'a in his Sultanate, Iltutmish not being a Islamic zealot, rejected the proposal by cleverly replying to them;

"But since at the moment, the land has just been conquered, the Hindus here are in such an (overwhelming) number that the Muslims in their midst are like salt (in a dish). If this injunction is enforced they may unite and raise a commotion."[5]

He was not ready to annoy either his Muslim population by rejecting Ullemas outright or Hindus by enforcing sharia'h, as they formed majority of his subjects. He was a practicing Muslim, indeed, but a monarch first. Governance never conformed to theocracy, especially in the circumstances when the State was inhabited by people with various faiths, sects and schools of thoughts. Babur, the founder of the Mughal dynasty, is said to advised his son Humayun;

> "O my son! people of diverse religions inhabit Hindustan, and it is a matter of thanksgiving to God that the King of Kings entrusted the government of this country to you, it therefore behoves you that: you should not allow religious prejudice to influence your mind and administer impartial justice...."

He advised Humayun, it is said, not to destroy the places of worship of any community and refrain from the killing of the cows. These words of the founder of the Mughal dynasty echoed throughout the reign of the Mughals. Aurangzeb is said to be drifted from that policy which resulted in the downfall of the Mughal Empire. Sher Shah, a contemporary of Humayun, constructed *sarais* (inns) by the sides of the various roads including Sadak-e-Azam at every two *kos*, for Hindus and Muslims separately. Sadak-e-Azam, initially built by Mauryans, was repaired, maintained and extended by him and this connected his empire from Mushidabad to Lahore. The road came to be known as Grand Trunk Road in British India. From the ascendency of the Turks (Mamluks) in thirteenth century to the capture of power by British in ninteenth century, majority of subcontinent was ruled by the Muslim kings but *Shariya* was seldom imposed by them on their non-Muslim subjects.

The Indianization of Muslim immigrants started as soon as the Turks established their rule on firm footing in northern India. The Hindavi or Rekhta came in existence to facilitate interaction between common people and the ruling class. Ab'ul Hasan Yamin-ud-din Amir Khusrau, composed a number of treatises, prose and poetry, in Hindavi. He was boastful of his Hindavi (Hindustani) identity. He is said to boast;

> *"Shakkar-e-Misarina daram kaz*
>
> *Arab guyam jawab Turk-e-Hindustaniyam dar hidawi guyam jawab"*

> (I have no Egyptian sugar with which to talk to an Arab,
>
> I am an Indian Turk, I respond in Hindavi.)[6]

The Sufi poetic verses, *'pahelis'* and *'masnavis'* composed by Khusrau have become an inherent part of the social life and conversation in today's northern India. Amir Khusrau, was a pure Indian, born in Patiyali in the present district of Kasganj in the state of UP (India) in the year 1253AD. He witnessed the ascendency and the down fall of the seven Sultans of Delhi sultanate during his life time (1253-1325AD). His literary works in Persian and Hindavi or Rekhta began the movement which later on developed in '*Ganga-Jamuni Tahzib'*. He invented a number of '*Ragas*' such as '*Yaman*', a new style of singing known as '*Qawwali'* with '*Qual'*, and musical instruments such as 'Tabla', a drum instrument and 'Sitar', a string instrument, which are inseparable to the present day Hindustani classical music. Khusrau's mystical verses imbibed with the highest order of Sufism, many of them written in the praise of his mentor Hazrat Nizam-ud-din Aulia, are still sung with great respect in India and Pakistan. A number of Pakistani singers, such as Nusrat Ali Khan, Sabri brothers, Sher Ali and Mehr Ali, Abida Parveen are best known in India for lending their powerfull and sonorous voices to the verses written by Khusrau[7]. In Hidustani music he cannot be equated to anyone else but to Mian Tansen. Tansen was known as Tanna Mishra before his arrival to the court of Akbar and eventual conversion to Islam. Very soon he was adorned with the honour of one of the Nine Jewels and the court musician of 'Akbar the Great' in the second half of the sixteenth century.

Most of the Delhi Sultans are credited with cultivating Indian Music. Alauddin Khalji (1296-1316AD) is said to persuade Nayak Gopal to translate *'Dhrupad'* from Sanskrit to the then spoken language. Sharqi Sultans of Jaunpur, and Zain-ul-Abidin of Kashmir are credited with the promotion of Indian classical music in the fifteenth Century, in their respective domains.

The Muslim Sultanates of south India not only promoted the languages of the masses such as Dakhani, Marathi, and Telagu, but many of them like Adilshahi Sultanate in Bijapur, Baridshahi Sultanate in Bidar and Qutubshahi Sultanate in Golkunda adopted them as their court languages. Many Sufi and ascetic cults like Gurzmars, Jalalis, Madaris and Haidaris adopted the Hindu practices which many a times were contradictory to the interpretation of Islam.[8] These forms were neither approved in orthodox Islam nor in the Brahmanical order of Hinduism, yet they contributed to the social assimilation and integration as they were equally revered both by Hindus and Muslims. The process of social assimilation was not a new phenomenon to India. After the demise of the Mauryan Empire in the first century BC, a number of people, such as Parthians, Scythians or Sakas, Kushans and Hunas invaded India, bringing their culture and practices with them and assimilated with the Indian society. Thus, while the rulers, though were from the dynasties outside of India, the subject and the officials at the lower levels, more or less remained same. The ancestors of the present day Hindu, Muslims, Sikhs, Christians, Buddhists and Jains were the same, many of them indeed switched over to the faiths irrespective to the place of their origin. Indian Muslims were one of them. Like all other immigrants to India, a few hundred thousands Muslims came from abroad, married local Hindu women and set the process of their Indianisation in motion.

As has been explained earlier, by 1858 AD, almost entire India had been subjugated by British. Failed in their attempt to bring Afghanistan and Tibet under their rule and pursuant to their policy of keeping them as buffer-States between British India and Imperialist Russia, the British drew the border lines at both the western and the northern frontiers of India. British apprehensions of southward expansion of Tsarist's Russia was instrumental to the independent status of Afghanistan and Tibet. In 1893, the British officer Sir Mortimer Durand sitting with Abd-ur-Rahman Khan, Amir of Afghanistan, across the table drew a line on a piece of paper with green ink, a symbol of Islamic truthfulness, saying to Amir 'this side is ours and that side is yours'. The Durand Line was based on no natural divide but the political expediency as well as compulsions, which divided the Pashto (also known as Pakhtoon in Indo-Pak region) people in two different political entities. This was a blatant action to cut the social fabric of the Pakhtoons.

As Britishers left India delivering the new state of Pakistan, the demand for unification of Pashto land falling in Afghanistan and Pakistan, was raised at both sides of the Durand Line. Majority of the Pakhtoons wanted a unified Pakhtoonkhwa. Afghan government did not approve the Durand Line. The inclusion of Sibi and Pishin to Baluchistan became another issue for Pakhtoon discontentment. In 1956, Afghan government asserted that there was no legitimacy of the Durand Line. In 1973, Sardar Muhammad Daud, just after overthrowing the government of King Zahir Shah, called the Pathans of Pakistan to secede and join Afghanistan. Again in 1979, the Afghan Prime Minister, Amin, reiterated the demand of a greater Afghanistan. Even the Taliban government that came to power in Afghanistan with Pakistan's help, in 1996, refused to ratify the Durand Line as the border between the two countries.

The border line at Pakistan's western front was as artificial and anti-Pashtoon, as the line of control (LoC) in Kashmir between India and Pakistan. But in today's world, borders between Pakistan and Afghanistan are as irrevocable as the existence of the two nations. Pakistan's fears of a hostile government in Afghanistan led Pakistan to interfere in the Afghan politics in the seventies of the last century. Pakistan's involvement in Afghan politics first through the support to Mujahideen and then to Taliban hardly earned any benefit to it. It brought a gun wielding culture and terrorism to home.

The north-eastern borders of the British India were demarcated by McMahan Line. The line named after the then British Foreign Secretary and the chief British Negotiator, Sir Henry McMahan, was drawn in compliance to the Shimla Convention in 1914. The McMahan Line which was agreed upon by Tibetans and British, determined the border which extends from Bhutan to NEFA, now Arunachal Pradesh. It stretches about 890 kms. (550 miles) all through the crest of Himalayan range in the East. China did not approve it on the ground that Tibet, being just a local government with sovereignty in China, was not authorized to sign the agreement.

In the north, the map drawn by William Henry Johnson, a Surveyor of the Trigonometric Survey of India, in 1865, became the Indo-China border of British India.[9] People's Republic of China (PRC), that came in to existence in October 1949, did not approve it. In 1951 the sovereignty of Tibet was passed over to China through an agreement under the pressure of Chinese military. Soon after that China started the construction of a road to join Tibet with its province of Xinjiang cutting through Aksai Chin in Ladakh[10]. The occupation of Aksai Chin by China brought the Indo China honeymoon under the banner of Panchsheel for about a decade, to a tragic end in 1962.

Apart from contributing to British economy the subcontinent contributed manpower to two World Wars to save the Britain from annihilation at the hands of advancing German forces in Europe and Africa and Japanese forces in south-east Asia. As many as 23,77,147 Indian soldiers drawing largely from Muslim and Hindu community took part in the First World War. 12,15,358 were sent overseas to fight on behalf of the British empire.[11] Indian Muslim soldiers fought against Turkish Muslim soldiers also. They did not hesitate to fight with their co-faith-followers to save the Empire, even the Turkish Sultan had issued a *fatwa* to Muslims for Jihad on 16 November 1914. Almost an equal number of soldiers from the subcontinent fought in the Second World War. About 74,000 Indian soldiers in the first and 87,000 soldiers in the Second World War were killed on the foreign lands in their efforts to save the British Empire. Many more were injured and suffered the odds in the hostile and alien lands, never known to them. Fighting as united soldiers of the British India in battle fields, at return they found themselves in two opposing camps of political ideologies at home. They had a common history till they were divided in 1947.

Chapter - VIII

The Beginning of the Beginning

The emergence of the two independent nations, Pakistan and India, and thereby, also, two political entities in the subcontinent was epoch making event in many respects. The independence of Pakistan and India was followed by the independence of scores of countries in Africa, Asia, and elsewhere in the world. The transfer of power was not smooth in the subcontinent. It was deeply infected with the self-interested malice of the power brokers, nearly always elites among the former slave-like subjects of the British. People of erstwhile India bore the brunt of the clashing interests of their political bosses. The country was partitioned to satisfy the whims of the power brokers. Whatever were the reasons and whosoever were responsible for the partition or whether partition was for good or bad, these issues have no worth in the context of the present millennium in which the world has travelled a long distance and has adopted an entirely different course since then.

At present, the existence of India, Pakistan and Bangladesh along with their neighbours, Nepal and Bhutan, in the landmass known as the Indian subcontinent, is as real as the existence of any the sovereign States in the world. Any attempt to disturb this arrangement would be perilous to the prosperity and wellbeing of the people of the subcontinent. Politics can attempt misadventures but people have to guard themselves against mischief. They have to respect territorial integrity, economic prosperity and the happiness of their neighbours, many of whom were once living in the same country about seven decades ago. Sovereignty belongs to the people, not to political entities.

People of these nations have many similarities in economy, society, culture and history, trespassing the boundaries of the political divide. They have to look beyond their political borders, shedding off the straightjacket sham-nationalism and adopt best practices from various continents and nations across the world.

Indian society has been enriched by Islamic beliefs of equality and simplicity. *'Namaskar'*, *'Namaste'* or *'As-Salaam-Alaikum'* and *'Wa-Alaikum-Salaam'* are the most common ways of greeting one another throughout the subcontinent.

Urdu is the national language of Pakistan, a language that originated and developed in Northern India, and hence is spoken in India's entire northern region and also in some parts of southern states.

The social ethos and practices are adapted to suit the area specific peculiarities owing to geographical and natural specialities and barriers as well. *'Kos-kos pe pani, do kos pe zabani'* (taste of water changes at every two miles and the language at every four miles), the Hindustani proverb represents the true state of varied social mosaics in the subcontinent. Yet, seen in broader aspect the social and cultural systems across the Indian subcontinent appear based on the ethos very close to all ethnic groups of the land. During the colonial rule the people were sharing almost everything from currency to communication, from governance to dissent, from army to civilian life and from rebellions to suppressions, in common. They were freely travelling to any part of the country as per their choice, need and convenience, unless restricted to them by law, interacting with the people of such regions. A unified India provided the opportunities to various social systems to be understood and embraced. Even today one would find difficult to differentiate between the villages of Indian Bengal and a village of Bangladesh or a socio-cultural mosaic of village of Indian Punjab and a village of Pakistani Punjab, at the other side of the borders.

Many a times being the followers of the same faith their places of worships and practices attached to them are also same. Several of the places are of equal reverence to all major communities, Hindu, Sikhs, Buddhist and Muslims across India, Pakistan, Bangladesh, Bhutan and Nepal. Interestingly, the Sikh shrine at Balakot, a city in which the training camps of terrorist outfit JeM were allegedly bombed by a dozen Miraj 2000 jets of India on 26 February in 2019, is a place of reverence for Sikhs, Muslims and Hindus alike. Balakot is named after Bhai Bala, one of the two disciples of Guru Nanak, other disciple being Bhai Mardana, a Muslim. The three saints visited the place in fifteenth century. As Bala stayed for a longer time preaching to people there, the place was named after him as Balakot. Later on, the place cultivated the legend of Bala Pir, a Muslim saint. The Sufi tradition of Kashmir kept alive the composite culture of Balakot.[1] More than a dozen of Sikh and Hindu shrines in Pakistan and Bangladesh and the Dargahs of Sufi saints across the subcontinent have always been the bridges of social harmony over the rivers of political hostilities. This cultural amalgamation is a common feature throughout the subcontinent.

Till recent years, India had the credit of having the second largest Muslim population in the world, only to be overtaken by Pakistan lately. Despite this demographic reality, it has not been accorded any status in the Organisation of Islamic Cooperation (OIC). This denial has its roots in Pakistan's longstanding objection to India's inclusion in any capacity in the OIC. Pakistan has always apprehended being wiped out by India. Both the nations have been using international forums and regional organisations to isolate each other. This politicking bars about twenty crore Muslims of India from being represented in world's largest forum for Muslims. Hypothetically, if India were to be admitted to OIC even in the relatively limited capacity of a Permanent Observer, if the same were to happen on the recommendation of Pakistan, a united subcontinent with a united voice of about fifty crore (half a billion) Muslims would be a potent force to be reckoned with all over the world. The potential development unlocked for this population would be immense. But unfortunately, for Pakistani politicians, the welfare of Muslims in the subcontinent is surmounted by the issue of 'Kashmir'. Kashmir is projected as the 'core issue' for Indo-Pak relations. The absence of India in OIC meetings and conferences enables Pakistan to raise this issue and get Resolutions condemning India's Kashmir policy discussed. This then becomes representational of the Islamic world's stance on the Kashmir question.

The people of Indian subcontinent have been divided through artificial borders into separate political entities, drawn by the erstwhile colonial masters. These borderlines have often been disputed by the succeeding states. The Durand Line, the Radcliffe Line, the McMahon Line, the borders based on the Johnson's Map, the legitimacy of all has been challenged in the past and has led to confrontations. The disputes have not still died down. The history of these borders hardly stretches to more than a hundred and fifty years. The Johnson's Map, developed on the basis of a survey done by a Junior Sub-Assistant of theTrigonometric Survey of India in 1865, was the earliest among all the above border demarcations that demarcated the boundaries between Jammu and Kashmir (under British suzerainty) and Imperial China[2]. The 1200 miles long[3] Durand Line, drawn by Sir Mortimer Durand in 1893, was the next. It was followed by the McMahon Line in 1914, that runs 550 miles along the crests of the Himalayas. Lastly, as important as the others, the Radcliffe Line drawn by Sir Cyril Radcliffe on 16 August 1947, runs 1802 miles (2900 kilometre) between India and Pakistan, and 2582 miles (4156 kilometre) between India and the then Eastern Wing of Pakistan, now known as Bangladesh. These Border Lines were not challenged with any seriousness by anyone till the British ruled India. The British were the masters of the world and no one had the courage to challenge them. But as soon as the British left India, all these boundary lines were disputed by one or another country.

After independence, India and Pakistan redefined their borders for their territorial exploits in their far north, Jammu and Kashmir. They fought a war which lasted for about a year and two months and came to an end with UN sponsored ceasefire on 1 January, 1949. The occupation positions became 'The Cease Fire Line' (CFL) to be admitted as Line of Control (LoC) about 23 years later in July 1972 by both the States under Shimla Agreement. This line runs a distance of 759 kilometre from Chhamb in south to the point NJ 9842 in the north.[4] They did not recognise each other's occupations, terming them illegal. India never accepted Gilgit and Baltistan and Azad Kashmir as part of Pakistan which it termed as Pakistan occupied Kashmir (PoK), unlawful acquisitions of Pakistan. Pakistan in its turn had always an eye on India Held Kashmir (IHK) harbouring all sorts of elements which could be helpful to its Mission Kashmir. Kashmir along with LoC became the mother of all disputes and disagreement at every platform, bilateral to international.

The sorry state of economy is a commonality to these States. This has been discussed earlier with facts and figures. The countries of the subcontinent are characterised by poor levels of Gross Domestic Product (GDP) PPP per capita and Gross National Income(GNI) PPP per capita. The GNI PPP per capita measured in US dollars in 2017 was $ 6353 for India, $ 5311 for Pakistan, $ 3677 for Bangladesh, $ 2471 for Nepal and $ 8065 for Bhutan, as against $ 54941 for US and $ 47766 for Sweden, $46136 for Germany, $ 39254 for France, $ 39116 for UK, $ 35299 for Italy, $ 24233 for Russian Federation and $ 15270 for China, all of them are also major arm suppliers to the third world countries, including the Indian sub-continent. The countries are indebted to foreign loans so heavily that every Indian is said to be indebted with $388, every Pakistani with $366 and every Bangladeshi with $149. These people include the people living below the poverty line set by their own countries who are 21.9% in India, 29.5% in Pakistan and 24.3% in Bangladesh.[5] Despite of their much publicised programmes related to food security they are not able to provide food for all. The starvation deaths are not unknown. Suicide by farmers is a testimony to the sorry state of those engaged in agricultural sector. Unemployment is quite high only to be camouflaged by underemployment ranging from unorganized labour to the service sectors. In a society where employment is a dear commodity, joining the hardliners or fundamentalist or radical organisations or terror groups seems a good opportunity to whom legitimate employment is next to impossible. This illegitimate sector promises them bread and butter and the recognition of their being.

There are other commonalities also, for bad reasons. One of them is with regard to gender discrimination, which is more or less equally followed throughout the subcontinent. The discrimination is reflected from the very start of the birth. Indian Hindu society is seriously infected with the virus of first choice to son which has brought discrimination against the girl child from the time of her birth. This has been one of the major contributing factors to the gender inequality in the subcontinent. A daughter owing to various religious and social beliefs and practices among Hindus is regarded as a burden on the parents. As per its own statistics (NFHS-4) the ratio of women per thousand men in India was 919 in 2017. Globly India was the eighth worst country in the world with 1.11 men per one woman in 2017. Due to discrimination to women on various counts in the whole subcontinent, 'The HDR-2016' enlisted all countries of the subcontinent in Group V, except Nepal which was in Group IV. The Group V countries are those which have an absolute deviation from gender parity from more than 10% and are at the bottom of all groups.[6] In 2018 Nepal slipped to this Group (Group V) to join others at the bottom. Domestic violence against women has the social sanction in the subcontinent. Not only men but women also find women- beating justified for the reasons such as if the wife burns the food, goes out without telling him or refuse sexual relations with him. The bride burning for dowry among Hindus and divorce (Talaq) to wife, Talaq-e-Biddat by Muslims, at personal whim and convenience, are common across the subcontinent. While Talaq-e-Biddat or instant triple talaq, contrary to the teachings of Islam, has been banned in many countries, yet its threat still looms large on the poor Muslim women. It is a matter of concern that a little has been done to improve the status of women in Pakistan, ranking it, just above the countries like Yemen, Niger and Afghanistan.

The countries of the subcontinent share another commonality in their failure to provide a quality life to their people. The UN sponsored Human Development Report (HDR) measures the state of human development in all of the countries of the world on the status of three basic dimensions of human development viz, a long and healthy life, knowledge and a decent standard of life. Various indexes such as IMR, U5MR, MMR, life expectancy, the incidence of communicable diseases, nourishment and the growth of the children, vaccination, children attaining education at various levels, their enrolment and retention, government expenditure on social sector and other interventions which are essential to bring a qualitative improvement in the life of human being are taken in to account and a ranking on the basis of above in order of best to worst is done and published every year since 1990. The assessment of the progress of a country is judged based on the concept that "the real wealth of a nation lies in its people", propagated by Dr. Mahboob ul Haq. The countries of his own subcontinent, however, did not accord much thought to this concept in practice. As per 'Human Development Report, 2019', the ranking of

India at 129, Bhutan at 134, Bangladesh at 135, Nepal at 147 and Pakistan at 152 out of a list of 189 countries speak itself about the pathetic state of the issues related to the human development in the subcontinent. In the HDR 1990, these countries were placed in the category of Low Human Development Category with Bhutan at 12; Nepal at 17; Bangladesh at 23; Pakistan at 36 and India at 37 in an order of from worst to the best in a list of 130 countries. The HDI rankings of the subcontinent's nations as per HDR 1995, HDR 2000, HDR 2005, HDR 2010, HDR 2016, HDR 2018 and HDR 2019 in order of highest to lowest is given in Box no. 12.

Box No. 12

Sl. No.	*Country*	*HDR 1995*	*HDR 2000*	*HDR 2005*	*HDR 2010*	*HDR 2016*	*HD 2018 update*	*HDR 2019*
1.	India	134	135	127	119	131	130	129
2.	Pakistan	128	128	135	125	148	150	152
3.	Bangladesh	146	146	139	129	139	136	135
4.	Nepal	151	144	136	138	144	149	147
5.	Bhutan	160	142	134	-	132	134	134
	Ranking in countries	174	174	177	169	188	189	189

The malady of backwardness of these states lies in the confrontational attitude within themselves and unfair treatment to their own people. India and Pakistan have been victims of this attitude since they came into existence in 1947. As has been stated in the earlier Chapters, misunderstanding, mistrust and mischief culminating in misadventures through state and non-state actors did not leave even a little space for the evolution of mutual understanding and cooperation for the mutual development of the people of the subcontinent.

There always remained two hostile nations across the borders suspicious to each other, modernising their armies to have leverage in case of an armed conflict. They have large armies in terms of numerical strength. To maintain these armies and keep them abreast to the most modern technology, India spent up to about 3% and Pakistan up to about 6% of their GDP on military during past years. In 2017, 9.07% in India and 16.65% in Pakistan, of the annual budget was allotted to the defence sector. From the point of view of weapons world is divided between two categories, i.e., weapon exporting countries and weapon importing countries. With a few exceptions, the weapon-exporting countries manufacture them also. They are in the category of developed countries while those who import them invariably are developing countries. While the developed nations mint money from the strife and conflicts between the developing nations by selling them arms and weapons at the exorbitant prices, the developing nations drain out their economic resources to purchase them. The countries of Indian subcontinent are some of them.

Out of the total imports of weapons world over in 1917, India with 12% was the largest buyer of the weapons. Pakistan was at ninth place with 2.8%. A good chunk of their budget goes on the purchases of weapons from the countries which have a PPP per capita in relation to GDP seven to nine times higher to India and Pakistan. Yet, there is no end to arms purchases. In the process, the economy of weapon supplying countries flourishes at the cost of weapon purchasing countries, keeping the economy of latter impoverished. India and Pakistan boast the robustness of their armies on the acquisition of such arms and challenge each other for a military showdown. Arms exporting countries never sell their latest generation weapons to the countries like India and Pakistan for the reasons best known to them and understood by everyone. Though India and Pakistan hardly manufacture any weapon of advance technique and are dependent on the mercy of other countries for their availability, the Chiefs of Staff of armed forces assure their countrymen of the forces' readiness to take on any country at war.

According to some estimates, by the first decade of the present century, Pakistan had achieved superiority in Air force over India. This means, Pakistan must have spent money several times higher than India on the updating of its air force. But this information rang alarm bells in the Indian military camps and political circles. India attempted to purchase Rafale fighter bombers from France in 2014, but as Dassault Aviation, the company that manufactures it, cited the price at about two times higher than it had offered seven years back, the then government of India dropped the purchase plan. However, within two years the Government of India revived the plan and despite of about a threefold increase in its price over the 2014 prices, Indian government put its seal to the contract. The opposition parties cried foul in the deal.

Both India and Pakistan are determined to have a superior military but the question remains to be answered- at whose cost?

There is a silent war seldom reported by media, going always in heights such as Siachen, where soldiers often encounter a common enemy, the hostile climate in a difficult terrain.

There goes a widely circulated lore in those heights.

'A contingent of soldiers led by a young captain is out on a patrol. It is a usual but an indispensable exercise by the soldiers guarding the borders of their nations. All of the soldiers are tied to each other with a rope, each lugging a heavy payload on their backs. Every breath becomes an additional burden, as the load gets even heavier with increasing altitude and thinning air. With the help of an ice axe, they move slowly but steadily ahead, maintaining a predetermined and calculated pace and space with each other. The rope is there to help them rescue their fellow soldier if they accidentally lose their footing. Suddenly, the patrol party is jerked to a halt. A soldier shouts as his foot gets trapped somewhere on the track.

The patrol party's worst fears have come true. The soldier's foot has gotten stuck in a crevice. The warmth of human movement has melted the ice over the crevice. The soldier in a reflex action, against all the advices in such a situation, tries to pull his leg out. As the ice melts, getting further heat from his leg, the opening of the crevice goes from wide to even wider, dragging the other leg into the crevice as well. The Captain orders all his fellow soldiers to pull their stuck brother with all their might, but all is in vain. He commands again and exhorts them to pull the rope to save the trapped soldier. As the party sees him slipping and sinking further, it also starts to feel a downward pull dragging them all into the crevice. The Captain also feels it. He makes a final call to pull the trapped soldier out. The fear of dragging all the soldiers in, one after the other, and thus losing the entire contingent to the crevice bears heavy. The Captain retreats and orders the rope be cut at both the ends of the trapped soldier. The soldiers follow the orders of their commander. Realising the reality, the sinking soldier requests the Captain, "Sir, I know that there is no other option but to cut the ropes and leave me to die in the crevice. But please fulfil my only and last wish." The fellow soldiers and the Captain look at him with a mix of despair, helplessness, and sorrow in their eyes with an obvious unspoken but well understood "Yes?". "Sir, don't tell my mother that I was lost to the crevice alive," says the sinking soldier, "Otherwise my mother will wait for me throughout her life."

Which nation do these soldiers belong to? A pertinent question, difficult to answer. "Pakistan probably." "No, No. Probably to India." With hundred percent surety one can say "to both the nations, in all certainty". Pakistan this time, India another or vice-versa, it's the same.

During the fights, the incompatibility of weapons too takes the life of soldiers at such heights of Kashmir. A true story about one such fight at Siachen glacier, an altitude of more than 22,000 feet, was narrated by a writer in following words:

"All these groups started climbing up and...(he) was the first to get behind the rocky outcrop and cut the rope after encountering a deep crevice. Subedar...reached the area of the saddle and started his journey to the top of the objective, moving along the razor thin ridge line. The progress was slow and deliberate with the party inching forward. They had barely moved 50 metres along the ridge when Nai..., the scout of the party observed some movement in front, and alerted the troops following close behind. Before they could even get down and take up firing positions, the enemy opened fire with his medium machine guns, instantaneously killing ...(him) and two others. The troops following behind immediately tried to return the fire, but not a single shot left the muzzle of the barrel as all the weapons malfunctioned due to extreme cold, despite the fact that the weapons had been tested a 1,000 feet below. However, the enemy weapons blazed away and we discovered later that their machine guns were firing because the weapons were being heated with a kerosene stove placed under the weapon. There was hardly any place at the top and the troops had to hide behind icicles and undulating ice beds to avoid being hit by the enemy fire."[i-n]

However, Bangladesh despite several constraints has been successful in containing its army at a very low strength of only 1.26 lakh compared to Pakistan's 6.19 lakh and India's 13.25 lakh and restrict the expenditure to a maximum of 1.5% of GDP on military. This paradigm shift from military to social sector in Bangladesh has resulted in a marked reduction from the level of 1990 to 2016 in U5 MR from 144 to 34.2, in MMR from 600 to 134 and in IMR from 96 to 28.2. During last fifteen years it brought down the level of stunted growth among children from 45% to 36.2%. This was the best performance among all of the countries of Indian subcontinent. A long duration of no major conflict since Bangladesh's birth in 1971 and its preference to socio-economic sector over military probably were the reasons behind its achievements in human development indicators.

The dispute resolution is not a difficult task. What the subcontinent needs, is a political will with altruist intentions, centred around the welfare of the people. People are just people. To divide them between "ours" and "yours" as commodities, is the negation of the right of living to fellow human beings.

The new millennium method of politicking needs to be centred around human welfare instead of territorial expansions. The signing of Indo-Bangladesh agreement on transfer of their enclaves and adverse possessions on each other's territory on 6 June, 1974 between the then Premiers of India and Pakistan, Indira Gandhi and Sheikh Mujib-ur-Rahman respectively, sailing through the troubled water remained defunct. A sincere effort was again made by Man Mohan Singh and Sheikh Haseena Wajed, the Premiers of India and Bangladesh respectively, in 2014, but failed to be linked with agreement owing to objections from some Indian regional politicians. Finally in 2016 an Indo-Bangladesh agreement was signed with the efforts of two Premiers, Modi at Indian side and Sheikh Haseena at Bangladeshi side, which provided relief to 51,549 people residing in these enclaves. With the travesty of destiny these enclaves as the popular say goes, had been used as pawns in the chess board of the rulers of Cooch Behar and Rangpur. Peoples living in these enclaves were forced to live in virtual landlocked Islands, belonging to other country. There were about 111 Indian enclaves covering about 6,940 hectares in Bangladesh and 51 Bangladeshi enclaves spread over 2880 hectares in the Indian territory.

The two governments took the bold decision, putting the question of territorial loss or gain, aside, for the benefit of more than half a lakh people. The people of these enclaves were living in the conditions of virtual housearrests, within the boundaries of enclaves, encircled by the territory of adverse political entities, since 1947. As per agreement the enclaves falling within the geographical boundaries of Bangladesh were transferred to Bangladesh while falling within Indian geographical boundaries were transferred to India. Moreover, they were given the options of choosing the citizenship of either nation. Most of them chose the citizenship of the nation to which the enclave was being transferred. A miniscule number, about 1,000 out of about 36,000 people of former Indian enclaves in Bangladesh, chose Indian citizenship. They were granted and relocated in the Indian Territory. Yet more has to be done to meet the aspirations of the Bangladeshi people of the enclaves, still falling in India. Land belongs to the people who are born there and by virtue of that, ownership lies to them only. The denial of citizenship and equality before law is the denial of human rights.

Outside the subcontinent the two 'All Weather Fiends' of India and Pakistan and the erstwhile rivals for centuries, Russia and China respectively, worked on defusing the border disputes by mutually agreeing to recognize each other's possessions or claims in a friendly manner. The process which started in the nineties of the last century reached to finality in 2008. The Sino-Russian accord of 2008 accorded the final closure to all earlier boundary agreements. The accord affected the cessation of 174 kms of Russian territory with two small islands on the mouth of two rivers to China. China relinquished its claim on about half of the territory under Russian possession. Many of the border disputes had already been solved in the last decade of twentieth century. Their desire to stand up against what they called American hegemony has almost secured their entire border with a length of 4,300 kms. Analysts did not forget to point out that China was the second largest consumer of the oil and Russia was the second largest exporter of it. The distance of the Russian oilfield in Siberia to China is astonishingly very short. Consequent to border settlement accord the 24 lakh strong

Chinese and 10.27 lakh strong Russian armies were relieved from the threats from across the Sino-Russian borders. In Indian subcontinent also India and Bangladesh have almost resolved their border issues making 4,156 kms long border free from any trouble, but the Indo-Pak borders still remain volatile.

There is no dispute in terms of their actual possessions, between India and Pakistan. As of Jammu and Kashmir, the PHK has become a part of Pakistan, as the IHK is the integral part of India, for all purposes, leaving no issue for further discussions or negotiations. Similarly, the northern areas of Gilgit and Baltistan are being administered by Pakistan since 1947. Likewise, Sir Creek has a historical legacy and be accepted keeping the interests of both in to consideration. The arrangement of geographical boundaries of the present day nations cannot be changed in any manner. Majority of the people of both the nations are unacquainted with the pre- bifurcation history and realities of Jammu and Kashmir. They are misled by their politicians and media (centred around the inhancement of their TRP rating) to join them in harping the conflicting issues. To raise the issues of the legitimacy of the possessions and indulge in conflicts is a sheer wastage of national resources including economic and human lives.

Borders of European countries came to be settled finally by the second half of the last century not through wars and conflicts but the consensus decision of the participating States, keeping the agenda of people's development at the foefront. A few countries got their name changed with their ethnicity at the centre stage. Once settled, they joined the group of nations for inclusion in EU. As of now four non-EU members (Iceland, Liechtenstein, Norway and Switzerland) have their own Union, 'European Free Trade Association'(EFTA), similar to EU in function.[ii-n] People of Europe, now are enjoying much better life than they were enjoying in the pre-Second World War era.

India and Pakistan fought many wars which brought no benefits except loss of lives, devastation and backwardness to their countries. The stockpile of about 300 nuclear heads, about 130 to 140 with India and 140 to 150 with Pakistan by 2017[7] and a race to increase them as a deterrent to each other is a foolish proposition, as they are not to bring any benefit either in storage or dropping on enemy lands, which would bring no economic development to the perpetrator but devastation to both. So far only one country, USA, is discredited with such madness. In the event of any of the country resorting to it would invite international condemnation and sanctions, throwing the life of its entire population to risk.

The policy of fomenting internal insurgency or support the terrorist outfits have boomeranged to Pakistan. This, as the facts tell us have resulted only in killings of the people by their own people, people of their own country, summarily people of erstwhile India. Terrorism can make a few cuts but cannot inflict death upon any nation. The brain and bravery of the youth engaged in militancy need to be invested in national reconstruction. All the people including security personnel, agitators and terrorists as well, are from within our society and politicians at the helm of affairs in both the countries have the responsibility to protect each and every life of the citizen of the subcontinent. The countries of Indian subcontinent have made laudable achievements in many fields such as energy, medicine, space, information technology, agriculture, science and art and culture. These achievements need to be shared with each other. India has made a great advance in space technology with its weather and communication satellites. India can share the benefits of this technology with other nations of the subcontinent. This does not involve any discernible additional cost. The fruit brought about by advancement of Indian scientists and doctors made in the field of medicine and health should be allowed to be enjoyed by the entire subcontinent.

Let these nations shut their irresponsible media, electronic or print, and politicians and communal groups from spitting venoms and repeating the past stories of humiliation and animosities against each other. Presently, differences are often exaggerated, sometimes cooked also, and war rhetoric are raised unwarrantedly. Let the people reach to the militants and terrorists along with their outfits to impress upon them the futility of killings of the people of rival groups, ideology and faiths or the innocent crowds.

Let the people understand that abstinence from killings is in the interest of peace, prosperity and development of their own people and communities.

Militants should also not be answered with violence but be responded by addressing their genuine problems. Craze for guns has to be replaced by longing for a better life. The individuals playing with the life of youths by indoctrinating them to shed their as well as others blood as suicide-bombers (*fidayeen*) need to be isolated from the society with the joint efforts of all the nations of the subcontinent.

Democracy is prerequisite for responsive and acceptable governance which needs to be made people-centric by making it accessible to all. No condition that prevents people's participation in the democratic governance, including educational, be imposed upon through election laws at any level. No government can have the trust of the people unless it is elected by the people themselves, in a free and fair manner without any prejudice to region, faith, religion, caste, sect or any sort of communal bias. Everybody should be provided with the facilities of state-sponsored educational institutions and medical facilities.

The official ceremonies at the borders which perpetuate or promote divide, such as 'Beating the Retreat' at Wagha, might be substituted by friendly exchanges with each side wishing good to each other. Many problems can be solved just by saluting each other's national flag and joining each other in reciting their national anthems.

The security of each and every country in the subcontinent lies within the subcontinent. Searching friends outside results, as Ayub had found, in masters. The outside friends as history tells us seldom come up to our expectations. Their own national political compulsions overshadow the accords and agreements signed with the nations of lesser importance. The frequent US missile strikes at the civilian habitations and the social congregations especially in the provinces of Khaiber Pakhtoonkhwa, Baluchistan and FATA in Pakistan, killing hundreds of innocent people are unpardonable crimes against humanity. The thumb rule for a super power, like US is 'let the people of other country die but keep the morale of its forces high'. This situation could have never been emerged in the absence of Pakistan's collusiveness with US to destabilize the Afghan Government.

Pakistan was virtually attacked on the night of May 2, 2011 by US, as America's stealth Black Hawk Helicopters with 25 Navy SEALS entered in its air space, and made a blitzkrieg at the hideout of Al Qaida leader, Osama bin Laden at Abottabad, about 50 kms (aerial) away from its capital, Islamabad. Not only this, Osama was picked up and killed by the US navy SEAL marines and his body was dumped in the sea while returning to their base as a part of 'Operation Neptune Spear'. Weakness of Pakistani dispensation became conspicuous beyond any doubt. Pakistan's sovereignty was violated but Pakistan with a few words of formal protests, chose to keep mum. How can a weak nation react against a nation to whom its leaders owe a number of obligations? Not only Pakistan, but no country in the subcontinent would have the courage and power to retaliate in similar circumstances.

America, to ensure the location of the hideout and presence of Osama therein committed one of the most deplorable crimes of misusing the UNICEF and WHO sponsored Polio-vaccination programme. The services of a government physician, Dr. Afridi, were secretly obtained. The DNA samples taken by Afridi to confirm Osama's presence, indeed benefited America but inflicted a great set back to Polio eradication from Pakistan and eventually from the world as by then Pakistan was one among the only four countries in the world who were experiencing Poliomyelitis.

Osama misused American Boeings to destroy the Trade Towers at New York; US misused polio vaccination drive to eliminate Osama. US was not criticised by anyone for torpedoing the programme of one of the highest human value. Muslims in the subcontinent were already harbouring many apprehensions about the vaccine - one of them making their children impotent. It must have strayed many Muslims away from vaccinating their children against many other widely prevalent communicable diseases also. There must have been an adverse effect on eradication of poliomyelitis in Pakistan, Even in 2020 Pakistan along with Afghanistan remained one of the last vestiges of the disease as even in 2018 and 2019, 132 and 144 Polio cases were reported from Pakistan.

The subcontinent is inflicted with internal discontentment often resulting in mass agitations, violent demonstrations and armed insurrections. This is often taken as State's failure to address the peoples' aspirations and expectations.

Political leaderships, unable to provide good governance, many a times, prefer to engage various groups in raising such demands which often hurt the interests of other communities. This results in creation of rifts between various sections and groups within the society which are exploited by the political parties to garner support from particular communities in their favour. Conflicts between Muhajirs, represented by Muttahida Quami Movement (MQM) and Sindhi inhabitants, and between various ethenic groups and sects (Shias, Sunnis and Ahemadias in particular) in Pakistan; cast consciousness and violent agitations to get reservation in jobes and seats and offices in the constitutional and statutory bodies by various communities in India; conflicting claims between Tharu and Madhesis at the one side and other Nepali communities at the other leading to violent demonstrations and clashes in Nepal; and between moderates and the uncompromising Islamists in Bangladesh and Pakistan, are some of the evidences of such conflicting interests.

In comparision to Pakistan India faced less problems of regional nationalism. The inflow of migrants did not change the demography of the areas where migrants settled themselves. Hence, their settlement generated no antipathy from the people living there from the pre-partition days. However, people of non-Hindi speaking areas reacted sharply when Hindi was imposed upon them as the national language.

South India burst in to anger and expressed its protest resorting to violent protests, damaging government property in sixties of the last century. Better sense prevailed upon the government and the government soon withdrew its policy of thrusting Hindi upon the non-Hindi speaking states. Indian government took corrective measures by initiating three-language formula (1968) in the school education. Gradually essentiality of Hindi was withdrawn from the school curriculum. People of non Hindi speaking areas began to learn and accept it as the most important and widely known language of India. English remained the first language for all official and legislative purpose. With no pressure from the Union government today, Hindi is understood by the people almost all over India.

Yet, discontentment among the people remains for the various reasons. The desire for independence or autonomy among the various communities of northeast India, Naxalite movement in the sixth and seventh decades of last century and the leftwing extremism in the specific areas of about more than half a dozen States, and continued unrest in J&K since nineties of the last decade are some of the instances of Indian government's failure to satisfy the people's aspirations of the Indian State.

Nepal was never subjugated by British colonial masters, but the life of the people was worse than the people of slave-India. It went through several political upheavals after British freed the subcontinent from its command, yet there was hardly any visible improvement in the living status of the masses. The last king Gyanendra, succumbed to the mass movement and Maoist insurgency, against the monarchy, in 2006. Later a comprehensive peace agreement (CPA) in 2007 paved the way for elections and a new constitution for Nepal. Much blood had already shed since Feb 1996, in the conflicts between the Maoists and Loyalists. The issues related to regions and communities were so conflicting that the law makers could not agree on a draft-constitution during their tenure, 2008-2012. The good thing was that the Constituent Assembly agreed on federalism, secularism and inclusive democratic republic.

A new Constituent Assembly elected in Novermber 2013, finalized the Constitution in 2015, "recognizing the multi-ethnic, multi-lingual, multi-religious, multi-cultural and diverse regional characteristics, resolving to build an egalitarian Society…" "by eliminating discrimination based on class, caste, region, language, religion and gender and all forms of castebased untouchability…" Going by the Preamble of the constitution, Nepal seemed to proceed far ahead of the best democracies of the world. But the promulgation of the new Constitution was received with protests from many communities in many regions. 'Madhesis' and 'Tharus' living in the Tarais (low lands) of the Himalayas found some of the provisions of the new Constitution against their interests. As a large number of Tharus live in India and the Madhesis have close relations with the people accross the borders living in India, the Indian government came under the pressure of its own people. An undeclared economic blockade of Nepal blocking the vehicular transport at all check points, was imposed by India. The citizenship provisions in the

Costitution were apprehended by many a people to put them in disadvantage. There were wide spread protests in low land of Nepal. However, the pressure-tactics adopted by the Indian government marred the Indo-Nepal relations.

Nepal, a land locked country, owing to its geography and culture, must be regarded an equal partner of India in all spheres of politico-socio-economic life. More than half a dozen large rivers and thousands of rivulets originating from Nepal irrigate the plains of India and during monsoons, when there are excessive rains, also play havocs. River water management and collaboration for various purposes between the two countries offers infinite opportunities for the mutual economic development of both the countries.

Nepalese and Indian people were expecting closer politico-socio-economic relations with each other in the newly emerged post monarchy-democratic set-up in Nepal. But their expectations received a serious blow from Nepal's new dispensation in 2020, which raised the issue of ownership of a piece of land, presently owned by India. On 9 August 2019, India abrogated the special status conferred upon its state of J&K, vide its Constitution (Art.370), changed the constitutional status of the State and subsequently issued its amended map. Nepal contested the Indian map by claiming a *Khukri* shaped 370 sq.kms Indian territory at its western borders, as its own.

Situated at an altitude of more or less 5200 mts, the disputed area has three important passes; Limpiyadhura, Kalapani and Lipulekh (LKL Triangle) at the Indian side of Indo-China border. These passes are in Dharchula Sub-division of District Pithoragarh in Uttarakhand State of India. River Kali (known as Mahakali in Nepal) makes the border of the two countries, India and Nepal, as per Article -III and V of the Treaty of Sugauli. The Treaty was signed about two centuries ago on 2 December 1815(ratified on 4 March 1816), between the then king of Nepal and the British East India Company. By virtue of the Treaty the area east to river Kali is held by Nepal and to the west belongs to India. Article-III of the Treaty envisaged as follows:

'The Rajah of Nepal hereby cedes to the Honourable the East India Company in perpetuity all the under-mentioned territories, viz.,-

First:-The whole of the lowlands between the Rivers Kali and Rapti. Second:-..............................' .

However, the source of river Kali has often been disputed by the Nepalese Government. The river in its upper reaches in Himalayas has several tributaries. Nepal asserted the western most tributary originating from Limpiyadhura as the main river Kali while for India the main river Kali originates from Kalapani, close to Lipulekh. According to the Government of India, the river that flows through Limpiyadhura is a tributary, Kuti-Yankit, which meets river Kali at Gunji, and thus, the easternmost tributary is the river Kali, drawing waters from other tributaries. The people living in the region, such as of the villages of Kuti, Navi and Gunji, who are Indian citizens for centuries, also hold the same view. Prime Minister KPS Oli led Nepalese government started a vigorous campaign to the Nepalese claim during the first half of 2020. Finally through a parliamentary process the *Khukri* (a traditional dagger like weapon kept by almost every Gorkha) shaped area as described above (Limpiadhura, Kalapani, Lipulekh - LKL Axis), administered by India since 1816, was included in the map of Nepal through a Constitutional Amendment on 13 June 2020. Interestingly, the people of the areas at both sides of the River Kali had not any problem with the present status and even after the Amendment, they, were freely interacting with each other, as before.

It is well known that given the strategic and commercial importance of the LKL Axis, India would never compromise with the Nepalese claim. Without any uncertainty, Nepalese politicians created a retrogressive issue, which has no concern with its people's welfare. It is unfortunate that a new instrument to keep people in a state of perpetual backwardness has been created, and that too by an elected government.

Bhutan has been successful in keeping its various communities largely satisfied with the State. Its Constitution does not allow monarchy to turn ifself in to a dictatorship and ensures that monarch is retired at the age of 65 years. Though, a tiny State in terms of population, Bhutan's geographical location is significant to the economy of its neighbours, India and Bangladesh. A number of rivers that water the plains of the two countries arise from its land.

Countries of the subcontinent had already road and rail interconnectivity during the British Raj. However, as the British left India, people were deprived from this mode of connectivity by the new masters. Instead of extending rail and road connectivity, existing ones too were blocked. Apart from commercial activities people also lost the opportunity of social and cultural interaction. The rail and road infrastructure need to be re-established and extended with new ways and means.

As the territory of Bangladesh intercepts the states of North East India (Assam, Meghalaya, Arunachal Pradesh, Nagaland, Mizoram, Manipur and Tripura) from being connected with rest of India through it, the two nations need to come forward to establish vibrant and robust road and rail links, through the territory of Bangladesh, to provide commercial and economic connectivity to North-East Provinces of India.

Water flowing in the rivers with their basins in India, originating from the Himalayas, and irrigating the plains of Bangladesh, could be harnessed to strengthen friendship and co operation to bring economic development to the people of both the States. Not much has been done in this direction, the reason is in their insistence on their political ideology based on false notions of separatism and focus on exploitation of the sentiments of particular sections of the society for their electoral advantages.

At the north-west end of the subcontinent in J&K, the trade, commerce and human relations have been sacrificed at the altar of hostile politics of the politicians of India, Pakistan and the J&K based local politicians. The economic and social development of the people living in IHK and PHK have seldom been given due importance. The mass exodus of Kashmiri Pandits from Kashmir did not begin till Zia-ul-Haq formulated-scheme of fomenting trouble in Kashmir was given a violent start in July 1988. Zia was neither a Kashmiri nor he had the slightest concern for Kashmiris. Neither 'a thousand-year war' slogan of Bhutto nor 'bleeding India through a thousand cuts' policy of Zia ul Haq could bring any economic gain to Pakistani people, yet the slogans enthralled them. The public discontent against the government in absence of the effective opposition, which had been denied to J&K

people, through unfair practices in the 1987 elections to the legislative assembly, allowed the militancy a hassle-free go ahead.

No one else, but the people of Kashmir suffered in the process. Their economy got road blocks. The dreams of Kashmiri youths for a prosperous and dignified life shattered. Their self-esteem was destroyed under the boots of gun and bomb-wielding terrorists at the one hand and security forces equipped with AFSPA provisions at the other. In a democracy laws are framed for the sake of the people but contrary to it, laws were framed to equip the security forces to shut any act or voice of dissent from the people. At the same time a handful of troublemakers could have not been allowed to terrorise the minorities and put the government at ransom. This is the security system followed more or less all over the subcontinent.

The land belongs to its inhabitants not the political masters. Jammu and Kashmir never belonged to Pakistan. The area known as AK in Pakistan and GK in India, addressed as PHK in this treatise, was annexed to Pakistan along Gilgit and Baltistan with force, leaving rest of the area to the ruler of J&K, compelling him to accede to India through an agreement. The often-repeated hyperboles, 'Kashmir runs in the blood of Pakistan', or 'wipe out Pakistan from the World-map' are not to yield any benefit to anyone, but are bound to continue the everlasting tragedy of backwardness in the subcontinent.

The two nations, India and Pakistan, have been responsible for spoiling peace and tranquillity of the entire subcontinent resulting in the backwardness of the people. Taken together a 22 lakh strong army of the subcontinent, should not be seen as a killing machine but a highly trained group of professionals serving the people in their most difficult circumstances and situations. Most of the countries are suffering from regional discontentment, internal insurgency, militancy and terrorism. The ruling dispensation is greatly responsible for not meeting the people's aspirations. The ruling classes see good opportunities in the troubles in neighbouring country to divert the attention of their people from the core issues of development, by fishing in its troubled water. This aggravates the situation. With a firm 'no' to the terrorism and militancy from the neighbouring country or the countries, the terrorism and the militancy would be deprived from their lifelines. Support to terrorism by any government has never brought any benefit to its people.

These countries have not learned any lesson from their terrible past and the present exploitive economic colonial world-regime. In the recent past in the first half of 2020, like other countries of the world, they were invaded by the corona-virus, identified as COVID-19 by the WHO. India and Pakistan were already facing another invader, locust, since the summers of 2019. By the end of July 2020, as per their official figures COVID-19 had taken more than 16.4 lakh people in India, 2.77 lakh people in Pakistan, 2.35 lakh people in Bangladesh, 19,543 people in Nepal and 102 in Bhutan under its grip, with a death count of 35,786; 5,924; 3,083 and 52 respectively, in the first four above-mentioned countries.

The swarms of locust had turned 38% of the agricultural land of Pakistan in to their breeding grounds. They had already crossed the Indo- Pak borders in 2019 and were flying eastward. By mid 2020 they had ravaged the harvests in about 10 states of India. No concerted effort was made by the two countries to prevent locust's migration from African (Kenya, Ethopia and Somalia-the Horn of Africa) deserts. Warnings from FAO's 'Desert Locust Watch' went unheard to the hostile sloganeering of those who were heading the governments. No joint effort was done to arrest locust's breeding and their free roaming resulting in the loss of crops of billions of Dollars worth at both sides of the borders.

With no worth-full preventive intervention coming from their governments, people resorted to primitive-era methods, such as banging utensils and playing loud music, to scare away the locusts from their farms and habitations.

Yet, despite the above-stated dangers looming large over them, cease-fire violations and intrusion of Pakistan-backed terrorists to IHK did not show any sign of decrease.

Nefarious designs found expressions in the speeches of the leaders at both the sides of the borders. Indian Premiere Narendra Modi, addressing a Rally of National Cadet Corps (NCC) in January 2020 at Delhi, asserted that Indian Armed Forces would not need more than a week to ten days to defeat the neighbouring country(an obvious reference to Pakistan), in case of another war (Source: Hindustan times, 28 January 2020). Pakistani leadership at the other hand never missed an opportunity to poke its nose in the internal affairs of India. In the background of Indian government revoking article 370 and 35-A of its Constitution that withdrew special status granted to J&K and changed the constitutional status of the State, Pakistan's leadership started a vigorous campaign to condemn the Indian government's move. Pakistan's Premiere Imran Khan tweeted on 2 April 2020, that, Pakistan stood with the Kashmiris in rejecting latest Indian attempt to alter the demography of IOJK. Further on 19 April, he termed Modi Government's policy as 'the deliberate and violent targeting of Muslims in India' and compared the same with, 'what Nazis did the Jews in Germany'.

The countries of the Indian subcontinent need to forget their bitter history of hostilities and forge their own Union, on the footsteps of European Union and develop a mechanism of Joint Defence System of the Indian subcontinent.

The road to prosperity of people passes through the economic development of each other. For any of the country of the subcontinent a weak neighbour is a danger to its own peace, progress and prosperity and also to the tranquillity of the entire subcontinent. The people of the subcontinent have no closer historical, social, economic and cultural ties with any other country's people of the world than with their own neighbours'; Pakistanis, Indians, Bangladeshis, Nepalis, and Bhutanese. Indian subcontinent has to compete with the industrialized world. The road to prosperity is not difficult but is in want of will, a will to combat the everlasting tragedy of enmity that has been perpetuated and resulted in the backwardness of the people.

HYPOTHETICAL - UNITED NATIONS OF INDIAN SUBCONTINENT

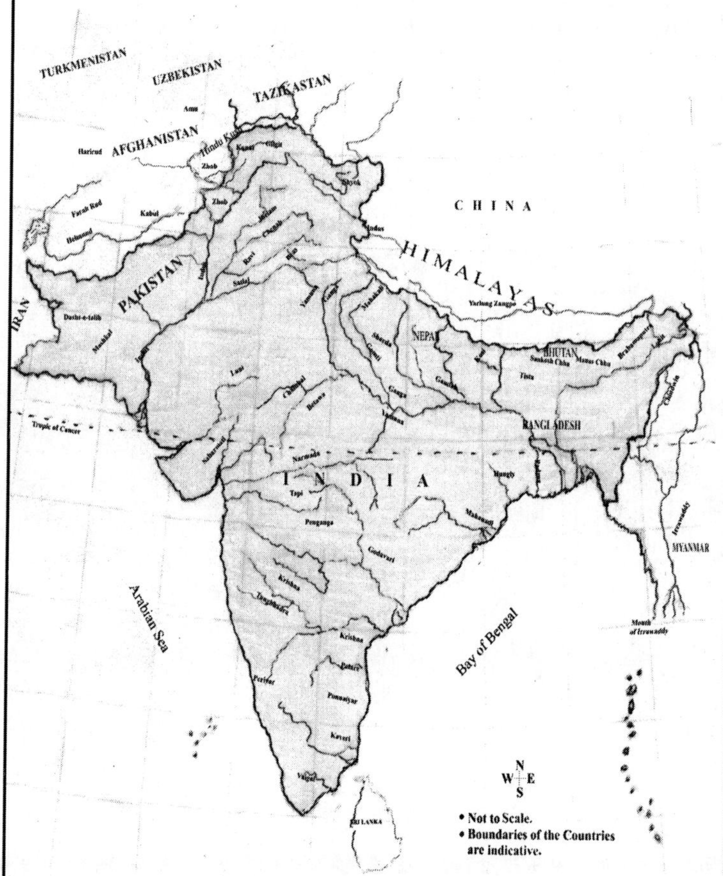

Annexures

Annexure - 1

Quaid-e-Azam Muhammad Ali Jinnah's presidential address to the Constituent Assembly of Pakistan

August 11, 1947

Mr. President, Ladies and Gentlemen!

I cordially thank you, with the utmost sincerity, for the honour you have conferred upon me - the greatest honour that is possible to confer - by electing me as your first President. I also thank those leaders who have spoken in appreciation of my services and their personal references to me. I sincerely hope that with your support and your co-operation we shall make this Constituent Assembly an example to the world. The Constituent Assembly has got two main functions to perform. The first is the very onerous and responsible task of framing the future constitution of Pakistan and the second of functioning as a full and complete sovereign body as the Federal Legislature of Pakistan. We have to do the best we can in adopting a provisional constitution for the Federal Legislature of Pakistan. You know really that not only we ourselves are wondering but, I think, the whole world is wondering at this unprecedented cyclonic revolution which has brought about the clan of creating and establishing two independent sovereign Dominions in this sub-continent. As it is, it has been unprecedented; there is no parallel in the history of the world. This mighty sub-continent with all kinds of inhabitants has been brought under a plan which is titanic, unknown, unparalleled. And what is very important with regards to it is that we have achieved it peacefully and by means of an evolution of the greatest possible character.

Dealing with our first function in this Assembly, I cannot make any well-considered pronouncement at this moment, but I shall say a few things as they occur to me. The first and the foremost thing that I would like to emphasize is this: remember that you are now a sovereign legislative body and you have got all the powers. It, therefore, places on you the gravest responsibility as to how you should take your decisions. The first observation that I would like to make is this: You will no doubt agree with me that the first duty of a government is to maintain law and order, so that the life, property and religious beliefs of its subjects are fully protected by the State.

The second thing that occurs to me is this: One of the biggest curses from which India is suffering - I do not say that other countries are free from it, but, I think our condition is much worse - is bribery and corruption. That really is a poison. We must put that down with an iron hand and I hope that you will take adequate measures as soon as it is possible for this Assembly to do so.

Black-marketing is another curse. Well, I know that blackmarketeers are frequently caught and punished. Judicial sentences are passed or sometimes fines only are imposed. Now you have to tackle this monster, which today is a colossal crime against society, in our distressed conditions, when we constantly face shortage of food and other essential commodities of life. A citizen who does black-marketing commits, I think, a greater crime than the biggest and most grievous of crimes. These blackmarketeers are really knowing, intelligent and ordinarily responsible people, and when they indulge in black-marketing, I think they ought to be very severely punished, because the entire system of control and regulation of foodstuffs and essential commodities, and cause wholesale starvation and want and even death.

The next thing that strikes me is this: Here again it is a legacy which has been passed on to us. Along with many other things, good and bad, has arrived this great evil, the evil of nepotism and jobbery. I want to make it quite clear that I shall never tolerate any kind of jobbery, nepotism or any any influence directly of indirectly brought to bear upon me. Whenever I will find that such a practice is in vogue or is continuing anywhere, low or high, I shall certainly not countenance it.

I know there are people who do not quite agree with the division of India and the partition of the Punjab and Bengal. Much has been said against it, but now that it has been accepted, it is the duty of everyone of us to loyally abide by it and honourably act according to the agreement which is now final and binding on all. But you must remember, as I have said, that this mighty revolution that has taken place is unprecedented. One can quite understand the feeling that exists between the two communities wherever one community is in majority and the other is in minority. But the question is, whether it was possible or practicable to act otherwise than what has been done, A division had to take place. On both sides, in Hindustan and Pakistan, there are sections of people who may not agree with it, who may not like it, but in my judgement there was no other solution and I am sure future history will record is verdict in favour of it. And what is more, it will be proved by actual experience as we go on that was the only solution of India's constitutional problem. Any idea of a united India could never have worked and in my judgement it would have led us to terrific disaster. Maybe that view is correct; maybe it is not; that remains to be seen. All the same, in this division it was impossible to avoid the question of minorities being in one Dominion or the other. Now that was unavoidable. There is no other solution. Now what shall we do? Now, if we want to make this great State of Pakistan happy and prosperous, we should wholly and solely concentrate on the well-being of the people, and especially of the masses and the poor. If you will work in co-operation, forgetting the past, burying the hatchet, you are bound to succeed. If you change your past and work together in a spirit that everyone of you, no matter to what community he belongs, no matter what relations he had with you in the past, no matter what is his colour, caste or creed, is first, second and last a citizen of this State with equal rights, privileges, and obligations, there will be on end to the progress you will make.

I cannot emphasize it too much. We should begin to work in that spirit and in course of time all these angularities of the majority and minority communities, the Hindu community and the Muslim community, because even as regards Muslims you have Pathans, Punjabis, Shias, Sunnis and so on, and among the Hindus you have Brahmins, Vashnavas, Khatris, also Bengalis, Madrasis and so on, will vanish. Indeed if you ask me, this has been the biggest hindrance in the way of India to attain the freedom and independence and but for this we would have been free people long long ago. No power can hold another nation, and specially a nation of 400 million souls in subjection; nobody could have conquered you, and even if it had happened, nobody could have continued its hold on you for any length of time, but for this. Therefore, we must learn a lesson from this. You are free; you are free to go to your temples, you are free to go to your mosques or to any other place or worship in this State of Pakistan. You may belong to any religion or caste or creed that has nothing to do with the business of the State. As you know, history shows that in England, conditions, some time ago, were much worse than those prevailing in India today. The Roman Catholics and the Protestants persecuted each other. Even now there are some States in existence where there are discriminations made and bars imposed against a particular class. Thank God, we are not starting in those days. We are starting in the days where there is no discrimination, no distinction between one community and another, no discrimination between one caste or creed and another. We are starting with this fundamental principle that we are all citizens and equal citizens of one State. The people of England in course of time had to face the realities of the situation and had to discharge the responsibilities and burdens placed upon them by the government of their country and they went through that fire step by step. Today, you might say with justice that Roman Catholics and Protestants do not exist; what exists now is that every man is a citizen, an equal citizen of Great Britain and they are all members of the Nation.

Now I think we should keep that in front of us as our ideal and you will find that in course of time Hindus would cease to be Hindus and Muslims would cease to be Muslims, not in the religious sense, because that is the personal faith of each individual, but in the political sense as citizens of the State.

Well, gentlemen, I do not wish to take up any more of your time and thank you again for the honour you have done to me. I shall always be guided by the principles of justice and fairplay without any, as is put in the political language, prejudice or ill-will, in other words, partiality or favouritism. My guiding principle will be justice and complete impartiality, and I am sure that with your support and co-operation, I can look forward to Pakistan becoming one of the greatest nations of the world.

I have received a message from the United States of America addressed to me. It reads:

I have the honour to communicate to you, in Your Excellency's capacity as President of the Constituent Assembly of Pakistan, the following message which I have just received from the Secretary of State of the United States:

On the occasion of of the first meeting of the Constituent Assembly for Pakistan, I extend to you and to the members of the Assembly, the best wishes of the Government and the people of the United States for the successful conclusion of the great work you are about to undertake.

Source: Dawn, Independence Day Supplement, August 14, 1999.

Transcribed from printed copy by Shehzaad Nakhoda

Links: Constitution of Pakistan/Legislation/www. pakistani.org

Annexure - 2

Speech of Quaid-e-Azam Muhammad Ali Jinnah on 14th August 1947

Your Excellency, I thank His Majesty the King on behalf of the Pakistan Constituent Assembly and myself for his gracious message. I know great responsibilities lie ahead, and I naturally reciprocate his sentiments and we are grateful for his assurance of sympathy and support, and I hope that you will communicate to His Majesty our assurance of goodwill and friendship for the British nation and himself as the Crown head of the British.

I thank you for your expressions of goodwill and good wishes for the future of Pakistan. It will be our constant endeavor to work for the welfare and well-being of all the communities in Pakistan, and I hope that everyone would be inspired by the idea of public service, and they will be imbued with the spirit of co-operation and will excel in their political and civic virtues which go to make a great nation and help to advance its greatness.

I once more thank you and Lady Mountbatten for your kindness and good wishes. Yes, we are parting as friends and sincerely hope that we shall remain friends.

I wish to emphasize that we appreciate the spirit in which those in the Government service at present and in the Armed Forces and others have so willingly and ungrudgingly volunteered themselves provisionally to serve Pakistan. As servants of Pakistan we shall make them happy and they will be treated equally with our nationals.

The tolerance and goodwill that great Emperor Akbar showed to all the non-Muslim is not of recent origin. It dates back thirteen centuries ago when our Prophet not only by words but by deeds treated the Jews and Christians, after he had conquered them, with the utmost tolerance and regard and respect for their faith and beliefs. The whole history of Muslims, wherever they ruled, is replete with those humane and great principles which should be followed and practiced.

Finally, I thank you for your good wishes for Pakistan, and I assure you that we shall not be wanting in friendly spirit with our neighbors and with all nations of the world.

Source: http://m-a-jinnah.blogspot.com/2009/09/inauguration-ofpakistan-constituent.html

Annexure - 3

'Tryst with Destiny' Speech of Mr. Jawahar Lal Nehru Prime Minister of India in the Constituent Assembly of India at Midnight of 14-15 August 1947 on the Eve of Independence

Long years ago we made a tryst with destiny, and now the time comes when we shall redeem our pledge, not wholly or in full measure, but very substantially. At the stroke of the midnight hour, when the world sleeps, India will awake to life and freedom. A moment comes, which comes but rarely in history, when we step out from the old to the new, when an age ends, and when the soul of a nation, long suppressed, finds utterance. It is fitting that at this solemn moment we take the pledge of dedication to the service of India and her people and to the still larger cause of humanity.

At the dawn of history India started on her unending quest, and trackless centuries are filled with her striving and the grandeur of her successes and her failures. Through good and ill fortune alike she has never lost sight of that quest or forgotten the ideals which gave her strength. We end today a period of ill fortune and India discovers herself again. The achievement we celebrate today is but a step, an opening of opportunity, to the greater triumphs and achievements that await us. Are we brave enough and wise enough to grasp this opportunity and accept the challenge of the future?

Freedom and power bring responsibility. That responsibility rests upon this Assembly, a sovereign body representing the sovereign people of India. Before the birth of freedom we have endured all the pains of labour and our hearts are heavy with the memory of this sorrow. Some of those pains continue even now. Nevertheless the past is over and it is the future that beckons to us now.

That future is not one of ease or resting but of incessant striving so that we might fulfil the pledges we have so often taken and the one we shall take today. The service of India means the service of the millions who suffer. It means the ending of poverty and ignorance and disease and inequality of opportunity. The ambition of the greatest man of our generation has been to wipe every tear from every eye. That may be beyond us but as long as there are tears and suffering, so long our work will not be over.

And so we have to labour and to work and work hard to give reality to our dreams. Those dreams are for India, but they are also for the world, for all the nations and peoples are too closely knit together today for anyone of them to imagine that it can live apart. Peace has been said to be indivisible, so is freedom, so is prosperity now, and so also is disaster in this one world that can no longer be split into isolated fragments.

To the people of India, whose representatives we are, we make appeal to join us with faith and confidence in this great adventure. This is no time for petty and destructive criticism, no time for ill will or blaming others. We have to build the noble mansion of free India where all her children may dwell.

I beg to move, Sir.

"That it be resolved that:

(1) After the last stroke of midnight, all members of the ConstituentAssembly present on this occasion do take the following pledge: At this solemn moment when the people of India, through suffering and sacrifice, have secured freedom, I,..., a member of the Constituent Assembly of India, do dedicate myself in all humility to the service of India and her people to the end that this ancient land attain her rightful

place in the world and make her full and willing contribution to the promotion of world peace and the welfare of mankind.

(2) Members who are not present on this occasion do take the pledge (with such verbal changes at the President may prescribe) at the time they next attend a session of the Assembly."

(*Source:* nehrumemorial.nic.in>gift-gallery, Tryst with Destiny-Speech Text.)

References & Notes

REFERENCES

Introduction

1. Quoted by Ashutosh Varshney in 'The Idea of Pakistan' contributed to the book, 'The Great Divide, India and Pakistan', edited by Ira Pandey, published by Harper Collins Publishers with a joint venture with The India Today group in 2009 Maulana Azad's speech as President of the Congress Party in 1940, reproduced in sources of Indian Tradition, edited by. Stephen Jay, pg. 237-41 New Delhi : Penguin 1991.
2. Hafeez Malik,Dilemmas of National Security and co-operation in India and Pakistan,St.MartinPress,USA/The Mc MILLAN Press,UK
3. Referred by Quaid-e-Azam Muhammad Ali Jinnah in his presidential address to the Muslim League Session from 22-24 March 1940 which adopted the Resolution in favour of a separate homeland for Muslims.
4. From the speech delivered by Quaid-e-Azam Muhammad Ali Jinnah on 22 March 1940 in the Lahore Session of Muslim League.

Chapter - 1

1. The narration between W Churchill and Roosevelt has been reproduced in an impressive manner by Kunal Verma and Brig Rajiv Williams, The Long Road to Siachen Pg. 259-263, Rupa Publications.
2. Drawn from www.legislation.gov.uk/ukpga/Geob/10-11/30#IDA3KLYlegislationgov.uk.IndianIndependenceACT, 1947.
3. Kunal Verma and Brig. Rajiv Williams, The Long Road to Siachen, pg. 187, Rupa Publications
4. Kunal Verma and Brig. Rajiv Williams, The Long Road to Siachen, pg. 273-281, Rupa Publications.
5. David Devadas, in Search of a future, the story of Kashmir, pg. 58, Penguin/ Viking.

6. Ramchandra Guha, India after Gandhi, pg. 65, Picador India.
7. Kunal Verma and Brig. Rajiv Williams, The Long Road to Siachen, pg. 198, Rupa Publications.
8. Sudhir S Bloria, PAKISTAN's INSURGENCY vs. INDIA's SECURITY, Tackling Militancy in Kashmir.
9. Ramchandra Guha., India after Gandhi, pg. 80, Picador India.
10. Ramchandra Guha., India after Gandhi, pg. 51, Picador India.
11. Ramchandra Guha., India after Gandhi, pg. 52, Picador India.
12. Ian Talbot, Pakistan a Modern History, pg. 112-113, C Hurst & Co (Publishers) Ltd, Distributer Foundation Books.

Chapter - 2

1. Ramchandra Guha, India after Gandhi, pg. 31, Picador India.
2. Larry Collins and Dominique Lapierre, Freedom at Midnight, The Greatest Migration in History, pg. 319, Vikas Publishing House.
3. Urvashi Butalia, The Other Side of the Silence, Honour page 153, Viking, Penguin Books India (P) Ltd.
4. Urvashi Butalia, The Other Side of the Silence, Facts, pg. 58, Viking, Penguine Books India (P) Ltd.
5. Larry Collins & Dominique Lapiere, Freedom at Midnight, the Greatest Migration in History, pg. 322, Vikas Publishing House.
6. Urvashi Butalia, The Other Side of the Silence, Facts, pg. 55-56, Viking, Penguin Books India (P) Ltd.
7. As referred by Urvashi Butalia in 'The Other Side of the Silence', pg. 112, Viking, Penguin Books India (P) Ltd.
8. Urvashi Butalia, The Other Side of the Silence, pg. 121, quoted from GD Khosala, Stern Reckoning: A Survey of the Events Leading up to and Following the Partition of India, pg. 75, Delhi Oxford University Press, 1949.
9. Ian Talbot, Pakistan a Modern History, Picking up the pieces: Pakistan 1947-49, pg 103-104, C Hurst & Co (Publishers) Ltd, Distributer Foundation Books.
10. Ian Talbot, Pakistan a Modern History, pg. 104, C Hurst & Co (Publishers) Ltd, Distributer Foundation Books.
11. Ian Talbot, Pakistan, A modern History, pg. 105, C Hurst & Co (Publishers) Ltd, Distributer Foundation Books.
12. Ian Talbot, Pakistan, A modern History pg. 108, C Hurst & Co (Publishers) Ltd, Distributer Foundation Books.

13. Tariq Rahman, Language and Politics in Pakistan, The Sindhi Language Movement, pg. 110-111, Orient Longman.
14. Ian Talbot, Pakistan a Modern History, pg. 13, C Hurst & Co (Publishers) Ltd, Distributer Foundation Books.
15. Ian Talbot, Pakistan a Modern History, pg. 108, C Hurst & Co (Publishers) Ltd, Distributer Foundation Books.
16. Jagmohan(2005) Soul and the structures of the governance in India, pg. 49, Allied publishers.
17. Ramchandra Guha, India After Gandhi, pg. 11, Picador India.
18. Ramchandra Guha, India after Gandhi, The History of The World's Largest Democracy, page 33. Macmillan Ltd.
19. Ramchandra Guha, India After Gandhi, The History of The World's Largest Democracy, page 15, Macmillan Ltd.
20. Col. Ranjeet Sen Gupta, The Indian Sepoys, Soldiers of the Raj, pg. 267.
21. Hafeez Malik, Dilemmas of National Security and Co-operation in India and Pakistant, 1993, St. Martin Press, USA/The Mc Millan Press Ltd-UK.
22. PD Reeves, BD Graham and JM Good man, Elections in Uttar Pradesh, 1920-51, pg. 252-53, Manohar, 1975.
23. Hafeez Malik, Dilemmas of National Security and Co-operation in India and Pakistant, 1993, St. Martin Press, a quote from B.R. Ambedkar, Pakistan or the Partition of India (Bombay, Thacker).
24. Hafeez Malik, Dilemmas of National Security and Co-operation in India and Pakistan, St. Martin Pess, USA/The MAC Millan Press Ltd, UK) who quoted it from Syed Shrifuddin Pirzada, Evolution of Pakistan.
25. Hafeez Malik, Dilemmas of National Security and Co-operation in India and Pakistan, 1993, St. Martin's Press Ltd. UK.
26. Ibid.
27. Col. Ranjit Sen Gupta, The Indian Sepoy, Soldier of the Raj, pg. 387.
28. Ramchandra Guha. India After Gandhi, pg 8, Macmillan Ltd.
29. PD Reeves, BD Graham, JM Goodman, Elections in Uttar Pradesh 1920-1951, Manohar, 1975.
30. English rendering from https://penguin.co.in.the penguinedigest.
31. Yousuf Saeed, Fled is that Music, an essay published in The Great Divide, India and Pakistan, edited by Ira Pande, pg, 240-243, Harper Collins.

Chapter - 3

1. Ramchandra Guha, India After Gandhi, pg.68, Macmillan Ltd.
2. Sudhir Bloria, Pakistan's Insurgency vs Indian Security, Tackling Militancy in Kashmir, and, 2) Kunal Verma and Brig. Rajiv Williams, The long road to Siachen, pg. 281. Rupa Publications.
3. Kunal Verma and Brig.Rajiv Williams, The Long Road to Siachen, pg.198, Rupa Publications. According to the authors Major Onkar Singh Kalkat had already informed the Indian officials about the Pakistan's army plan two days ahead of the tribalmen's invasion. Major Kalkat was serving in Bannu Frontier Group, which was being commanded by a British officer, Brigadier CP Murray. As Murray was out a DO letter marked 'Personal/Top Secret' from C-in-C of Pakistani army to Murray was received and opened by Kalkat. The letter contained the plan of invasion of Kashmir. As soon as Murray came to know about the leak of the plan, Kalkat was put under house arrest which he managed to escape. He reached Delhi on 19 of October and apprised acting Chief of General Staff, acting DGMO and the Defence Minister, Sardar Baldev Singh. None of them believed Kalkat's revelations and no action was taken on his information.
4. Kunal Verma & Brig. Rajiv Williams, The Long Road to Siachen, pg. 209. Rupa Publications.
5. Owen Bennett Jones, Pakistan Eye of the Storm, pg. 74-75, Viking.
6. Ramchandra Guha, India After Gandhi, pg. 409-410.
7. PR Chari, Parvez Iqbal Cheeman and Stephen P. Cohen, Four Crisis and a Peace Process-American Engagement in South Asia.
8. Ramchandra Guha, India After Gandhi, pg. 399.
9. Owen Bennett Jones, Pakistan Eye of the Storm pg. 152-153 (PENGUIN/ VIKING) who sourced the figures from Keith Collard, Pakistan: Political Study, George Allen & Unwin, Oxford 1957.
10. Tariq Rahman, Language and Politics in Pakistan, pg. 96, Orient Longman.
11. Tariq Rahman, Language and Politics in Pakistan, Page 96, Publisher Orient Longman.
12. Tariq Rahman, Language and Politics in Pakistan, pg. 97-98, Publisher Orient Longman.
13. Tariq Rahman, Language and Politics in Pakistan, pg. 90, Publisher Orient Longman.
14. Tariq Rahman, Language and Politics in Pakistan, pg. 101, Publisher Orient Longman.

15. Ramchandra Guha, India after Gandhi, The History of The World's Largest Democracy, Page 455. Macmillan Ltd.
16. Owen Bennett Jones, Pakistan Eye of the Storm, page 179 - 183, Penguine/Viking.
17. Ian Talbot, Pakistan a Modern History, pg. 212, C Hurst & Co (Publishers) Ltd, Distributer Foundation Books.
18. PR Chari, Parvez Iqbal Cheema and Stephen P Cohen. Four Crises and a Peace Process - American Engagement in Southeast Asia.Harper Collines with India Today Group.
19. Tariq Rahman, Language and Politics in Pakistan, pg. 120, Orient Longman.
20. Owen Bennett Jones, Pakistan, Eye of the Storm pg. 92-93, Viking Publication Penguin Book India.
21. Owen Bennett Jones, Pakistan, Eye of the Storm pg. 92, Viking Publication Penguin Book India.
22. Owen Bennett Jones, Pakistan, Eye of the Storm pg. 95, Viking Publication Penguin Book India.
23. Kuldip Nayar, Wall at Wagah, India-Pakistan Relations p. 285, Gyan Publishing House.
24. Bruce Riedel, Avoiding Armageddon,America, India and Pakistan to the brink and back, pg. 131. Harper Collins, who quoted it from 'Kargil from Surprise to Victory' by VP Malik, D elhi, Harper Collins 2006, pg. 146-147.
25. Bruce Riedel, Avoiding Armageddon,America, India and Pakistan to the brink and back, pg. 132. Harper Collins.
26. Owen Bennett Jones, Pakistan Eye of the Storm, pg. 100, Viking.
27. Kuldip Nayar, Wall at Wagah, India-Pakistan Relations p. 285, Gyan Publishing House.
28. Kuldip Nayar, Wall at Wagah, India-Pakistan Relations p. 285, Gyan Publishing House.
29. Kunal Verma and Brig. Rajiv Williams, The Long Road to Siachen, The Question Why, pg. 50-51, Rupa Publications.
30. Kunal Verma and Brig. Rajiv Williams, The Long Road to Siachen, The Question Why, pg. 361, Rupa Publications.
31. Ian Talbot, Pakistan a Modern History, pg. 284, C Hurst & Co (Publishers) Ltd, Distributer Foundation Books.
32. Bruce Riedel, Avoiding Armageddon, pg. 78. Harper Collins.
33. Stephen Cohen,The Idea of Pakistan, page 80, Oxford University Press.
34. Owen Bennett Jones, Pakistan Eye of the Storm, pg. 193, Viking.

35. Owen Bennett Jones, Pakistan Eye of the Storm, pg. 187, Viking.
36. Bruce Riedel, Avoiding Armageddon, pg. 140, Harper Collins.
37. Zahid Hussain, Frontline Pakistan, pg. 61-62, Penguine/Viking.
38. Bruce Riedel, Avoiding Armageddon, pg. 141, Harper Collins.
39. Wikipedia.
40. Zahid Hussain, Frontline Pakistan, pg. 107, Penguine/Viking and Bruce Riedel, Armageddon pg. 148, Harper Collins.
41. (1) Zahid Hussain, Frontline Pakistan, pg. 106 -107, Penguine /Viking, and (2) PR Chari, Parvez Iqbal Cheema and Stephen P Cohen, Four Crisis in the Peace Process- American Engagement in South Asia, Harper Collins publishers Limited.
42. Bruce Riedel, Avoiding Armageddon, pg. 151, Harper Collins.
43. Mary Anne Weaver, Pakistan In the Shadow of Jihad and Afghanistan, pg. 250,Viking.
44. Zahid Hussain, Frontline Pakistan, pg. 108. Penguine/Viking.
45. Zahid Hussain, Frontline Pakistan, pg. 109. Penguine/Viking
46. Zahid Hussain, Frontline Pakistan pg. 110-111. Penguine/Viking.
47. Amit Baruah, The Fourth Party, an essay published in 'The Great Divide, India and Pakistan, edited by Ira Pandey, pg. 197, Harper Collins Publisher India with India Today Group.
48. Amit Baruah, The Fourth Party, an essay published in 'The Great Divide, India and Pakistan, edited by Ira Pandey, pg. 198, Harper Collins Publisher India with India Today Group.
49. The Hindu, Friday, 15 February 2019.

Chapter - 4

1. CJH Hayes, Modern Europe to 1870, pg. 227-242.
2. CJH Hayes, Modern Europe to 1870, pg. 321-322.
3. Handbook of Public Administration and Policy in the European Union, edited by M Peter van der Hock, published by Taylor and Francis, Year 2005.
4. David Devadas, In Search of a Future, The Story of Kashmir, pg. 58-59.
5. Ian Talbot, Pakistan a Modern History, pg. 112-113.
6. The Year Book of the World Affairs, 1958, Vol. 12 Essay on Britain, the Common Market and the Free Trade Area by GDN Worswick.
7. The European Union and the Global South, pg. 2, edited by Fredrik Soderbaum and Patric Stalgren.

Chapter - 5

1. https://data.worldbank.org/indicator/SP.POP.Total.
2. Global Economic Governance, IMF Quota Reform by Arvind Virmani.
3. https:www.imf.org.sec.member
4. HDR-2016 pg. 141-142.
5. Adapted from e paper Dawn, 1 August, 2018, Karachi, Pakistan.
6. https//economicsclubimi.wordpress.com/2018/07/15minimum-support-price-isthe-support-enough/Article dated 15 July, 2018Author: The Economics Club IMI.
7. World Bank Report, modelled on ILO estimates in 2017.
8. UNHDR-2005, Chapter-4, International Trade-unlocking the potential for human development, pg. 131.
9. www.worldstopexports.com>cotton-export, Cotton Exports by Country-World's Top Exports.
10. www.worldstopexports.com>rice-export, Rice Export by Country-World's Top Exports.
11. The Hindu, 2 October 2018, pg. 12.
12. HDR-2005 pg 131-132, Chapter-4, International Trade-Unlocking the Potential for Human Development, pg. 131-132.
13. HDR, 2005, Chapter 4, International Trade-unlocking the potential for Human Development, pg. 132.
14. HDR, 2005, Chapter 4, International Trade-unlocking the potential for Human Development, pg, 132.
15. HDR, 2016, human development for every one.

Chapter - 6

1. For figures not for percentage https://data.worldbank.org/ indicator/ SP.Pop. (Also referred in hdr.undp.org/sites,HDStatisticalupdate2018)
2. As per respective national portals
3. HDR- 1990, Chapter 1, Defining and Measuring human Development, pg. 9. Also reproduced in HDR-Pakistan, 2017 in its beginning.
4. Based on the information published in HDR 2006 published for UNDP, Table 22.
5. Based on the information published by world Bank (data.worldbank.org/ Country).
6. HDR, 2003.
7. HDR, 2003.
8. SIPRI Year Book, 2018 Armaments, Disarmament and International SecurityInternational Arms Transfers and Development in Arms Production, pg. 8.

9. Ibid.
10. HDR 2006.
11. Tariq Rahman, Madarsas in Pakistan, pg. 14, compiled in Sampark, a Journal of Global Understanding, edited and published by Sunandan Roy Chaudhury.
12. HD, 2018, Statistical Update.
13. SIPRI Year Book, 2018 Armaments, Disarmament and International Security, Summary, pg. 11. According to this report Pakistan had 140-150 and India had 130-140 nuclear heads out of a total of 14,465 nuclear heads in the world.
14. HD- 2018 Statistical Update.
15. HD-2018, Statistical Update.
16. HDR 2016 Table8-Health Outcomes.
17. Economic Growth and Human Development, HDR, 1990 pg. 59.
18. HDR-2003, Table 17.
19. Indian nuclear forces, January 2018.
    (a) Aircraft range is for illustrative purposes only; actual mission range will vary according to flight profile and weapon loading. Missile payloads may have to be reduced in order to achieve maximum range.
    (b) The yields of India's nuclear warheads are not known. The 1998 nuclear tests demonstrated yields of up to 12 kt. Since then it is possible that boosted warheads have been introduced with a higher yield, perhaps up to 40 kt. There is no open-source evidence that India has developed 2-stage thermonuclear warheads.
    (c) Aircraft and several missile types are dual-capable. Cruise missile launchers carry more than 1 missile. This estimate counts an average of 1 warhead per launcher. Warheads are not deployed on launchers but kept in separate storage facilities. All estimates are approximate.
    (d) Other fighter-bombers that could potentially have a secondary nuclear role include the Su-30MKI.
    (e) Each Dhanush-equipped ship is thought to have possibly 1 reload.
    (f) Some sources have referred to the K-15 submarine-launched ballistic missile (SLBM) as Sagarika, which was the name of the missile development project.
    (g) The K-15 and K-4 use the same 4 launch tubes on the INS Arihant nuclearpowered ballistic missile submarine (SSBN). Each launch tube can hold either 3 K-15s contained in a triple-missile canister or 1 of the larger K-4 SLBMs (once the K-4 becomes operational). Thus, according to the US AirForce National Air and Space

Intelligence Center (NASIC), the K-15 has 12 possible launchers and the K-4 has 4.

(h) There are reports that the Nirbhay, which is in development, might have a nuclear capability, but the Indian Government has not confirmed them.

(i) In addition to the 124 warheads estimated to be assigned to fielded launchers, warheads for additional Agni-III and future Agni-IV medium-range ballistic missiles may already have been produced giving a total stockpile of 130– 40 warheads.

20. Pakistani nuclear forces, January 2018

(a) Aircraft range is for illustrative purposes only; actual mission range will vary according to flight profile and weapon loading. Missile payloads may have to be reduced in order to achieve maximum range.

(b) The yields of Pakistan's nuclear warheads are not known. The 1998 nuclear tests demonstrated a yield of up to 12 kt. Since then it is possible that boosted warheads have been introduced with higher yields. There is no open-source evidence that Pakistan has developed 2-stage thermonuclear warheads.

(c) Aircraft and several missile types are dual-capable. Cruise missile launchers carry more than 1 missile. This estimate counts an average of 1 warhead per launcher. Warheads are not deployed on launchers but kept in separate storage facilities.

(d) There are unconfirmed reports that some of the 40 F-16 combat aircraft procured from the USA in the 1980s were modified by Pakistan for a nuclear delivery role.

(e) Some launchers might have 1 or more reloads of missiles.

(f) It is unclear whether the Shaheen-IA has the same designation as the Shaheen-I.

(g) It is unclear whether the Shaheen-III has the same designation as the Shaheen-II.

(h) According to the Pakistani armed forces, the missile is 'capable of delivering multiple warheads', using MIRV technology.

(i) The Pakistani Government claims the range is 700 km, double the range reported by the US Air Force, National Air and Space Intelligence Center (NASIC).

(j) The Babur-2, which was first test launched on 14 Dec. 2016, is an improved version of the original Babur GLCM.

(k) The first test launch of a Babur-3 SLCM was carried out from an underwater platform on 9 Jan. 2017.

21. HD Indices and Indicators, 2018 Statistical Update.

Chapter - 7

1. DN Jha, Ancient India, in historical Outlines.
2. Abul Fazl Allami, Ain-i-Akbri, The Sayings of His Majesty, Vol. II, translated in to English by Col. HS Jarrett, pg. 429, New Taj Office.
3. Abul Fazl Allami, Ain-i-Akbri, The Sayings of His Majesty, Vol. II, translated in to English by Col. HS Jarrett, pg. 449, New Taj Office.
4. Abul Fazl Allami, Ain-i-Akbri, The Sayings of His Majesty, Vol. II, translated in to English by Col. HS Jarrett, pg. 426, New Taj Office.
5. Muzaffar Alam, The Language of Political Islam in India c.1200-1800, pg. 83, Permanent Black.
6. Muzaffar Alam, The Language of Political Islam in India C.1200-1800, pg. 148, By Muzaffar Alam, Permanent Black.
7. Yousuf Saeed, Fled is That Music, an essay in 'The Great Divide', pg. 245-46, Edited by Ira Pandey.
8. Muzaffar Alam, The Language of Political Islam in India C.1200-18000, pg. 90, Permanent Black.
9. Kunal Verma and Brig. Rajiv Williams, The Long Road to Siachen, pg. 78, Rupa and Co Publication.
10. Kunal Verma and Brig. Rajiv Williams, The Long Road to Siachen, pg. 83, Rupa and Co Publication.
11. Col. Ranjit Sen Gupta, The Indian Sepoy, Soldier of the Raj, pg. 267.

Chapter - 8

1. Adapted from 'The little known regions, History of Balakot by Haroon Khalid, Published in Dawn (www.dawn.com) 6 March 2019.
2. Kunal Verma and Brig. Rajiv Williams The Long Road to Siachen, the Question Why, pg. 78, Rupa and Co Publication.
3. Mary Annie Weaver, Pakistan in the shadow of Jihad and Afghanistan, page 60 publisher VIKING, 2430 kilometres according to an article published in Dawn dated 1 May 2019 see https//www.dawn.com.
4. Kunal Verma and Brig. Rajiv Williams, The Long Road to Siachen, pg. 52, Rupa and Co Publication.
5. Human Development, 2018, Statistical update.
6. HDR-2016, Table 4.
7. SIPRI Year Book, 2018, Armaments, Disarmament and international SecuritySummary, page 11.

NOTES

Chapter - 1

i-n. As per details given in the wikipedia 'sudhans' (also known as Sudhozai), tribe traces its ancestry to Jassi Khan who arrived in Poonch about 500 years ago. He is said to be a Sudhozai Pathan, one of the most respected tribes in Afghanistan. The name Sudhan was supposedly drawn from the Sanskrit word 'Sudhan' which means justice, fair and honest. *Sudhans* of Poonch had traditional rivalry with the Dogras and the Sikhs of the region.

ii-n. The total strength at the British Indian army in 1947 was about 4.50 lakh. In accordance to the agreement on divison of army between two dominions the army was divided in a ratio of 1 : 2 between Pakistan and India. This led transfer of about 1.5 lakh personnel to Pakistan, with 3.00 lakh staying in India. Though the military had about 58% Muslim soldiers, the share of Muslim officers was very low. Out of a strength of 22,000 officers, only 8,500 were Indians. While India too needed extra officers, Pakistan got only about 2,000 officers out of a requirement of 4,000. Both the countries had the shortage of officers, hence a good number of British officers were retained and were serving the armies of both the dominions. (Source : Ilhan Niaz, the culture of power and governance of Pakistan, 1947-2008, pg. 142-143, Oxford Pakistan Paperbacks). When the Kashmir invasion took place Pakistani army was under the command of General Frank Messervy who had been appointed the C-in-C of Pakistani army on 15 August, 1947. He was succeeded by another British General Sir Douglas Gracy on 11 February 1948, who remained C-in-C till 16 January 1951. In India, army was under the command of General Bob Lockhart from 15 August 1947 to 31 December 1947. He was succeeded by General Roy Bucher on 15 January 1947, who remained C-in-C of Indian army till 15 January 1949.

Chapter - 3

i-n. In India secularism had not been specifically mentioned in its Constitution till 1976, when the words 'SOVEREIGN DEMOCRATIC REPUBLIC' in the original Preamble were substituted by the words, 'SOVEREIGN SOCIALIST SECULAR DEMOCRATIC REPUBLIC' by the Constitution (Forty Second Amendment) Act, 1976 (w.e.f. 3-1-1977). However, most important components of secularism which are as follows had already been incorporated by various provisions in the original Constitution:

(i) *Samanata* (equality) was incorporated in article 14;

(ii) Prohibition against discrimination on the ground of religion, caste, etc., was incorporated in articles 15 and 16;

(iii) Freedom of speech and expression and all other important freedoms of all the citizens were conferred under articles 19 and 21;

(iv) Right to practise religion was conferred under articles 25 to 28;

(v) Fundamental duty of the State to enact uniform civil laws treating all the citizens as equal, was enshrined in article 44;

(vi) Sentiment of majority of the people towards the cow and against its slaughter was incorporated in article 48. (Source: P.M. Bakshi: The Constitution of India, pg. 4)

ii-n. In Bangladesh the present status of the Secularism along with the Islam as the State religion is one of the prudent amalgamation of two contradictory features in the modern polity. Its Preamble reads as follows:

'We, the people of Bangladesh, having proclaimed our independence on the 26th day of March, 1971 and through historic struggle for national liberation established the Independent, Sovereign People's Republic of Bangladesh.

Pledging that the high ideals of nationalism, socialism, democracy and secularism, which inspired our heroic people to dedicate themselves to, and our brave martyrs to sacrifice their lives in, the national liberation struggle, shall be the fundamental principles of the Constitution.'

Article-2A provides that, "The State Religion".

The State religion of the Republic is Islam, but the State shall ensure equal status and equal right in the practice of the Hindu, Buddhist, Christian and other religions.

The Secularism is again reiterated in article-12 as follows : Secularism and freedom of religion.

'The principle of Secularism shall be realised by the elimination of –

(a) communalism in all its forms;

(b) the granting by the State of political status in favour of any religion;

(c) the abuse of religion for political purposes;

(d) any discrimination against, or persecution of persons practicing a particular religion;'

It leaves no doubt about the 'Freedom of religion'. Article 41 provides that,

'(1) Subject to law, public order and morality –

(a) every citizen has the right to profess, practice or propagate any religion;

(b) every religious community or denomination has the right to establish, maintain and manage its religious Institutions.

(2) No person attending any educational institution shall be required to receive religious instruction, or to take part in or to attend any religious ceremony or worship, if that instruction, ceremony or worship relates to a religion other than his own.'

iii-n. Clause (1) of Article 352 of the Constitution of India provides, "If the President is satisfied that a grave emergency exists whereby the security of India or of any part of the territory thereof is threatened, whether by war or external aggression or [armed rebellion,] he may, by Proclamation, make a declaration to that effect [in respect of whole India or such part of the territory thereof as may be specified in the Proclamation]."

When Indira Gandhi resorted to Emergency, the words in the first bracket were "internal disturbance" which were substituted by the words "armed rebellion" by the successive government in 1978 through Constitution (Forty-fourth Amendment) Act . The provision was exploited to its fullest. The other clauses of the Art. 352, set the terms and conditions and the procedure for proclamation of emergency, which Mrs. Gandhi was blamed to ignore.

iv-n. The two representatives were R.K. Mishra, an editor of Bombay newspaper from the Indian side and Niaz Naik, a retired diplomat from Pakistani side. The meeting between the two representatives in May 1999 at New Delhi's Imperial Hotel was kept a top secret. They agreed that they would have to go beyond their governments public positions over the issue. (Owen Bennet Jones, Pakistan, Eye of the Storm.)

v-n. The Gwadar Sea Port is situated on the Arabian Sea, which is now in Baluchistan province of Pakistan. It is at a distance of about 170 kms from the Chabahar Port in Iran in the west and about 533 km from Karachi in the east. Gwadar is just 120 km from the Iran's border (https://en.m.wikipedia.org wiki). Till 1958 it belonged to Oman as about two centuries ago it had been given by the Khan of Kalat to Sultan of Oman. It was purchased by Pakistan from the Sultan of Oman for $10 million in 1958 (Mary Anne Weaver, Pakistan in the Shadow of Jihad and Afghanistan pg.116, Penguin/Viking). The agreement provided the recruiting rights to Oman's Navy and Army. Gwadari people own the dual nationality with Oman which serves a good source of employment to them.

In 2015 Gwadar became the south-eastern extremity of the proposed China-Pakistan Economic Corridor (CPEC) which is to connect Gwadar to the Karrakoram Highway providing it the access to the area as far as Gilgit Baltistan and the Chinese region of Xinjiang. The locals believe that its inclusion in CPEC will give more political and economic access to China rather than to benefit them.

At the time of the Kargil war, the entire area was so backward that Marry Anne Weaver, who visited the area in early years of present century wrote in her book, 'Pakistan, In the shadow of Jihad and Afghanistan, that "We travelled nearly a thousand miles, during the last part retracing the route of Alexander the Great, zig zagging between the desert and the sea. There was no coastal road inAlexander's time, and there was none now."

vi-n. A concept paper with regard to Kashmir Policy intercepted by the Indian intelligence and attributed to Zia-ul-Haq was published in Indian Defence Review (July, 1989), which laid down that: "...we whip up anti Indian feelings amongst the students and peasants preferably on some religions issues, so that we can enlist their active support for rioting and anti-government demonstrations. Organize and train subversive elements and armed groups with capabilities initially to deal with para military forces located in the valley. Adopt and develop the means to cut off lines of communications between J & K and within Kashmir and Ladakh by stealth without recourse of force. In collaboration with Sikh extremists create chaos and terror in Jammu to divert attention from the valley at a critical juncture and discredit the regime even in the Hindu mind." Quoted from Sudhir S. Bloria, Pakistan's Insurgency vs. India's Security, Tackling Militancy in Kashmir.

vii-n. On 28 June in 1914 Archduke Francis Ferdinand, the heir apparent to the Austrian throne, and his wife were killed when they were passing through the streets of Sarajevo. Sarajevo was the capital of Bosnia, which had been annexed by Austro-Hungarian Empire. The assassin was a member of a group of Serbian secret society, 'Union of Death', that wanted to unite all Serbians in in to a single Serbian State. Serbia was accused of the complicity in the plan of murder by the Austrian ruler. Austria in view of subjugation of Serbia to its empire, served an ultimatum with eleven demands on 23 July. Austria set a timeline of forty eight hours for their compliance. Serbia agreed with most of the demands except those which would have resulted in loss of its sovereignty. On the pretext of Serbia not fulfilling the Austrian demands, Austria declared war on Serbia on 28 July 1914.

Chapter - 5

i-n. The Finance Minister proposed an allocation of Rs. 1.60 lakh crore for agriculture, irrigation and allied activities and 1.23 lakh crore to the activities under Rural Development and Panchayati Raj (see: Dr. Jagdeep Saxena,Action Plan for Prosperity of Farmers,Yojana (March 2020), pg. 65, Published by Ministry of Information and Broadcasting, GoI) out of a total Budget proposal of Rs. 30.42 lakh crore for 2020-21.

As per Press Information Bureau of MoIB Press-Release, the proposed expenditure on agriculture and Allied Activities was 1.55 lakh crore and on rural Development and Panchayati Raj was Rs. 1.45 lakh crore.

Chapter - 6

i-n. Israel having a HD ranking at 22 spent 7.7% of GDP in 2001)

ii-n. During the presidency of Parvez Musharaff in 2002 through the section 8A of the Conduct of General Election Order 2002 (the CGEO), and Section 99(1) (C) of ROPA, the bachelor's degree or an equivalent degree was made essential to contest an election to the Parliament. This requirement was later removed through the Election Laws (Amendment Act), 2009 with effect from 21 April 2008.

Chapter - 8

i-n. The vivid account of an operation of Indian forces in Siachen is given by Kunal Verma and Brigadier Rajeev Williams in 'The Long Road to Siachen' - The Questions Why, pg. 367-370, Rupa & Co., The names of the soldiers have deliberately omitted in view of bringing such eventualities and the haplessness of the soldiers at the face of sure death, by the authors of this book, to the readers notice.

ii-n. EFTA was launched in 1960 by the Stockholm Convention. It was created by the States which for reasons of sovereignty or neutrality-either did not want to or could not join the European Economic Community (EEC). Five member-States, Austria, Denmark, Portugal, Sweden and the UK have left it since then to join the European Union. (William Rossier, Secretary General of EFTA, EFTA Bulletin 2.2006).

Index